Business Data Analysis Using Excel

# Business Data Analysis Using Excel

David Whigham

OXFORD

UNIVERSITY PRESS

# OXFORD
UNIVERSITY PRESS

Great Clarendon Street, Oxford OX2 6DP

Oxford University Press is a department of the University of Oxford.
It furthers the University's objective of excellence in research, scholarship,
and education by publishing worldwide in

Oxford New York

Auckland Cape Town Dar es Salaam Hong Kong Karachi
Kuala Lumpur Madrid Melbourne Mexico City Nairobi
New Delhi Shanghai Taipei Toronto

With offices in

Argentina Austria Brazil Chile Czech Republic France Greece
Guatemala Hungary Italy Japan Poland Portugal Singapore
South Korea Switzerland Thailand Turkey Ukraine Vietnam

Oxford is a registered trade mark of Oxford University Press
in the UK and in certain other countries

Published in the United States
by Oxford University Press Inc., New York

British Library Cataloguing in Publication Data

Data available

Library of Congress Cataloging in Publication Data

Data available

Typeset by Laserwords Private Limited, Chennai, India
Printed in Great Britain
on acid-free paper by
Ashford Colour Press Limited, Gosport, Hampshire

ISBN 978-0-19-929628-6

10 9 8 7 6 5 4 3 2

To my family

# ■ PREFACE

The aim of this text is to provide a thematic introduction to the use of the Excel spreadsheet in introductory business data analysis. No prior knowledge of Excel is required.

The text has been designed to provide both an explanation of the overall nature of *what* is to be achieved and also instruction in *how* it is to be done with Excel.

Each chapter is therefore structured as follows:

- Each problem is defined in general terms—i.e. what is it that we want to do?

- A template data file is prepared. Data files can also be downloaded from the dedicated online resource centre—these are not simply Excel files but include numerous embedded comments and tips. The online resource centre can be found at www.oxfordtextbooks.co.uk/orc/whigham/. Further details can be found on page xv.

- Each objective is achieved by following the text's instructions.

- To ensure the correct understanding of each objective by students, an exercise focusing on each objective should be completed.

- Solutions to the exercises are given to allow comparison and further extension. A number of solution data files can also be downloaded from the online resource centre.

The learning approach is highly interactive and enables students to develop an understanding of the power of Excel in allowing both analysis of business data sets and in the flexible preparation of graphs, charts and tables for inclusion in reports and essays.

The material in the text has been extensively live-tested with thousands of students. It proved to be very popular and student evaluation was extremely positive. This was true even for students with no prior knowledge of Excel.

# ■ ACKNOWLEDGEMENTS

The author would like to thank students and staff at Glasgow Caledonian University for many corrections and suggestions for improvement.

# ■ CONTENTS

# ■ ONLINE RESOURCE CENTRE

Visit the Business Data Analysis online resource centre at

**www.oxfordtextbooks.co.uk/orc/whigham/**

to find an extensive range of teaching and learning resources, including:

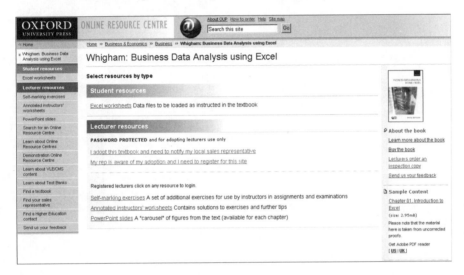

*For Students:*

Excel files: All the data files referred to in the text are available to download from the online resource centre. They are arranged by chapter. They should be downloaded as and when instructed in the textbook. These are not simply Excel files but also include numerous embedded comments and tips.

*For Lecturers:*

PowerPoint slides: A set of PowerPoint slides containing the figures and diagrams for each chapter.

Excel files: A set of annotated worksheets containing solutions to the exercises and additional tips/comments for lecturers.

Self-marking exercises: A set of exercises, marked by the computer, for use within a virtual learning environment to provide formative and summative assessment.

The Economics Network website allows instructors to download free software that automates the process of compiling and marking a wide range of Excel assessments.

# 1

# Introduction to Excel[1]

The following files from the online resource centre should be loaded as instructed:

W1_5A.xls    W1_7.xls    W1_8.xls
W1_9.xls

## 1.1 Terminology and navigation

An Excel **workbook** is simply a three-dimensional stack of **worksheets** consisting of **rows** and **columns**. In any sheet the columns are identified by letters:

$$(A, B, C, \ldots, Z, AA, AB, AC, \ldots, AZ, BA, BB, \ldots, IV)$$

and the rows by numbers:

$$(1, 2, 3, \ldots, 8000).$$

The intersection between a row and a column is known as a **cell** and therefore has a unique **cell address** or **cell reference**. Hence, the cell in the 5th row of column C has the cell address C5. Notice that the column letter *always comes first* in the cell address, followed by the row number. Thus 5C is **not** a valid cell reference.

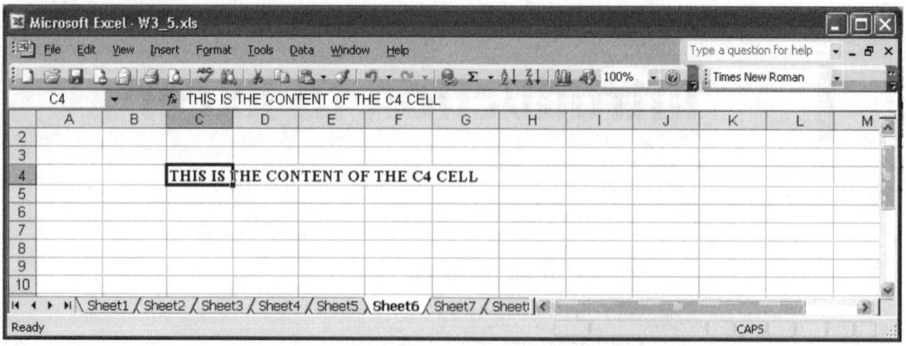

**Figure 1.1**

You therefore have what amounts to a three-dimensional electronic card index box at your disposal.

By default, the sheets of the workbook are numbered as Sheet1, Sheet2 and so on, but it is an easy matter to change this nomenclature to one that is more personal to your own work. More on this later.

*Access an Excel workbook now and read on.*

When Microsoft Excel is accessed for the first time a worksheet similar to the one shown in Figure 1.1 will be observed. If this is not exactly what you see then your version of Excel may have been configured in a different way. Consult an experienced user to assist in setting up Excel in the way indicated so that you can follow the argument. Alternatively, select View from the Menu bar and experiment with the various options there until you obtain the desired effect—Formula bar and Status bar should both be ticked (click on them once if no tick shows) and under the Tool bar option the Standard and Format options should be ticked.

Navigation around the worksheet or selection of Menu or Tool bar options is usually done by placing the **mouse pointer** over the desired option and clicking the **left-hand** button of the mouse **once**.

*Try a few clicks for yourself to appreciate how it works.*

Notice that when the mouse pointer is in the area of the actual worksheet it appears as a **white cross**, but when it is moved out of this area (into the Tool bar area or onto a Scroll bar for example), it turns into a **white arrow**.

At the very top of the screen is the **File name indicator**. This shows the name of the file that is in use at the moment, although if a new worksheet has just been opened it will always indicate 'Book1' since Excel automatically assigns the file that name **until you change it**. This is what is known as the default status.

Below the file indicator is the **Menu bar**. This contains a number of programmed facilities that will be explained in due course. Basically, they allow such things as saving, opening, printing or creating workbooks, altering the appearance of the worksheet, inserting or removing rows and columns, and a large number of useful tools and accessories. Click once with the left-hand button of the mouse on any of the topics to obtain further options in this category.

*Try it now and then click again on the Menu bar topic to restore the original screen.*

Above the Menu bar are the **Tool bars**. These duplicate many of the features of the Menu bar in the form of **icons**. If their meanings are not immediately obvious, place the mouse pointer over the icon but **do not** click the mouse button.

*Do this now.*

After a few seconds a brief explanation of the icon's purpose will appear either beside the icon itself or at the bottom left-hand corner of the screen. More will be said on these icons later when their features are required.

Below and to the right of the toolbars, is the **Formula bar**. This is where the contents of any cell will be displayed. If the cell is empty the Formula bar will be blank, otherwise its contents are displayed.

*Click on any cell now and enter your name. Press enter.*

Your name should appear both in the cell and on the Formula bar.

Next below, are the letters identifying the columns of the worksheet and then comes the actual worksheet itself with grids indicating the cells, a solid white cross indicating the mouse pointer and a solid border indicating the **active cell**. The active cell's address is also shown in the bar to the left of the formula bar.

Any cell in the worksheet is made **active** by pointing to it with the mouse and clicking the left-hand button once. A bold or coloured border will appear around the cell, indicating that it is now the active cell. **Only** when a cell is active can information be entered to it, or its contents altered.

*Practise this by making the C4 and then the E6 cell active.*

To the right of, and also below the actual worksheet area are the **Scroll bars**. These allow the screen to be moved up, down, to the right or to the left. Simply click once on the appropriate **solid arrow** of the Scroll bar to move one row or one column in the desired direction. If larger movements are required place the mouse pointer on the button **between** the arrows of the scroll bars, depress the left hand mouse button and drag the button to the arrow at the **opposite** end of the scroll bar. This will create a movement of one full screen in any direction.

*Confirm this for yourself by using the Scroll bars to move around the worksheet in a clockwise direction.*

Movement around the worksheet can also be effected from the keyboard. The **cursor arrows** move the active cell up, down, right or left by one row or column at a time.

The **Page Down** and **Page Up** keys move one full screen up or down at a time, while **Tab** and **Shift Tab** move one full screen to the right or left, respectively.

Next, pressing the Ctrl and Home keys simultaneously makes the A1 cell active, while pressing function key five (F5) activates the Goto command. Enter the cell address of the cell that is to be made active and then click OK.

Finally, pressing the End key and then one of the cursor arrows will cause the active cell to move up, down, right or left to the **last occupied** cell in the column or row. For example, if the active cell is currently A1, and if the cells A1 to A60 are all occupied, then End and down arrow will move to the end of this range and make the A60 cell active. If all of the cells are unoccupied then End and down arrow goes to the last row of the sheet while End and right arrow would go to the last column of the sheet.

*Practise using these movement keys now.*

To the left of the bottom scroll bar are the **Sheet tabs**. 'Tab' is simply Excel no-menclature for a 'clickable' device. When you click on any tab either an action is performed directly, or another tab or dialogue box appears requesting the user to enter information. The Sheet tabs are used to select a particular sheet from the list of sheets available. For example, when a new Excel workbook is opened for the first time, Sheet1 will be the **active sheet** and this will be indicated by its having a light background. The other available sheets appear with a dark background but they are **not active** unless you click once on them with the left-hand button of the mouse.

To the left of the sheet tabs are the **Sheet Scroll bars**. These allow the user to display the names of all the sheets available in the workbook. Click on the left-hand arrow of the bar to display the first sheet in the list of those available, or on the right-hand arrow to move to the last sheet in the list. The middle two arrows move one sheet at a time in either direction throughout the list of sheets.

*Check for yourself that this is the case by moving through the list of sheets.*

Finally, at the very bottom of the screen is the **Status indicator bar**. Various messages will appear here and provide information upon what tasks the worksheet is performing, as well as which of several default settings has been selected.

*For example, press the Caps Lock key on the keyboard and the letters CAPS will appear on the right-hand side of the Status indicator bar.*

Any text entered to the worksheet will now be upper-case (capital letters).

*Press Caps Lock again and the CAPS indicator will disappear.*

Text entries will now be lower-case.

Finally, notice the icon on the Tool bar in the form of a curved left-pointing arrow. This is the **Undo** facility and can cancel the last action that you performed. Since mistakes are inevitable, and can be very time-consuming to rectify, Undo is one of the most helpful routines provided by Excel. Use it immediately you suspect that something has gone wrong in your worksheet.

*Now attempt Exercise 1.1.*

## 1.2 **Entering data**

The information entered to a cell is known as **data** and can adopt four basic forms—text, number, formula or function.

A **text** entry is characterized by its first character being a letter, a space or a punctuation mark. Text entries (often known as **labels**) are used to enter descriptive comments to the worksheet. This could be your name at the top of the sheet, or a descriptor of the worksheet's purpose, or a list of names of clients about whom you have information. The fundamental feature of a text entry is that arithmetic calculations **cannot** be performed on them. They are **for descriptive purposes only**.

*To practise entering textual data click on C1 and type your first name into this cell of your sheet and include a spelling mistake. When you have finished typing press Enter or click on another cell.*

To **edit** the contents of a cell, first make the cell active by clicking on it with the mouse. The contents of the cell will be shown in the Formula bar between the Tool bar and the letters of the column identifiers. Now click once with the mouse on this Formula bar and again use the mouse to move to the section of the text that is to be altered. Then use the Backspace key or the Delete key to remove superfluous characters and type in the amendment(s) that you want to make. Press the Enter key, or click on another cell when you have finished.

*Use this procedure to correct the spelling mistake that you included in your name as efficiently as possible.*

**Numerical** data entries, on the other hand, commence with a positive or negative numeric character and contain **only** numerical characters thereafter. They are the raw data to which calculations can subsequently be applied and are entered **directly** to the sheet in the form:

$$23 \text{ or } -19 \text{ or } 167.$$

It is important to note that text characters, spaces or punctuation marks **must not be included before or after** numeric characters if the contents of the cell are to be used for calculations. For example, 23 is a valid numeric entry that could be subjected to an arithmetic process (squared, cubed, etc.), but 23rd (as in the 23rd of June) is a text entry that cannot be manipulated mathematically. As long as Excel receives numbers, and **only** numbers, then the entry will be treated numerically, but once a non-numeric character such as a letter of the alphabet is introduced the **whole** entry usually becomes textual.[2]

*Practise entering numerical data in your sheet by typing 31 in C2 and 193.5 in C3.*

**Formula** entries are what distinguish a spreadsheet from a calculator. They are *algebraic* rather than *arithmetic* concepts and allow **general** rather than **specific** computations to be performed.

For example, suppose your annual salary is £20000 and your partner's is £25000. Your combined income is clearly £45000.

*Enter your salary (as a number) into the A1 cell of your worksheet and your partner's to the A2 cell.*

The task to be undertaken is to write an expression (in A3, say) that will compute the combined income.

At first sight you might be tempted to write, in A3:

$$A1+A2$$

but if you do, then you will find that it appears as text rather than as the required numerical answer of 45000.

*Try it now.*

The reason for this is that, as we saw above, any entry that commences with a letter will be treated by Excel as text and will **not produce a numerical result**.

Clearly the problem being faced is to distinguish, for example, the 'A' of the cell reference A1 from 'A' as in the first character of a text label such as Asset value.

Excel allows this to be done quite simply by placing an equals sign (=) in front of any entries that require arithmetic computation on the basis of formulae using cell addresses. Thus,

$$=A1+A2$$

when entered to A3, will return 45000 if A1 and A2 contain 20000 and 25000, respectively.

*Do this now and confirm that it works.*

Importantly, however, if either your or your partner's annual salary should change, then all that is required is to alter the contents of A1 and/or A2 appropriately. The computed result in A3 will change **automatically**.

*Try it for yourself on the sheet that you are using. Change the values in A1 and/or A2 and confirm that A3 computes the correct result automatically.*[3]

This is what was meant when it was previously said that formulae were **algebraic** rather than **arithmetic concepts**. This is because the formula

$$=A1+A2$$

is to be thought of as 'whatever is in A1' plus 'whatever is in A2' rather than 20000 plus 25000.

This is an algebraic process rather than an arithmetic one.

It should also be noted that if numbers as well as cell addresses are to be used in formulae then the entry **must also** be preceded by an equals sign. For example, an entry of 4 to a cell is a perfectly valid numerical entry if it simply represents the number four (a raw data item). However, if you want to add 4 to the contents of A1 then the following entry will **not work**:

$$4+A1$$

*Try this now in any vacant cell of the sheet and notice that it appears as text.*

The equals sign at the start is now **essential** since the entry contains subsequent parts that are not *automatically* treated as numeric. Consequently, it must be written as either

=4+A1   or   =A1+4

*Type both of these entries into vacant cells of your sheet to confirm that they work.*

Now observe that in this last formula there are effectively *four* distinct terms—the equals sign to tell Excel that a numerical operation is to be performed, the number four, the plus sign, and the cell reference A1 representing the contents of the A1 cell. Clearly this implies that the contents of A1 must itself be a raw number, or the result of some other numerical calculation, otherwise no numerical answer can be obtained.

Also, the plus sign is what is known as an **operator** since it instructs Excel as to which mathematical operation is to be performed (addition in this case).

There are, however, a number of further mathematical operators that can be used in Excel formulae. The full list is:

| Purpose | Operator symbol |
| --- | --- |
| Addition | + |
| Subtraction | - |
| Multiplication | * |
| Division | / |
| Powering | ^ |
| Equal to | = |
| Greater than | > |
| Greater than or equal to | >= |
| Less than | < |
| Less than or equal to | <= |
| Not equal to | <> |

These operators, in conjunction with cell references and numbers, allow very complex formulae to be written, provided that the rules governing operator use are fully appreciated. This proviso is necessary because Excel, in conjunction with all other spreadsheet packages, uses a strict system of **priorities** with regard to the order in which it evaluates operators in a formula. Furthermore, since expressions can become very complex, it will not always be immediately obvious whether the result obtained is in fact correct, and so it is essential that the priorities are understood and obeyed at all times.

The **priority** of an operator is quite simply an indication of which operation will be carried out **first** by the spreadsheet, when there is more than one mathematical operation defined by a formula.

Powering has the highest priority and so Excel will perform any powering operation in a formula first. Then it will perform multiplication and division operations at the same level of priority and lastly it will perform addition and subtraction operations, also at the same level of priority.

For example, the expression

$$=A1+A2*A3^A4$$

will be evaluated by Excel in the following step-by-step way:

A3^A4 Powering has the highest priority.

A3^A4 is then multiplied by the contents of A2.

The product of A3^A4 and A2 is then added to the contents of A1.

**Hence with A1 = 10, A2 = 4, A3 = 3 and A4 = 2**, the formula above is equivalent to

$$10 + 4*3^2$$

which evaluates to

$$3^2 = 9$$
$$4*9 = 36$$
$$10 + 36 = 46$$

*Now take a new sheet (click on Sheet2 on the Sheet tabs bar) and enter the above values to the A1 to A4 cells. Then, in A5 type the expression*

$$=A1+A2*A3^A4$$

*and confirm that a result of 46 is obtained*

A **completely different** result would have been obtained if, for example, the multiplication operation had been carried out first. Then we would obtain:

$$4*3 = 12$$
$$12^2 = 144$$
$$10 + 144 = 154$$

Clearly, the operator priority system imposes a constraint upon how formulae can be written and from the discussion above it would appear that nothing can be done to overcome this predefined set of priorities. For example, suppose it were the case in the last illustration that we **actually did** want the 4 to be multiplied by the 3 before the powering by 2 took place. How could we override the default priority of powering first?

The answer is to place brackets around any terms that the user wishes to be evaluated first. Hence, while we have already seen that the expression

$$10 + 4*3^2$$

will be evaluated by Excel as 46, the expression

$$10+(4*3)^2$$

will be evaluated by Excel as:

$$4*3 = 12$$
$$12^2 = 144$$
$$10 + 144 = 154$$

*Confirm that this is the case by making the contents of A6 contain*

$$=A1+(A2*A3)^\wedge A4$$

The difference between the two expressions should now be clear.

The use of brackets in the context of the last example can be further illustrated by the following two illustrations:

$$(a): (10+4)*3^\wedge 2 = 14*3^\wedge 2 = 14*9 = 126$$
$$(b): (10+4*3)^\wedge 2 = (10+12)^\wedge 2 = 22^\wedge 2 = 484$$

*Confirm both of these results by entering the following formulae to the A7 and A8 cells:*

$$=(A1+A2)*A3^\wedge A4$$
$$=(A1+A2*A3)^\wedge A4$$

Now compare the results obtained in A5, A6, A7 and A8 and remember that the numbers in A1 to A4 have *not changed*, though four numerically different results have been obtained.

Notice that inside the brackets of a formula the normal default priorities again apply. For example, in the last expression the higher priority of the multiplication process ensures that the numbers inside the brackets are evaluated as

$$4*3+10 = 12+10 = 22$$

**rather than**

$$10+4*3 = 14*3 = 42$$

If this last operation was **in fact** what was required then we would have to add a **second** set of brackets around the 10+4 term to ensure that it was evaluated first. In other words, it should be written as:

$$((10+4)*3)^\wedge 2 = (14*3)^\wedge 2 = 42^\wedge 2 = 1764$$

*For final confirmation of this, use the A9 cell to contain*

$$=((A1+A2)*A3)^\wedge A4$$

*and check that the correct result of 1764 is obtained*

Also notice that if there is more than one set of brackets then Excel works on an 'inside-out' basis. That is, the innermost brackets are evaluated first, then the next innermost and so on.

Finally, to appreciate the role that brackets can play in modelling practical business problems, consider the following situation.

Individual income tax is charged at a rate of 25% on the difference between gross income and the statutory tax allowance. How can a worksheet be prepared that will compute the tax due for any entered levels of gross income and tax allowance?

The solution is shown in Workbook 1.1.

| | A | B | C |
|---|---|---|---|
| 1 | | | Formulae used in Column B |
| 2 | Tax Rate | 25% | None |
| 3 | Gross Income | 2500 | None |
| 4 | Tax Allowance | 5000 | None |
| 5 | Tax Due | -625 | =B2*(B3-B4) |

**Workbook 1.1**

*To follow the argument yourself click on the Sheet1 tab and make the model up as indicated in the illustration.*

Note that the entries in Column C are for information only. They indicate the formula contents of the adjacent cells in column B. You do not need to make these entries. Also note that throughout the text important formulae will be shown on the Formula bar along with their cell address (the one in B5 in this case).

Notice the role played by the brackets here. If the difference between gross income and the tax allowance had **not** been enclosed in brackets then the tax rate (in B2) would **only** have been applied to the gross income (in B3) if the formula had been written as:

$$=B2*B3-B4$$

Alternatively, the tax rate (in B2) would **only** have been applied to the tax allowance (in B4) if the formula had been written as:

$$=B3-B4*B2$$

Only by placing brackets around the difference between gross income and the tax allowance can the correct result be obtained. That is:

$$=B2*(B3-B4) \text{ or } =(B3-B4)*B2$$

*Now attempt Exercise 1.2.*

The final form of entry to an active cell is an Excel **function**.

Excel contains a large number of pre-programmed functions that can perform sophisticated tasks as required. In Excel, a function, like a formula, is **always** preceded by an equals sign if it is the first entry to a cell. Then the name of the function must be supplied, followed by an opening bracket. There then follow the **arguments** of the function. Some functions only have one argument, but others have several, in which case each argument is separated by a **comma**. Also, if an argument represents a **range** of cells then the required syntax is to type the address of the first cell in the range, then a colon (:) and then the address of the last cell in the required range. Finally, after all the arguments have been entered the brackets are closed. A full list of all the functions available can be obtained from the **Function Wizard** ($f_x$ icon on the tool bar) along with prompts as to the arguments that they require. For the moment, however, reconsider the formula that was written earlier for the combined income of the two individuals. That was:

$$=A1+A2$$

The same result could have been obtained by using the **SUM** function. This contains only one argument—the range of cells to be summed; and so we could write:

$$=SUM(A1:A2)$$

*To see this, click on the Sheet2 tab and re-enter the two incomes to A1 and A2 (20000 and 25000). Now, in A3, enter:*

$$=SUM(A1:A2)$$

The result will be the same as the one obtained earlier from the expression

$$=A1+A2$$

Now, while typing =SUM(A1:A2) is in fact slightly less efficient than typing =A1+A2, this would not be the case if we were required to sum, say, the first 100 rows of column A. Using a formula we would have had to type:

$$=A1+A2+A3+ \ldots \text{ and so on until } \ldots \text{ A99+A100}$$

Clearly, this is very tedious, especially in comparison with the functional alternative:

$$=SUM(A1:A100)$$

Appropriate Excel functions will be introduced throughout the text as and when they are required. Some are indispensable for serious quantitative analysis, but in other cases there may be no alternative to writing a formula of your own, in which case you have created what is known as a **user-defined function**.

Finally, Excel functions and user-defined functions can be used together without difficulty. For example, suppose that you wanted to find the square of the sum of the numbers contained in A1 to A100. There is no predefined Excel function that will do this, but the SUM function and the power operator can be combined to produce the required result as follows:

$$=SUM(A1:A2)\hat{\ }2$$

*Confirm that such a procedure would work by using the A5 cell of the current sheet to contain:*

$$=SUM(A1:A2)\hat{\ }2$$

If A1 and A2 still contain 20000 and 25000 respectively, then a value of 2025000000 should be returned to A5.

If this is not what is shown then it is probably because the column width is too small. Excel will return the number as something like 2.03 E+09, which means 2.03 times 10 to the power of 9. But you can widen the column by selecting Format, Column and then

Width. The default width (8.5) will usually show, so change this to 13 say, and the result will now show in conventional form.

Alternatively, place the cursor on the vertical line separating the A column identifier from the B column identifier, depress the left-hand mouse button and drag to the right. The A column will be widened.

*Now attempt Exercise 1.3.*

## 1.3  Selecting an area of the worksheet

*To follow the subsequent discussion open a new workbook and proceed as instructed.*

Selecting an area of the worksheet in Excel is most easily done with the mouse.

*Place the mouse pointer in the first cell that is to be selected, depress the left-hand button and then drag down and/or across until the required area has been highlighted.*

This area has now been **selected** and can be subjected to a variety of processes.

*For example, with an area selected (A1:C9 say), click once on the B icon on the toolbar.*

All entries to this area will now appear in bold lettering.

*To deselect an area click on a cell outside the selected area. To remove the bold formatting that was created above select the area once again by clicking and dragging (if you have deselected it) and then choose Edit from the Menu bar. Now select Clear and then All and the formatting will return to normal.[4] Now enter your first name, middle name and surname to the A1, A2 and A3 cells respectively and select the area A1:A3. Format this area to bold and italic by clicking click the B and then the I icon on the toolbar.*

Then suppose that you wanted to move these data to the area C6 to C8.

*With the area A1:A3 still selected choose Edit from the Menu bar and then Cut.*

The border around the selected area will start flashing.

*Now activate the C6 cell by clicking on it, choose Edit from the menu bar and then Paste.*

It should be found that the selected area has been moved (cut and pasted) to the new desired area. Also notice that the bold italic formatting has also been carried over to the new area and that any entry to the A1:A3 cells will **no longer** be bold italic.

*Now attempt Exercise 1.4.*

# 1.4 Saving, closing and opening files

The information that you enter to an Excel workbook is contained in units known as **files**. Files can be saved, closed and then opened again provided the correct procedures are followed.

*To follow the arguments involved in these procedures more closely, begin a new session in Excel by selecting File and then Exit from the Menu bar. Click on 'No' to any Save prompts that appear and then re-access Excel from your computer's main list of options.*

The first thing to note is that when Excel is accessed for the *first* time in a *new* session a workbook with the title 'Book1' appears. This is the **File name** that Excel has *automatically* assigned to the new workbook.

Now activate the A5 cell and enter your name.

This information must now be **Saved** and to do this select **File** from the menu bar. There are three 'Save' options on the list that now appears: **Save, Save As and Save Workspace**. The first two of these will be used most frequently in the discussion.

The distinction between Save and Save As is as follows.

**Save** will save the workbook with whatever name is currently displayed in the File name bar immediately above the column letters. Thus, selecting Save would save this worksheet with the default file name of Book1.

**Save As**, on the other hand, allows users to choose a name for the file that is appropriate to their filing system and usually mnemonic. Once a user-selected name has been given, however, subsequent use of the Save command will save the workbook with that **given** name.

*Consequently, select Save As from the File menu.*

A screen resembling the one indicated in Figure 1.2 will appear.

This screen indicates the **default** settings for the saving procedure which will be determined by the configuration of the system that you are using.

Normally, however, we will want to supply our **own** name for the file and save it to our **own** storage area.

Clearly, depending upon the system being used, there are simply too many possibilities to illustrate each and every one.

Consequently, the following general rules of thumb should be employed.

At the bottom of the screen is the File name tab box and the default name will be showing. Usually we will simply type over this to supply the new name that we have chosen. Sometimes, however, we may want to use an existing file name and if this is the case click on the arrow tab to see a list of those available. Be careful, however, since if you select an existing file name from the available list then the saving procedure will overwrite the old file information with that contained in the new one.

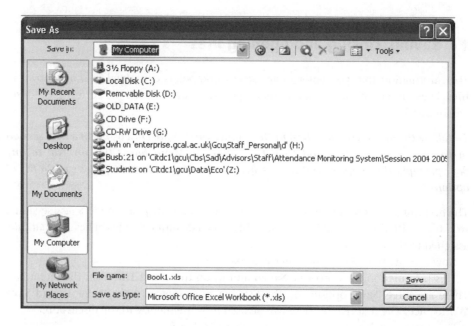

**Figure 1.2**

Below the File Name box is the Save as Type box. This allows you to save the file in a different format such as an older version of Excel or another spreadsheet package such as Lotus 1-2-3. Usually we will accept the default setting.

Now that you have selected your file name and file type the last step is to choose a location in which the file is to be saved.

The options available are shown in the Save in box at the top of the screen.

As can be seen from Figure 1.2 there can be a large number of these. The general principle, however, will be to use the arrow tab to select a location to which you have read and write access privileges. Normally this would be a network drive allocated to you by your administrator, or a removable device such as a floppy disc (drive A) or a CD drive.

In any event, once you have selected your preferred location, click Save and the file will be saved.

For example, in the case illustrated in Figure 1.2 the file would be saved as a Microsoft Excel Workbook with the name Book1 to the location known as My Computer.

## 1.5 Copying data

The ability to copy text, formulae and functions from one cell of the worksheet to another chosen range of cells is one of Excel's most powerful features. It is also quite a sophisticated process that needs careful explanation.

|   | A | B | C | D | E | F | G |
|---|---|---|---|---|---|---|---|
| 1 | BRITFUEL PLC PRICE, COST AND PROFIT DATA | | | | | | |
| 2 | | | | | | | |
| 3 | Item Code | Price | Unit Cost | Unit Profit | | | |
| 4 | Item 1 | £2.65 | £2.21 | | | | |
| 5 | Item 2 | £3.56 | £3.02 | | | | |
| 6 | Item 3 | £1.45 | £1.04 | | | | |
| 7 | Item 4 | £0.99 | £0.78 | | | | |
| 8 | Item 5 | £1.24 | £1.02 | | | | |
| 9 | Item 6 | £0.56 | £0.35 | | | | |
| 10 | Item 7 | £1.29 | £0.99 | | | | |
| 11 | Item 8 | £3.76 | £2.99 | | | | |
| 12 | Item 9 | £4.56 | £3.99 | | | | |
| 13 | Item 10 | £4.12 | £3.56 | | | | |
| 14 | Item 11 | £0.68 | £0.41 | | | | |
| 15 | Item 12 | £0.92 | £0.80 | | | | |
| 16 | Item 13 | £0.83 | £0.75 | | | | |

**Workbook 1.2**

To appreciate the issues involved in the copying process consider the illustration shown in Workbook 1.2.

*To create this worksheet for yourself take a blank workbook (File and then New from the Menu bar) and proceed as follows.*

*First enter the title of the sheet:*

BRITFUEL PLC PRICE, COST AND PROFIT DATA

*to the C1 cell.*

*Next, in the A3 to D3 cells enter the following labels to identify the data in each column:*

Item Code   Price   Unit Cost   Unit Profit

Some of the columns may not be wide enough to contain these labels.

*If so, place the mouse pointer on the vertical line to the right of the column letter at the top of the sheet. When the solid white cross of the pointer turns into a black cross with arrows pointing left and right, depress the left-hand mouse button and drag to the right until the column width has increased sufficiently to allow all of the label's text to appear.*

*Now, in A4 type the label:*

Item 1

*and press enter once.*

*Now click on the A4 cell to make it active again.*

Then notice that the bold or coloured border indicating that A4 is the active cell has a small 'blob' on its bottom right-hand corner. This 'blob' is known as a **handle** and can be activated by placing the mouse pointer over it, whereupon the normal white cross of the pointer will become finer and black. The handle is **only** active if this black cross is showing.

*Provided this is the case, depress the left-hand mouse button and then drag down column A until you reach row 16. Let go of the left-hand mouse button and you should find that column A has been filled with the labels shown in the illustrative worksheet.*

This is a very clever piece of copying, since although the source cell is a text entry (Item 1), the fact that the last term is a number means that when it is copied into the cells below Excel adds one each time to produce Item 2, Item 3, etc.[5]

*Now you must enter the raw data on price and unit cost into columns B and C.*

Since there is no obvious pattern to these data there is no quick way of doing this, just enter them as quickly as possible, **but do not try to include the £ signs—these will be produced later by a special formatting procedure**.

*Once these data have been entered click on the B4 cell[6] and while depressing the left-hand mouse button drag down to row 16 and then three columns right into column E.*

The area B4:E16 has now been selected, and we are now going to format this area to currency.

*With the B4:E16 area still highlighted, select Format from the main Menu bar and then Cells from the list of options that follows.*

There then appears a list of options governing the numerical appearance of the cells in the worksheet.

*So select Currency and from the next set of option boxes that appears select £ and 2 decimal places (usually this will be the default).*

*Now click OK.*

What this has done is to format all the selected cells to show a £ currency symbol with two decimal places.

Column D is where we are going to compute the unit profit on Item 1 as the difference between its price and its unit cost.

*Hence in D4 we should enter:*

=B4-C4

Now notice that the appropriate entry in D5 for the unit profit on Item 2 would be

$$=B5-C5$$

and, by extension,

$$=B6-C6$$

in D6 for Item 3.

This logic would continue until we obtained

$$=B16-C16$$

in D16 for Item 13.

We *could* type in each of these expressions individually, but thanks to the copying facility there is no need.

*Provided there is a recognizable pattern* all we need to do is to provide *one* formula in a **source** cell and then copy this source down the sheet.

*So, with the D4 cell active and containing the formula*

$$=B4-C4$$

*activate the handle and, keeping the left-hand mouse button depressed, drag down from row 4 to row 16.*

If this has been done properly then the result should be the same as that shown in Workbook 1.3.

|   | A | B | C | D | E | F | G |
|---|---|---|---|---|---|---|---|
| 2 |   |   |   |   |   |   |   |
| 3 | Item Code | Price | Unit Cost | Unit Profit |   |   |   |
| 4 | Item 1 | £2.65 | £2.21 | £0.44 |   |   |   |
| 5 | Item 2 | £3.56 | £3.02 | £0.54 |   |   |   |
| 6 | Item 3 | £1.45 | £1.04 | £0.41 |   |   |   |
| 7 | Item 4 | £0.99 | £0.78 | £0.21 |   |   |   |
| 8 | Item 5 | £1.24 | £1.02 | £0.22 |   |   |   |
| 9 | Item 6 | £0.56 | £0.35 | £0.21 |   |   |   |
| 10 | Item 7 | £1.29 | £0.99 | £0.30 |   |   |   |
| 11 | Item 8 | £3.76 | £2.99 | £0.77 |   |   |   |
| 12 | Item 9 | £4.56 | £3.99 | £0.57 |   |   |   |
| 13 | Item 10 | £4.12 | £3.56 | £0.56 |   |   |   |
| 14 | Item 11 | £0.68 | £0.41 | £0.27 |   |   |   |
| 15 | Item 12 | £0.92 | £0.80 | £0.12 |   |   |   |
| 16 | Item 13 | £0.83 | £0.75 | £0.08 |   |   |   |

**Workbook 1.3**

However, before we leave this worksheet it is important to appreciate exactly what has taken place.

*Activate the D4 cell and observe the formula that appears in the Formula bar just above the column letters.*

It should show:

$$=B4-C4$$

This was the formula that was entered to D4.

*Now click on the D5 cell and note that*

$$=B5-C5$$

*shows in the Formula bar.*

*Keep on clicking down this column until you are satisfied that each cell contains the appropriate formula entry.*

Then remember that only **one** formula was actually typed into the sheet. This source formula (in D4) was copied down the column and produced, with incredible ease, exactly what was required.

The upshot of this is the observation that when Excel is instructed to copy a formula (or a function) it does so in a **fully relative manner**. By this, we mean that a source formula such as

$$B1+C1$$

when copied down the sheet produces:

$$=B2+C2 \quad =B3+C3 \quad =B4+C4 \text{ and so on.}$$

On the other hand, when the same formula is copied across the sheet it produces:

$$=C1+D1 \quad =D1+E1 \quad =E1+F1 \text{ and so on.}$$

In effect, fully relative copying means that the row numbers in an formula **update** by 1 as the formula is copied **down** the sheet and the column letters **update** by 1 as the formula is copied **across** the sheet.

*Now save this file with the name:*

$$W1\_3.xls$$

*since it will be used again later in the discussion.*

*Now attempt Exercises 1.5, 1.6 and 1.7.*

However, although fully relative copying is an exceptionally powerful tool, there can be circumstances in which it is **too** powerful for the requirements of our model. In other words, there may be circumstances in which we want to **restrain** the process.

To appreciate the nature of such circumstances consider the illustration in Workbook 1.4.

Here, we have taken the model constructed in Workbook 1.3 and added the information that the unit profit on each item is subject to tax at a rate of 15%.

|   | A | B | C | D | E | F | G |
|---|---|---|---|---|---|---|---|
| 1 | BRITFUEL PLC PRICE, COST AND PROFIT DATA | | | | | | |
| 2 | Tax rate | £0.15 | | | | | |
| 3 | Item Code | Price | Unit Cost | Unit Profit | Unit Net Profit | | |
| 4 | Item 1 | £2.65 | £2.21 | £0.44 | £0.37 | | |
| 5 | Item 2 | £3.56 | £3.02 | £0.54 | £0.46 | | |
| 6 | Item 3 | £1.45 | £1.04 | £0.41 | £0.35 | | |
| 7 | Item 4 | £0.99 | £0.78 | £0.21 | £0.18 | | |
| 8 | Item 5 | £1.24 | £1.02 | £0.22 | £0.19 | | |
| 9 | Item 6 | £0.56 | £0.35 | £0.21 | £0.18 | | |
| 10 | Item 7 | £1.29 | £0.99 | £0.30 | £0.26 | | |
| 11 | Item 8 | £3.76 | £2.99 | £0.77 | £0.65 | | |
| 12 | Item 9 | £4.56 | £3.99 | £0.57 | £0.48 | | |
| 13 | Item 10 | £4.12 | £3.56 | £0.56 | £0.48 | | |
| 14 | Item 11 | £0.68 | £0.41 | £0.27 | £0.23 | | |
| 15 | Item 12 | £0.92 | £0.80 | £0.12 | £0.10 | | |
| 16 | Item 13 | £0.83 | £0.75 | £0.08 | £0.07 | | |

**Workbook 1.4**

*To follow the argument open Workbook 1.3 (if it has been closed) and make the following additions.*

*First, in A2 enter the label*

Tax rate

*and in B2 enter*

0.15  or  15%

*Now, in E3 enter the label*

Unit Net Profit.

This will be the profit after tax.

We now need to write a formula in E4 that will compute the Unit Net Profit on the basis of the Unit Profits made by each item and the tax rate that is applied to those unit profits.

Logically, we should argue that

Net Unit Profit = Unit Profit − Tax rate × Unit Profit.

Hence, in E4 we can translate this into a formula of the form

**=D4-B2*D4**

This represents the Unit Profit on Item 1 minus the Tax rate times the Unit Profit on Item 1.

**As far as Item 1 is concerned** this is a completely valid formulation and would produce the correct result, but if we try to copy such a formula into the cells below, **difficulties will ensue.**

This is because fully relative copying means that the tax rate (in B2) will be row-updated in the copying process. In other words, B2 will become B3, B4, B5 and so on, when copied down the sheet. Yet B3, B4 and B5 **do not** contain tax rate information. **Only** B2 contains this information.

Consequently, we require that the B2 cell reference in the formula is **always B2 and does not update in the copying process.**

The two D4 references in the formula, on the other hand, **must update** when copied down the sheet since they relate to each of the items that the company sells and to which the tax rate must apply.

To deal with these different requirements we must add a dollar sign ($) in front of the row number in the B2 cell address. That is, we rewrite the formula as:

$$=D4-B\$2*D4$$

The dollar sign ensures that when the formula is copied down the sheet, the row number will **not** be updated. It will **always remain as B2**. The D4 references, on the other hand, without their dollar signs, will update in a fully relative manner. This will produce a formula that can be copied consistently and that will serve our purpose.

*Consequently, in E4 enter:*

$$=D4-B\$2*D4$$

*then activate the handle and drag down to row 16.*

The correct results will be obtained and if you inspect each of the cells then you will find that the references to column D have been row-updated as required but the one to B2 has remained fixed.

*Save this model now as* W1_4.xls *for future reference.*

*Now attempt Exercise 1.8.*

Correct use of the $ symbol in copying is of such crucial importance to the efficient creation of worksheet models that it deserves further discussion. Consequently, consider the illustration shown in Workbook 1.5.

*Create this now in a new workbook in line with the instructions below.*

*The first step is to enter the raw data to the A1:C3 range as indicated in the illustration.*

*Next, in A5 enter the formula:*

$$=A1*2$$

This is going to be the source cell for the copying process and will be copied into the adjacent two columns and the adjacent two rows. In this case, however, instead of dragging the handle as before, we are going to use the Copy command from the Menu bar.

*To do this, click on A5 to activate the cell. Then select Edit from the Menu bar and then click on Copy from the options that will have appeared.*

The border around the active cell should change from solid to flashing, indicating that this particular cell has been selected for copying.

| | A | B | C | D | E | F | G |
|---|---|---|---|---|---|---|---|
| 1 | 4 | 6 | 10 | | | | |
| 2 | 5 | 2 | 1 | | | | |
| 3 | 9 | 11 | 7 | | | | |
| 4 | SOURCE DATA | | | | | | |
| 5 | 8 | 12 | 20 | | 8 | 12 | 20 |
| 6 | 10 | 4 | 2 | | 8 | 12 | 20 |
| 7 | 18 | 22 | 14 | | 8 | 12 | 20 |
| 8 | FULLY RELATIVE COPYING | | | | SEMI RELATIVE COPYING ROW FIXED | | |
| 9 | 8 | 8 | 8 | | 8 | 8 | 8 |
| 10 | 10 | 10 | 10 | | 8 | 8 | 8 |
| 11 | 18 | 18 | 18 | | 8 | 8 | 8 |
| 12 | SEMI RELATIVE COPYING COLUMN FIXED | | | ABSOLUTE COPYING | | | |

**Workbook 1.5**

*Now depress the left-hand mouse button and drag down two rows and then across two columns.*

This will select the cells A5:C7 as the range that is to be **copied to**.

*Now press the Enter key, or select Edit and then Paste from the Menu bar.*

By either method, the result of the copying process should be the same as the A5:C7 range of the illustrative worksheet.

The first thing to note is that the copying has been done in a fully relative manner, with the result that each element in the A5:C7 range is exactly double the corresponding element in the A1:C3 range. This is because the copying process that has been performed can be thought of as follows:

$$=A1*2 \text{ BECOMES } =A1*2 =B1*2 =C1*2 \text{ FULLY RELATIVE COPYING}$$
$$=A2*2 =B2*2 =C2*2$$
$$=A3*2 =B3*2 =C3*2$$

*Now move to E5 and enter*

$$=A\$1*2$$

*Then use the same method as above to copy this into the E5:G7 range.*

In this case the dollar sign attached to the row number means that the latter will *not* update when copied down the sheet, but the column letter *will* update as copying is performed across the sheet. This has the effect of making each of the three rows in E5:G7 identical, with each element being twice the corresponding element in the A1:C1 range. The whole process can be visualized as follows:

$$=A\$1*2 \text{ BECOMES } =A\$1*2 =B\$1*2 =C\$1*2 \text{ SEMI-RELATIVE COPYING}$$
$$=A\$1*2 =B\$1*2 =C\$1*2 \text{ COLUMN RELATIVE}$$
$$=A\$1*2 =B\$1*2 =C\$1*2 \text{ ROW ABSOLUTE}$$

*Next, move to A9 and enter*

$$=\$A1*2$$

*and copy this into A9:C11.*

The results should be the same as in the illustrative worksheet and represent the following process:

=$A1*2 BECOMES =$A1*2 =$A1*2 =$A1*2 SEMI-RELATIVE COPYING

=$A2*2 =$A2*2 =$A2*2 COLUMN ABSOLUTE

=$A3*2 =$A3*2 =$A3*2 ROW RELATIVE

*Finally in E9 enter*

$$=\$A\$1*2$$

*and copy this into E9:G11.*

The appearance of dollar signs in front of **both** the row number and the column letter means that in the copying process the A1 cell address is **absolutely fixed**. Neither columns nor rows will update, since the process is equivalent to:

=$A$1*2 BECOMES =$A$1*2 =$A$1*2 =$A$1*2 ABSOLUTE COPYING

=$A$1*2 =$A$1*2 =$A$1*2

=$A$1*2 =$A$1*2 =$A$1*2

*Save this model now as W1_5.xls for future reference.*

 *You should also load the W1_5A.xls file which provides an interactive demonstration of the process explained above.*

## 1.6 Creating and using named cells

Excel allows users to define their own names for cells and to use these names thereafter in formulae instead of the conventional cell address (A1, B4, etc.).

For example, **if the B1 cell has been named as X**, then the following two formulae are equivalent:

$$=B1+2 \text{ and } =X+2$$

Naming cells can be very useful for memory purposes. For instance, if a firm's profit for the first quarter of the year is located in the C6 cell say, then naming this cell as Q1 is a lot easier to remember (since it has a mnemonic connotation) in subsequent formulae that need to refer to first-quarter profits.

The process and effects of naming a cell are illustrated in Workbook 1.6.

| B3 | ↓ | =Y-X | | | | | | | | |
|---|---|---|---|---|---|---|---|---|---|---|
| | **A** | **B** | **C** | **D** | **E** | **F** | **G** | **H** | **I** | **J** |
| **1** | INCOME | 15900 | | | | | | | | |
| **2** | EXPENDITURE | 13500 | | | | | | | | |
| **3** | SURPLUS | 2400 | =Y-X IS THE FORMULA IN B3 | | | | | | | |
| **4** | | | | | | | | | | |
| **5** | | | | | | | | | | |

Sheet1 / Sheet2 / Sheet3 / Sheet4 / Sheet5 / Sheet

**Workbook 1.6**

*Make this model up for yourself in a new workbook.*

Here, the B1 and B2 cells will be named as Y and X respectively.

*To do this, first activate the cell to be named (click on B1 first of all) then select Insert from the Menu bar and then Name and Define.*

The Name dialogue box will appear and will indicate any names that have previously been defined.

*Click on the Names in Workbook tab at the top of the box and enter Y as the name and then check that the Refers To: tab at the bottom of the box indicates Sheet1!$B$1.[7] Select OK and the B1 cell is now known to the workbook as Y. Now click on B2 and repeat this process for the B2 cell—naming it as X. With B1 and B2 named as Y and X respectively, the Surplus (Income − Expenditure) can be obtained by activating the B3 cell and entering:*

$$=Y-X$$

This is **completely** equivalent to:

$$=B1-B2$$

when B1 and B2 have been named as Y and X respectively.

*Confirm this now and then save the file as* W1_6.xls.

*Now attempt Exercises 1.9 and 1.10.*

## 1.7 Inserting or deleting rows or columns

Rows or columns can be inserted in the worksheet as required. Importantly, however, any insertion will cause all formulae to adjust **automatically** to take account of the relevant insertions. To appreciate the importance of this point consider Workbook 1.7.

| | A | B | C | D | E |
|---|---|---|---|---|---|
| 1 | Area | Sales (£) | | | |
| 2 | Region 1 | 23500 | | | |
| 3 | Region 2 | 41367 | | | |
| 4 | Region 3 | 52987 | | | |
| 5 | Region 5 | 28106 | | | |
| 6 | Region 6 | 34871 | | | |
| 7 | Region 7 | 52010 | | | |
| 8 | Region 8 | 31065 | | | |
| 9 | Region 9 | 19823 | | | |
| 10 | Region 10 | 41921 | | | |
| 11 | Region 11 | 27103 | | | |
| 12 | Total all Regions | 352753 | | | |

**Workbook 1.7**

*Make this model up for yourself in a new workbook or load it (W1_7.xls) from the online resource centre.*

Here, it is to be supposed that the sales information for Region 4 has been inadvertently omitted. We clearly need to insert a row between row 4 and row 5 to allow the data for Region 4 to be entered.

Before we do this, however, inspect the totalling formula that was entered to the B12 cell and which is indicated on the formula bar in the illustrative worksheet. It shows:

$$=SUM(B2:B11)$$

but if we insert a new row and enter some data for that row the totalling formula *should* become:

$$=SUM(B2:B12)$$

Fortunately, there is no need to perform this adjustment *manually* since the insertion procedure does it **automatically**.

*To insert the required row, activate any cell in row 5 (B5 will do) and then select Insert from the Menu bar and then Rows.*

The new row will be inserted.

*Now click on the B13 cell you will find that the totalling formula has been adjusted as required. Also confirm that it operates correctly by entering a value for Region 4's sales.*

The column total should automatically increase by exactly the amount that you entered.

The process for inserting columns to the worksheet is identical with the exception that **Columns** is chosen from the **Insert** menu.

*Practise this now by inserting a new column between column A and column B.*

Lastly, if **more than one** row or column needs to be inserted activate the first cell in the insertion range and then drag down or across for as many rows or columns as are required. Then select Insert and Rows or Columns as before.

Removing rows or columns from the worksheet is done from the **Edit** option on the Menu bar. First of all, place the mouse pointer in the row or column that is to be removed, then select **Edit** and then **Delete** and then **Entire Row** or **Entire Column**. Click OK to effect the deletion.[8]

*Practise this now by removing the column that you inserted between column A and column B.*

*Now attempt Exercise 1.11.*

## 1.8 **Working with multiple sheets**

As was said earlier, the sheets of a workbook are automatically named Sheet1, Sheet2 and so on, but you will often want to customize them with names *of your own* that relate to their purpose.

*To follow the argument open a new workbook. With Sheet1 active double-click quickly with the left-hand mouse button on the Sheet1 tab. Press the Delete key once to remove this name and then enter:*

2003DATA

*and hit enter.*[9]

The new name of the sheet, 2003DATA, will now appear on the sheet tab.

*Now double-click rapidly on the Sheet2 tab and use the procedure explained above to rename it as 2004DATA.*

Clearly you can continue with this process until all of the sheets that you intend to use are named appropriately, and if you need more than the usual default number of three use Insert from the main menu and then Worksheet from the submenu.

The information contained in the various sheets of the workbook can be linked in a variety of ways. To see this proceed as follows:

*Activate the 2003data sheet by clicking once.*

*Then in A1 enter the label:*

Quarterly profits

*Next, in A2:A5 enter the numbers:*

15000    21000    12500    and    8250

*Now activate the A1 cell and select Edit from the Menu bar and then Copy.*

The A1 cell will flash.

What we are going to do is copy this label from the 2003data sheet into the 2004 data sheet.

*So click on the 2004data sheet tab and then click on the A1 cell of this sheet to activate it. Now press enter, or select Edit and Paste from the Menu bar and the label will appear in the A1 cell of the 2004data sheet.*

We now need some profit data for 2004.

*So, ensuring that the 2004data sheet is selected and active, enter the following numbers to the A2:A5 cells:*

13000     26000     15900     and     12350.

What we have, therefore, is the firm's 2003 quarterly profits in the range A2:A5 of the 2003data sheet and its 2004 profits in the same area of the 2004data sheet.

We are now going to name a new sheet as 2003–4data where we will get Excel to compute the **combined** profits for the two years.

*First, double-click on Sheet3 and rename it as:*

2003-4data

*Then, in A1 enter the label:*

Combined profits 2003-4

*Now activate the A2 cell of the 2003–4data sheet.*

This is where the linking of the two sheets is going to take place.

The logic is as follows. The combined annual profits for the first quarter of 2003 and 2004 are clearly the contents of A2 in the 2003data sheet plus the contents of A2 in the 2004data sheet.

Excel allows you write this logic as follows:

**=2003data!A2+2004data!A2**

Notice the use of the exclamation mark to separate the *sheet* reference from the *cell* reference in that sheet.

*Enter this formula now to the A2 cell of the 2003-4data sheet.*

A result of 28000 should be returned (i.e. 15000+13000).

*Now activate the A2 cell of 2003-4data, activate the handle and drag down to A5.*

When you let go of the mouse button the appropriate formulae for the remaining three quarters will have been entered.

*Check this by inspecting each cell.*

Finally, although in this illustration there were only two sheets to be combined it is not hard to imagine circumstances where there are several sheets covering data for a large number of years. In such circumstances it is needlessly tedious to sum all the sheets *individually* as was done above—in other words to enter something like:

=2003data!A2+2004data!A2+ ...    and so on until    ... +2010DATA!A2

To overcome this tedium all we have to do is make use of the SUM function as follows:

=SUM(2003data:2010DATA!A2:A2)

or, since we only have two sheets named in this way in our illustration,

=SUM(2003data:2004data!A2:A2)

This will sum the A2 cells of all the sheets that are specified on either side of the first colon sign in the formula.

*Confirm that this works by replacing the formula that you previously entered to the A2 cell of 2003-4data with this new version and then copying it down into A3:A5 to obtain the 2nd, 3rd and 4th quarter totals.*

## 1.9 Avoiding errors and mistakes

It is never possible to avoid making mistakes when using Excel. Even the most experienced user will make elementary errors under various circumstances. However, the difference between experienced and novice users is that the former can quickly recognize and rectify thein errors. So how do novice users become experienced? Obviously, by gaining experience. Nevertheless, there are a few pointers that can be given to accelerate the gathering of this experience. To see this, consider the following simple illustration.

Suppose that we are set the task of adding the contents of the A1 cell to those of the A2 cell. Although clearly a very simple task it is nonetheless true that we can make a mistake in either of two categories, viz.

(a) An error of logic, i.e. in the algebraic integrity of our Excel representation of the set task.

(b) An error of syntax, i.e. in the form in which we enter our formula or function to a particular cell—a spelling error.

This means that Table 1.1 can be used to represent all possible outcomes from the ability to make either of these two types of mistake.

The top left cell of Table 1.1 shows two equally correct (equivalent) ways of achieving the designated task.

However, in the top right cell the first attempt is syntactically incorrect because the equals sign has been omitted, while the second uses a function, SAM, instead of SUM that Excel does not recognize. In both cases the logic is correct but it has been expressed in faulty syntax.

**Table 1.1**

|  | SYNTAX CORRECT | SYNTAX INCORRECT |
|---|---|---|
| LOGIC CORRECT | =A1+A2    =SUM(A1:A2) | A1+A2    =SAM(A1:A2) |
| LOGIC INCORRECT | =A1*A2    =SUM(A1:A1) | A1*A2    =SIM(A1:A1) |

In the bottom left cell, however, the syntax is perfect in both cases but the logic fails to achieve what is required since the first expression multiplies rather than adds, while the second omits the A2 cell from the range to be summed.

Finally, the bottom right cell combines both types of error—missing equals sign and multiplication rather than addition, unrecognized function name (SIM) and insufficient range of cells to sum.

Interestingly, errors of syntax are usually easier to fix than errors of logic. This is because with syntax mistakes Excel will produce error messages in the offending cell(s), thus providing a clear indication that something is wrong (#NAME, #ERR for example).

With errors of logic, however, this will rarely be the case.[10] A result will be obtained but there can be no guarantee of its logical validity in relation to the set task.

*Now attempt Exercise 1.12.*

## 1.10 Exercises

### Exercise 1.1

(a) The intersection between a column and a row in a worksheet is known as what?

(b) What is the cell address of the 21st row of column H?

(c) An Excel workbook is a three-dimensional stack of what?

(d) What is the indication that a cell is active?

(e) When can data be entered to a cell?

(f) Name three ways in which a cell can be made active.

(g) How many rows and columns are there in an Excel worksheet?

(h) Where are the contents of the active cell displayed?

(i) With the A1 cell currently active, what is the quickest way of making the bottom right cell of the sheet become the active cell?

(j) What is the quickest way of making the BZ9999 cell active?

### Exercise 1.2

Indicate how the following expressions would be evaluated by Excel

(a) =10+2^3      (b) =4*5+3^2      (c) =5+18/3^2

(d) =(9+18)/3^2      (e) =(1+18/3)^2      (f) 6/2+5*4

(g) =(3+2*6)*4      (h) =3+2*6*(3+7)      (i) =((3+2)*5)^2

(j) =((3+2)*5^2)      (k) =(3^2+1)*2^(2+1)      (l) =104/2^3

(m) =4^2/2^3      (n) =4^(2/2)^3

## Exercise 1.3

Identify each of the following cell entries as being one of text, number, formula, function or a mixture of the last three.

(a) 23      (b) '96      (c) Excel

(d) 2times2      (e) A1+A2      (f) =A1*3

(g) 6*A2+A3      (h) =9*A1      (i) =SUM(H5:H55)

(j) 7*SUM(Y56:Z99)      (k) =A1*SUM(D12:D32)

(l) =9+10+A1-B1+C1-SUM(A2:C2)

## Exercise 1.4

Enter some data to the A1:C6 range of a worksheet—anything will do—text and/or numbers are easiest.

(a) Format the range to underlined italics.

(b) Move the contents of A1:C6 into A8:C13.

(c) Delete the contents *only* of A8:C13.

(d) Remove the underlined italics formatting from A8:C13.

(e) Make A8:C13 bold formatted and then make an entry in this range to confirm that it has worked.

## Exercise 1.5

In a blank worksheet use the A1 cell to contain:
  January
Now copy A1 down to A12 and observe the effects.

## Exercise 1.6

Use the copying facility to create the following list in column A:
  Profits 1980
  Profits 1981
and so on until:
  Profits 2020

| | A | B | C | D | E | F |
|---|---|---|---|---|---|---|
| 1 | | | Interest | | Interest | |
| 2 | | | rate 1998 | | rate 1999 | |
| 3 | | | 7.20% | | 8.40% | |
| 4 | | Balance @ | Interest | Balance @ | Interest | Balance @ |
| 5 | Account No. | 31st Dec1997 | 1998 | 31st Dec 1998 | 1999 | 31st Dec 1999 |
| 6 | 1236 | 2045 | | | | |
| 7 | 1469 | 11213 | | | | |
| 8 | 1578 | 23198 | | | | |
| 9 | 1789 | 3578 | | | | |
| 10 | 1791 | 4901 | | | | |
| 11 | 1810 | 5109 | | | | |
| 12 | 1919 | 17451 | | | | |
| 13 | 1945 | 21997 | | | | |
| 14 | 1989 | 16718 | | | | |
| 15 | 2012 | 13109 | | | | |
| 16 | 2367 | 1098 | | | | |
| 17 | | | | | | |

**Workbook 1.8**

## Exercise 1.7

Use the copying facility to produce an efficient way of creating the following series of numbers in the A1:A20 range:

4, 9, 14, 19, 24, 29, 34, 39, 44, 49, 54, 59, 64, 69, 74, 79, 84, 89, 94, 99

## Exercise 1.8

Prepare the model shown in Workbook 1.8 or load it (W1_8.xls) from the online resource centre.

Now write formulae to complete the model in line with the requirements of the column headings.

Save the completed model as W1_8.xls for future use.

## Exercise 1.9

Use the Insert Name command to name the A1 cell of a blank worksheet as AONE and the A2 cell as ATWO.

Now enter any two values to the A1 and A2 cells and then using these names write a formula in A3 that will multiply these two values together.

## Exercise 1.10

The accumulated amount (A) after N years, of a principal of £P compounded at an annual interest rate of I% per annum is given by:

$$A = P*(1+I)\hat{}N$$

| | A | B | C | D | E | F | G |
|---|---|---|---|---|---|---|---|
| 1 | | Sales volume (units) | | | | | |
| 2 | | Region 1 | Region 2 | Region 3 | Region 6 | Region 7 | Total all regions |
| 3 | Product 1 | 2034 | 1056 | 8256 | 478 | 2045 | |
| 4 | Product 2 | 3012 | 2356 | 7145 | 721 | 2903 | |
| 5 | Product 3 | 1034 | 1691 | 6918 | 319 | 1402 | |
| 6 | Product 7 | 1298 | 1732 | 7024 | 408 | 1382 | |
| 7 | Product 8 | 3678 | 4891 | 12579 | 800 | 3819 | |
| 8 | Product 9 | 5612 | 3215 | 9120 | 792 | 4956 | |
| 9 | Product 10 | 4301 | 3710 | 9818 | 653 | 4642 | |
| 10 | Product 11 | 2981 | 2198 | 8156 | 812 | 3001 | |
| 11 | Total all products | | | | | | |

**Workbook 1.9**

Enter the following labels to the A1:A4 range of a worksheet:

Principal   Interest Rate   Number of years   Amount

Now enter the following data to the B1:B3 range:

2500   8.5%   25

Name the cells B1, B2 and B3 as P, I and N respectively and then use these names to write a formula for the accumulated amount in B4.

## Exercise 1.11

Prepare the model shown in Workbook 1.9 or load it (W1_9.xls) from the online resource centre.

Write and copy formulae for the totals in row 11 and column G.

Now insert as many rows and columns as are required to make the product and region numbers continuous.

Check that the formulae for the totals have adjusted appropriately.

## Exercise 1.12

In each of the following cases identify the exact nature of the error committed.

(a) Task: to make the value in A1 (100 say) increase by 20% of its value
    Formula 1:   =A1*0.2
    Formula 2:   0.2*A1
    Formula 3   A1+0.2*A1

(b) Task: to sum all the values in A1:A4
    Formula 1:   =SUM(A1:A3)
    Formula 2:   SUM(A1:A4)
    Formula 3:   =SUM(A1:A6)
    Formula 4:   A1+A2+A3+A4

(c) Task: to write a formula in B1 that can be copied down B20 and will multiply each
of the values in A1:A20 by whatever value is contained in the C1 cell.
Formula 1   =A1*C1
Formula 2   =A1*$C1
Formula 3   =A1+C$1

(d) Task: to write a formula in B1 that can be copied down to B20 and will calculate the
running total[11] of whatever values are contained in A1:A20.
Formula 1:   =SUM(A1:A20)
Formula 2:   =SUM(A1:A$20)
Formula 3:   =SUM(A$1:A20)
Formula 4:   =SAM(A$1:A1)

## 1.11 Solutions to the exercises

### Solutions to Exercise 1.1

(a) A cell

(b) H21 (not 21H)

(c) Worksheets

(d) A bold or different coloured border

(e) Only when it is active

(f) Click on the cell with the mouse, or use the cursor keys, or any of Goto, Home, End
down arrow

(g) 256 columns and 16384 rows

(h) In the cell itself and on the Formula bar

(i) End and then down arrow and then End and right arrow

(j) F5 (Goto) and then type BZ9999

### Solutions to Exercise 1.2

(a) $10 + 8 = 18$

(b) $20 + 9 = 29$

(c) $5 + 18/9 = 5 + 2 = 7$

(d) $27/9 = 3$

(e) $(1 + 6)\hat{}2 = 7\hat{}2 = 49$

(f) This is a text entry, but if the equals sign were there, then $3 + 20 = 23$

(g) $(3 + 12)*4 = 15 * 4 = 60$

(h) $3 + 2*6*10 = 3 + 120 = 123$

(i)  $(5*5)^2 = 25^2 = 625$   ('inside-out' evaluation of the brackets)

(j)  $5*5^2 = 5*25 = 125$   ('inside-out' evaluation of the brackets)

(k)  $(9 + 1)*2^3 = 10*8 = 80$

(l)  $104/8 = 13$

(m)  $16/8 = 2$

(n)  $4^1{}^3 = 4^3 = 64$

## Solutions to Exercise 1.3

(a)  Number

(b)  Text

(c)  Text

(d)  Text

(e)  Text

(f)  Formula and number

(g)  Text

(h)  Formula and number

(i)  Function

(j)  Text

(k)  Formula and Function

(l)  Number, formula and function

## Solutions to Exercise 1.4

(a)  Click on A1, depress the left hand mouse button and *with it still depressed*, drag down to A6 and then across to C6. Select the **I** icon and then the **U** icon from the toolbar.

(b)  With A1:C6 still selected, Choose **Edit** and then **Cut**. Now click on the A8 cell and press enter or select **Edit** and then **Paste**.

(c)  Select A8:C13 and then **Edit** and **Clear**. Thereafter, choose **Contents**.

(d)  Select A8:C13 and then **Edit** and **Clear**. Now choose **All**.

(e)  Select A8:C13 and click on the **B** icon on the toolbar.

## Solution to Exercise 1.5

With A1 containing the text entry:

  January

Click on A1, use the mouse to activate the handle by clicking on the bottom right hand corner of the cell until a black cross appears. Then drag down to A12.

The sequence January February etc. will be generated.

## Solution to Exercise 1.6

In A1, enter:

Profits 1980

Click on A1 and then point to the handle on the bottom right hand corner with the mouse. When the solid white cross turns to less solid black, depress the left hand mouse button and drag down to row 41.

## Solution to Exercise 1.7

In A1 enter:

4

In A2 enter:

=A1+5

Click on A2, activate the handle, and drag down to A20. The series:

=A1+5; =A2+5; =A3+5 . . . =A19+5

will be created in A2:A20.

## Solution to Exercise 1.8

The formulae in C6, D6, E6 and F6 should be:

**in C6: =C\$3\*B6**

**in D6: =B6+C6**

**in E6: =E\$3\*D6**

**in F6: =D6+E6**

Now select C6:F6, activate the handle and drag down this block of cells to row 16. The four source formulae will be copied.

The results should resemble those shown in Workbook 1.10

## Solution to Exercise 1.9

Select A1 and then from the main menu select Insert and then Name and Define. At the prompt enter the required name as AONE. Now select the A2 cell and repeat this process. Enter values of 10 and 15 to A1 and A2 respectively and then in A3 enter:

=AONE\*ATWO

The result should be 150.

|   | A | B | C | D | E | F |
|---|---|---|---|---|---|---|
| 1 |  |  | Interest |  | Interest |  |
| 2 |  |  | rate 1998 |  | rate 1999 |  |
| 3 |  |  | 7.20% |  | 8.40% |  |
| 4 |  | Balance @ | Interest | Balance @ | Interest | Balance @ |
| 5 | Account No. | 31st Dec1997 | 1998 | 31st Dec 1998 | 1999 | 31st Dec 1999 |
| 6 | 1236 | 2045 | 147.24 | 2192.24 | 184.15 | 2376.39 |
| 7 | 1469 | 11213 | 807.34 | 12020.34 | 1009.71 | 13030.04 |
| 8 | 1578 | 23198 | 1670.26 | 24868.26 | 2088.93 | 26957.19 |
| 9 | 1789 | 3578 | 257.62 | 3835.62 | 322.19 | 4157.81 |
| 10 | 1791 | 4901 | 352.87 | 5253.87 | 441.33 | 5695.20 |
| 11 | 1810 | 5109 | 367.85 | 5476.85 | 460.06 | 5936.90 |
| 12 | 1919 | 17451 | 1256.47 | 18707.47 | 1571.43 | 20278.90 |
| 13 | 1945 | 21997 | 1583.78 | 23580.78 | 1980.79 | 25561.57 |
| 14 | 1989 | 16718 | 1203.70 | 17921.70 | 1505.42 | 19427.12 |
| 15 | 2012 | 13109 | 943.85 | 14052.85 | 1180.44 | 15233.29 |
| 16 | 2367 | 1098 | 79.06 | 1177.06 | 98.87 | 1275.93 |
| 17 |  |  |  |  |  |  |

**Workbook 1.10**

## Solution to Exercise 1.10

Click on B1 and then select **Insert** then **Name** and then **Define** from the Menu bar. Enter P as the name for B1.

Click on B2 and repeat the process only this time supply the name I.

Click on B3 and repeat for the name N.

Click on B4 and enter:

$$=P*(1+I)^\wedge N$$

A result of 19216.91 will be returned.

## Solution to Exercise 1.11

The formula in B11 should be:

$$=SUM(B3:B10)$$

and must be copied along into C11:G11.

The formula in G3 should be:

$$=SUM(B3:F3)$$

and must be copied down into G4:G10.

This procedure produces the row and column totals as well as the grand total in G11.

There are three rows missing, (Products 4, 5 and 6), so click on A6 and drag down to A8. Select **Insert** and then **Rows** from the Menu bar. Three rows will be inserted.

There are two columns missing, (Regions 4 and 5), so click on E1 and drag along to F1. Select **Insert** and then **Columns** and two columns will be inserted.

Click on B14 and then I3 to confirm that the range of rows to be summed has changed from B3:B10 to B3: B13 and the range of columns to be summed has changed from B3:F3 to B3:H3.

The rest of the totalling formulae have also adjusted appropriately and will automatically accommodate any new data that are entered to the cells that have been created.

## Solutions to Exercise 1.12

(a) Task: To make the value in A1 (100 say) increase by 20% of its value

Formula 1:  =A1*0.2   Syntax correct   Logic incorrect since this only calculates the increase to be made (20) not the result of applying the increase (120).

Formula 2:  0.2*A1   Syntax incorrect   since equals sign is missing,
Logic incorrect for the same reason as above

Formula 3   A1+0.2*A1   Syntax incorrect since equals sign is missing,
Logic correct i.e. the value in A1 plus 0.2 times that value.
The correct solution would be:
=A1+0.2*A1   or its equivalent:=0.2$*A1+A1    or even =A1*0.2+A1

(b) Task: To sum all the values in A1:A4

Formula 1:  =SUM(A1:A3)   Syntax correct   Logic incorrect since this only calculates the sum of three cells. It would therefore only be correct if A4 always contained zero

Formula 2:  SUM(A1:A4)   Syntax incorrect since equals sign is missing, Logic correct

Formula 3:  =SUM(A1:A6)   Syntax correct   Logic incorrect since this calculates the sum of two extra cells. It would therefore only be correct if A5 and A6 always contained zero

Formula 4:  A1+A2+A3+A4   Syntax incorrect since equals sign is missing.   Logic correct although inefficient in comparison to the SUM function.
The most succinct solution is:  =SUM(A1:A4)

(c) Task: To write a formula in B1 that can be copied down B20 and will multiply each of the values in A1:A20 by whatever value is contained in the C1 cell.

Formula 1  =A1*C1   Syntax correct   Logic incorrect since this will allow both the A1 and the C1 references to update when copied. It would produce =A2*C2 in B2, =A3*C3 in B3 and so on. Clearly we require the column A references to update in this way but not the one in column C. That is, we always want to refer to C1.

Formula 2  =A1*$C1   Syntax correct   Logic incorrect since this will allow both the A1 and the C1 references to update when copied. The dollar sign in front of the column letter has no effect when copied down rows. In other words $C1 will update when copied down rows in exactly the same way as C1.

Formula 3   =A1+C$1   Syntax correct   Logic incorrect since this adds the fixed row reference in C1 to the values in column A instead of multiplying them. However, if we change operator from plus to multiply the required result is obtained. That is: =A1*C$1   When copied this will produce =A2*C$1 in B2, =A3*C$1 in B3 and so on.

(d) Task: to write a formula in B1 that can be copied down to B20 and will calculate the running total of whatever values are contained in A1:A20.

Formula 1:   =SUM(A1:A20)   Syntax correct   Logic incorrect since both the A1 and the A20 references will update when copied to produce: =SUM(A2:A21) in B2, =SUM(A3:A22) in B3 and so on.

Formula 2:   =SUM(A1:A$20)   Syntax correct   Logic incorrect since the A1 reference will update when copied to produce: =SUM(A2:A20) in B2, =SUM(A3:A20) in B3 and so on.

Formula 3:   =SUM(A$1:A20)   Syntax correct   Logic incorrect since the A20 reference will update when copied to produce: =SUM(A1:A21) in B2, =SUM(A1:A22) in B3 and so on.

Formula 4:   =SAM(A$1:A1)   Syntax incorrect since SAM is not a recognized function Logic correct since copying will produce: =SUM(A1:A2) in B2, =SUM(A1:A3) in B3, =SUM(A1:A4) in B4 and so on. This is exactly what is required for a running total. Consequently the solution is: =SUM(A$1:A1)

## ■ NOTES

1. This chapter may be omitted, browsed or read selectively by those readers who are experienced Excel users.

2. There are a few exceptions to this: £, $ and % characters for example.

3. If the result is not correct then the chances are that the formula in A3 has not been entered correctly. There must be no spaces before the equals sign and no spaces between any of the subsequent characters.

4. If you simply want to erase the contents of a range of cells while retaining any formatting (bold, currency or whatever) then select **Contents** instead of **All**. The data in the cells will be removed but the formatting will remain.

5. Excel also allows you to copy text entries such as Mon or Monday, or Jan or January in a 'clever' way. When either of the former two is copied the days of the week are produced, while copying either of the latter two produces the months of the year.

6. **Do not activate the handle.**

7. If it does not show this, erase what is there and then click on B1,or type in the reference as =Sheet1!$B$1.

8. More care has to be exercised with deletion of rows or columns than with insertions. This is because the removal of a row or column can erase data that need to be used by some formulae or functions elsewhere in the sheet. If this happens one or more #REF! messages will appear and the first thing to do is click on the Undo icon on the toolbar (a curved left-pointing blue arrow). This will undo the deletion and restore the integrity of the model.

9. **Do not** include a space between the 3 of 2003 and the D of DATA.

10. An exception to this would be the expression:

$$= 5/0$$

which is perfect syntax but runs up against the mathematical problem that anything divided by zero is infinity and so Excel returns the error message: DIV0!

11. A running total is simply the sum to date of the numbers used. For example, the running totals of the numbers 1, 2, 3, are 1, 3, 6, i.e. 1, $1 + 2$, $1 + 2 + 3$.

# 2 | Understanding data

The following files from the online resource centre should be loaded as instructed:

W2_1.xls     W2_2.xls

## 2.1 What are data?

Regardless of the field of study undertaken, there will always be a need to provide various types of evidence in support of the statements, propositions and conclusions contained in essays, presentations, reports or dissertations.

The basic constituent of this evidence base is known as **data**, and it is the main function of data analysis to develop methods of transforming raw data into usable information. This is because data and information are not really the same thing.

To use an analogy, a data element can be thought of as a single building brick and a collection of such bricks is a data set. When these bricks are first delivered they are without structure, but once ordered and assembled they can become a house or a monument or suchlike. Returning to the analogy, therefore, it is this process of ordering and assembling data sets that can convert data into something usable, i.e. information. This information can then be used as supportive evidence for the logical statement(s) being proposed as part of the study.

A **data element** is simply the recorded observation of a specific property possessed by a member of a particular group of individuals or objects. Some examples are:

**Table 2.1**

| Record Number | Age | Gender |
|:---:|:---:|:---:|
| 6 | 23 | F |
| 121 | 37 | M |

Individual Number 121 was 37 on his last birthday.

Car Number 102346 had 9 faults at pre-delivery.

Individual Number 6 was 23 on her last birthday.

Country 4 had a 5.6% unemployment rate.

Here, the data in each line are what is known as a **record**, and each record contains data on one or more **field variables**. For example, Individual Number 121 is a record, and it contains data for one extra field—'Age last birthday'.

When data elements are *consistently* gathered together then a **data set** is obtained, although it is important to understand what is meant by 'consistent'. Clearly some data elements cannot be combined sensibly—'Individuals' and 'Cars' in our example.

On the other hand, it may be possible to combine the data elements of the 'Individuals' field consistently. To see this suppose it was observed that:

Individual Number 121 was 37 on *his* last birthday.

Individual Number 6 was 23 on *her* last birthday.

This produces a two-record data set with data on three field variables—Record Number, Age Last Birthday, and Gender.

In Excel this could appear as in Table 2.1.

From this it should be clear that any one record contains data for all of the fields, while any one field contains data for all of the records (apart from any missing values, of course).

Furthermore, the intersection between any individual field and any individual record is a data element and in Excel will occupy one single cell.

There are many different types of data, but before discussing them in detail the fundamental distinction between **qualitative** and **quantitative** data sets must be understood.

The basis of the distinction is measurability—or more precisely, what properties of the variable can be measured and in what way.

## 2.2 Quantitative data

For quantitative data, measurement is precise (although not necessarily accurate).[1] A precise number will be obtained such as 34, 15.2 or 12.345.

Importantly, the significance of precise numerical measurement is that it allows any two or more data elements to be compared with an equivalent precision. For example, suppose that there are two interest rate observations, 5.4% and 6.0%, for two different banks. These data not only allow us to say that the second bank's interest rate is higher than the first's, but also allows us to quote the magnitude of the difference (0.6%). They also allow us to perform various other arithmetic operations such as sorting and counting with the expectation of sensible results.

As we will see later, this is not always the case for other types of data.

It should now be noted that quantitative data can be classified into a further two types—**discrete** and **continuous**.

## 2.2.1 **Discrete data**

A data set is said to be discrete if the values that can be adopted are separate and distinct.

Often, discrete data sets will consist of whole numbers (integers) and can represent variables such as:

(a) The number of children under 16 in a group of households.

(b) The number of students enrolled on a suite of university degree programmes.

(c) The number of accidents on a stretch of motorway over a given number of days.

Clearly the prominent feature in each of these cases is that non-integer values such as 0.5 or 1.5 can never be observed.

Now suppose that for the variable in (c) above we obtained the data shown in Table 2.2. This is a discrete data set containing the number of accidents occurring on each of nine recorded days. Importantly, it can be analysed in a variety of ways that will be detailed later. For the moment it is enough to note that the maximum number of accidents occurring on any one day was four and the minimum was zero. This gives us some information on the *range* of accident occurrences.

## 2.2.2 **Continuous data**

When the elements of a data set are capable of being measured to a large number of decimal places, then the data are said to be continuous. This means that there are no 'gaps' between whole-number values.

Very few real data sets are truly continuous, since there are always limitations on measurement precision. However, variables measured in units of time, weight or temperature are usually taken to be more or less continuous, given modern measuring devices. Nevertheless, truly continuous data implies that if observation one has a recorded value of 5.123456, and observation two has a value of 5.123457, it will still be theoretically possible to obtain a value for observation three that is between these two values (5.1234565, for example).

**Table 2.2**

| Day | 1 | 2 | 3 | 4 | 5 | 6 | 7 | 8 | 9 |
|---|---|---|---|---|---|---|---|---|---|
| No. of Accidents | 3 | 0 | 1 | 2 | 0 | 4 | 2 | 1 | 2 |

## 2.3 Qualitative data

Qualitative data are usually in text form, and will often be the result of interview or questionnaire responses to a range of questions that have been asked.

In simple cases this may be no more than a simple Yes/No option (or Yes/Unsure/No), but in other cases it may be a letter corresponding to the respondent's preferred choice from a list of offered options (A, B, C, D, E, F, etc.)

In either of these cases the possible responses are highly *structured* in the sense that there are only a few legitimate categories allowed for responses. For this reason data such as these are known as **categorical**.

### 2.3.1 Categorical data

A categorical data set is one in which the data elements belonging to it can be arranged according to their membership of various non-overlapping categories. Consequently, categorical data are discrete.

We have already encountered such data in the Yes/No illustration, but other examples would be Marital Status—D(ivorced), M(arried), S(ingle); or Nationality—E(nglish), I(rish), W(elsh), S(cottish).

With categorical data, counting the number of responses in each category is really the only sensible calculation that can be done. Ranking and measurement are not possible since the values do not measure anything, and therefore do not allow us to say that one value is greater or less than any other is.

With small categorical data sets counting the responses in each category will usually be a simple task. However, as the number of observations in the data set increases the counting task becomes ever more tedious. This is where Excel can help.

To follow the discussion, take a blank Excel worksheet and then make the following entries:

A1: Respondent No.      B1:Response (N/U/Y)[2]

Note that these entries are merely identification labels.

Now place the numbers 1 to 10 in A2:A11, and the following hypothetical responses in B2:B11:

Y N U Y Y Y N Y Y N

Simple inspection allows us to say that there were 3 N responses, 1 U response and 6 Y responses, but the question arises of how to get Excel to produce these results.

First of all, place the labels Total N, Total U, Total Y and Total All in A13:D13.

Now, since we want to count the number of responses in each category, we are going to use an Excel function called **COUNTIF**. The general syntax of this function is:

$$= \text{COUNTIF(Data range in which to count, ``Indicator of}$$
$$\text{which values are to be counted'')}$$

**Table 2.3**

|          | A       | B       | C       | D         |
|----------|---------|---------|---------|-----------|
| Row 13   | Total N | Total U | Total Y | Total All |
| Row 14   | 3       | 1       | 6       | 10        |

Applying this syntax to the current example means that we should use A14 to contain:

$$=COUNTIF(B2:B11,"=N")^3$$

*Do this now.*

When this has been done the correct answer of 3 will be returned.

*Now make the following further entries in B14:D14.*

In B14     =COUNTIF(B2:B11,"= U")   In C14     =COUNTIF(B2:B11,"= Y")

In D14     =SUM(A14:C14)

Notice that the function in D14 simply adds up (sums) the values in A14:C14 to give the total number of responses.

Rows 13 and 14 of your worksheet should now resemble Table 2.3, and clearly indicate the power of the COUNTIF function if large data sets are being used.

We should now note that the data in row 14 are known as **absolute** in the sense that they are not related to the total number of responses. In many cases, however, it will be wise to convert these absolute values into **relative** ones, by expressing each category total as a proportion or percentage of the Grand Total (10 in the example).

*To do this, place the labels Total N%, Total U%, Total Y% and Total All%, in*

**A15:D15.**

*Then use A16:D16 to house the following formulae and functions:*

In A16     =A14/D14

This expresses B14 (the number of N responses) as a proportion of D14 (the total number of responses), and should return a value of 0.3 (3/10). This is the decimal equivalent of 30%, but if we want to show all of the proportions in percentage format, select A16:D16 then from the main menu select:

Format, Cells, Number, Percentage, OK

*Do this now.*

The already computed value in A16 (0.3) will now appear as 30.00% since the default setting of two decimal places was accepted, and the next three cells will be formatted to percentage when calculated.

**Table 2.4**

|        | A          | B          | C          | D          |
|--------|------------|------------|------------|------------|
| Row 13 | Total N    | Total U    | Total Y    | Total All  |
| Row 14 | 3          | 1          | 6          | 10         |
| Row 15 | Total N %  | Total U %  | Total Y%   | Total All% |
| Row 16 | 30.0%      | 10.0%      | 60.0%      | 100.0%     |

*To perform these calculations place the following expressions in the remaining three cells*

    In B16     =B14/D14   In C16     =C14/D14
    In D16     =SUM(A16:C16)

The end result should resemble Table 2.4.[4]

Clearly, the result of these calculations has been to turn raw categorical data into information that can more easily be reported. This is because we could now propose statements such as:

    'The data show that more than half of the respondents agreed with the question posed'

    'Only 10% of the respondents were unsure whether they agreed or disagreed with the question posed'.

*Now attempt Exercises 2.1 and 2.2.*

### 2.3.2 Ordinal data

**Ordinal** data sets occur when the observation values they contain can be interpreted in terms of a respondent's preferred choices from a list of options. For example, suppose that a respondent was asked to rank the five terrestrial television channels in terms of those that they like best, to those that they like least. Clearly the respondent must have been told what responses can be made and also what they mean, so the question posed should have been phrased along the following lines.

    'With 1 representing "like best", 5 representing "like least" and 2, 3, 4 representing intermediate evaluations, rank the following terrestrial television channels in order of preference.'

    Now suppose that an individual responded as shown in Table 2.5

The rank variable is discrete and consists of the five allowed values. However, unlike most categorical data the responses allow us to order or rank the data in terms of preference.

**Table 2.5**

| Channel | BBC1 | BBC2 | ITV1 | C4 | C5 |
|---------|------|------|------|----|----|
| Rank    | 2    | 5    | 1    | 3  | 4  |

**Table 2.6**

| Channel | ITV1 | BBC1 | C4 | C5 | BBC2 |
|---------|------|------|-----|-----|------|
| Rank | 1 | 2 | 3 | 4 | 5 |

Hence a reordering of the table from left to right in order of most preferred would produce the results shown in Table 2.6.

From this it might be thought that ordinal data are in fact quantitative rather than qualitative, but this is to forget the crucial importance of measurement. In other words, although ordinal data support ranking they do not allow us to say by *how much* one ranking is superior or inferior to another. To be sure, a rank difference could be computed, such as BBC2 rank (5) minus BBC1 rank (2) = 3. Yet it should be clear that this figure is difficult to interpret since there are no units of measurement involved. In effect we are asking the question: 'How much is BBC1 preferred to BBC2?', to which there is no sensible numerical answer.

All we can legitimately say is that this respondent prefers BBC1 to BBC2, with the extent of this preference being immeasurable (and certainly not equal to three).

## 2.4 Exercises

### Exercise 2.1

Load the file called W2_1.xls.

Here the values in column A are 200 numbers produced by a roulette wheel with numbers zero to thirty-six.

(a) Use Excel to determine the number of spins in which the selected number was more than 18.

(b) Calculate the percentage of all numbers selected that were greater than 18.

### Exercise 2.2

Using the data from Exercise 2.1 devise a method of getting Excel to calculate how many selected numbers were odd. Hint: the feature of an odd number is that when divided by two a remainder of one is obtained, whereas the remainder is zero if the number is even. Excel can calculate the remainder from the =MOD function:

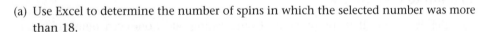

$$=MOD(Value, Divisor)$$

This should allow each number that occurred to be reclassified as either 1 or 0 depending upon whether it is odd or even.

## 2.5 Solutions to the exercises

### Solution to Exercise 2.1

(a)  Use the B1 cell to contain:

$$=COUNTIF(A2:A4000,`` > 18'')$$

Notice that we have used the range A2:A4000 in this function to allow for the results of subsequent spins to be entered in A202 and below.

For the data being used this should return a value of 78 for selections that are greater than 18.

(b)  The simplest solution would be to use B2 to contain:

$$=COUNTIF(A2:A4000,`` > 18'')/200$$

However this would only be correct if subsequent spins could not take place.

Better is to count the total number of values in column A with the following function:

$$=COUNT(A2:A4000)$$

and replace the fixed value of 200 with this function.
That is, use B2 to contain:

$$=COUNTIF(A2:A4000,`` > 18'')/COUNT(A2:A4000)$$

In this way additional data from subsequent spins will be accommodated automatically by Excel without and need to edit formulae.

A result of 39.00% should be obtained and implies that there would appear to be a slight bias in favour of numbers lower than 19.

### Solution to Exercise 2.2

The trick is to note that the property distinguishing odd from even numbers is that when divided by two odd numbers have a remainder of one whereas even numbers do not—the remainder is zero.

Now we should note that Excel has a dedicated function that will calculate the remainder of any number divided by any other. It is called MOD and has the following syntax:

$$=MOD(Value,Divisor)$$

Consequently, use the F2 cell say of the W2_1.xls file to contain:

$$=MOD(A2,2)$$

Then copy this down to F201.

Column F will now contain either 1 or 0 depending upon whether the number is odd or even.

Finally, use G1 say, to contain:

$$=COUNTIF(F2:F201,"=1")$$

For the data being used this should return a value of 86 for the number of odd numbers, implying that there were $200 - 86 = 114$ even numbers.

A completed version of this procedure is contained in the W2_2.xls file on the online resource centre.

■ **NOTES**

1. To appreciate this distinction think of a watch that keeps erratic time—the quoted time will be precise but it is unlikely to be accurate.

2. N(o), U(nsure), Y(es).

3. As another example =COUNTIF(B1:B11,">7") would count the number of values in the B1:B11 range that were greater than 7.

4. We could have used the Copy facility here. In A16 enter :
=A14/$D14
and then copy into B16:D16

# 3

# Data handling

The following files from the online resource centre should be loaded as instructed:

W3_1.xls   W3_2A.xls   W3_3.xls
W3_3A.xls   W3_4.xls   W3_5.xls
W3_6.xls

## 3.1 Sorting data

One of Excel's most powerful features is the ability to perform sophisticated data sorting. This was done manually in the previous chapter when the rankings of the TV channels were reordered from their original order to an order of most preferred channels.

To follow the argument consider the illustration shown in Workbook 3.1.

***Make this model up for yourself or load it from the online resource centre (W3_1.xls).***

Here, we have selected financial data for a list of hypothetical shares. The column headers at the top of the sheet identify what are known as **fields** and the individual share names are known as **records**. Thus, each field contains information on **all** the records and each record has information from **all** the fields.

Before proceeding to the sorting procedure, it will be useful to note the field data types. Share Name is a text variable and, as long as each share has a different name, can be used as a unique identification index for any record.

Share Price and Dividend are semi-continuous quantitative variables which may in fact have been truly continuous but like most currency data have been quoted to two decimal places.

| | A | B | C | D |
|---|---|---|---|---|
| 1 | Share Name | Share Price (£) | Dividend (£) | Capital gain % |
| 2 | Pandora | 0.95 | 0.19 | 5.60% |
| 3 | Pan-europe | 2.5 | 0.26 | 15.60% |
| 4 | IFI | 0.95 | 0.19 | 7.10% |
| 5 | MBI | 0.99 | 0.18 | 1.30% |
| 6 | Gloxo | 3.21 | 0.5 | 10.10% |
| 7 | PR&W | 2.03 | 0.49 | 2.90% |
| 8 | AM&M | 1.5 | 0.31 | 6.80% |
| 9 | Devoors | 1.5 | 0.31 | 8.90% |
| 10 | Brutus | 2.5 | 0.35 | 14.50% |
| 11 | Cathedral Life | 2.43 | 0.34 | 3.50% |
| 12 | Spoolers | 0.95 | 0.19 | 9.70% |
| 13 | Costcut | 2.5 | 0.35 | 12.40% |
| 14 | Credit Alpha | 12.21 | 1.65 | 5.20% |
| 15 | Commercial Plus | 1.67 | 0.21 | 9.10% |
| 16 | Agricola | 0.65 | 0.12 | 10.50% |
| 17 | Regal Bank | 1.56 | 0.4 | 5.80% |

**Workbook 3.1**

Capital Gain is a continuous variable that measures the difference between the selling price and the purchase price of the share expressed as a percentage of the purchase price.

For example, if the purchase price of the Pandora share were £ 0.90, and if it can now be sold for £ 0.95, then the capital gain per share would be calculated as:

$$(0.95 — 0.9)/0.9 = 0.05555 = 5.6\% \text{ when rounded up.}$$

Inspection of the data indicates that there are several groups of shares with the same price.

It should also be clear that *of those shares with the same price* some also have the same dividend payment. However, in this illustration there are *no* shares with the same price **and** the same dividend payment **and** the same percentage capital gain.

Next, it will be observed that the data have not been sorted into any kind of order.

The task to be undertaken is to sort the data in descending order of Share Price and then, since some of these prices are the same, to use the Dividend payment to distinguish between shares that are tied in terms of price. Once again, descending order will be used, so in the eventual sorted list two or more shares with the same price will subsequently be ranked from high to low in terms of their dividend payment.

Even then, as we have seen, there are some shares in the list that cannot be distinguished **either** on their price **or** on their dividend payment. Consequently, we will use their capital gain as the third way of separating tied ranks—once again on the basis of descending numerical value.

*To initiate the sorting procedure the first thing to do is select the entire area from A1 to D17 as the range to be sorted. This is crucial.*

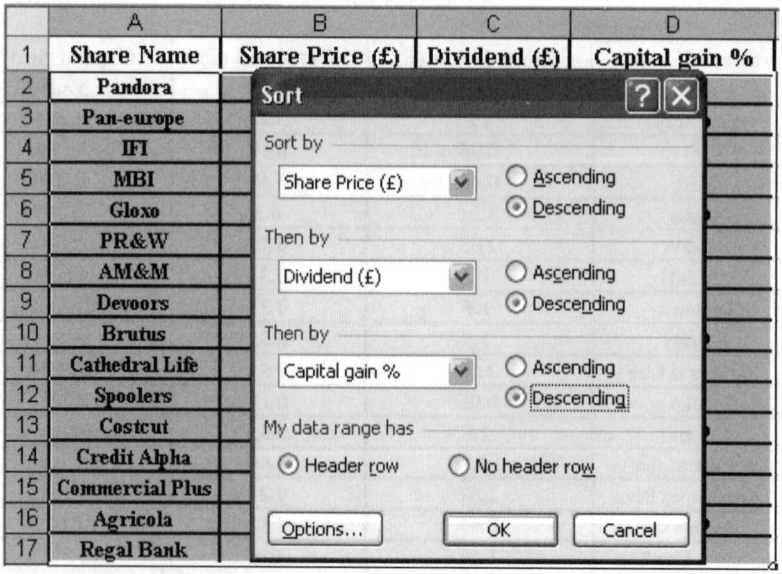

**Figure 3.1**

To understand the importance of this point remember that although we are **not** going to use the share names as a way of sorting, if they are **not** included in the sort area they will become **detached** from their field data on price, dividend and capital gain once we use this last information as the basis of the sorting process. Detaching one or more field values from their rightful owner in the sorting process is the commonest cause of what is euphemistically called 'computer error' and is usually enough to explain how, for example, Joe Lectric, who uses gas only to cook with, receives ICI's quarterly gas bill.

Put simply, if your worksheet contains 8 fields and 20 records, say, and even if you intend sorting those records only on the basis of **one** of those fields, **all** 8 fields and **all** 20 records must be included in the range selected for the sort.[1]

*Consequently, with the A1:D17 range selected, choose Data and then Sort from the Menu bar.*

The dialogue screen shown in Figure 3.1 should appear.

The illustrated dialogue box was created by clicking on the **Sort By** tab and selecting Share Price as the basis of the **primary** sort from the list of available fields that then appears. The **Descending** button alongside was also clicked. The **secondary** sort, to differentiate tied ranks, was defined by clicking on the first **Then By** tab and then selecting Dividend from the list and also choosing Descending. Finally, the **tertiary** sort, to differentiate between records that are tied on both the primary and the secondary sort, was defined by clicking on the second **Then By** tab and selecting Capital Gain from the list. Descending order was again selected.

| | A | B | C | D |
|---|---|---|---|---|
| 1 | Share Name | Share Price (£) | Dividend (£) | Capital gain % |
| 2 | Credit Alpha | 12.21 | 1.65 | 5.20% |
| 3 | Gloxo | 3.21 | 0.5 | 10.10% |
| 4 | Brutus | 2.5 | 0.35 | 14.50% |
| 5 | Costcut | 2.5 | 0.35 | 12.40% |
| 6 | Pan-europe | 2.5 | 0.26 | 15.60% |
| 7 | Cathedral Life | 2.43 | 0.34 | 3.50% |
| 8 | PR&W | 2.03 | 0.49 | 2.90% |
| 9 | Commercial Plus | 1.67 | 0.21 | 9.10% |
| 10 | Regal Bank | 1.56 | 0.4 | 5.80% |
| 11 | Devoors | 1.5 | 0.31 | 8.90% |
| 12 | AM&M | 1.5 | 0.31 | 6.80% |
| 13 | MBI | 0.99 | 0.18 | 1.30% |
| 14 | Spoolers | 0.95 | 0.19 | 9.70% |
| 15 | IFI | 0.95 | 0.19 | 7.10% |
| 16 | Pandora | 0.95 | 0.19 | 5.60% |
| 17 | Agricola | 0.65 | 0.12 | 10.50% |

**Workbook 3.2**

Finally, since in the range we defined (A1:D17) the first row contains headers, we make sure that the Header Row box is checked.

*Carry out these procedures now and click OK.*

The results of this three-way sort are shown in Workbook 3.2.

*Save this sorted worksheet now as* W3_2.xls *since we will be using it again in the next section.*

As you can see, Brutus, Costcut and Pan-europe are all tied on Share Price, but Brutus and Costcut are placed above Pan-europe as a result of their higher dividend. Finally, although Brutus and Costcut are tied on both Share Price and Dividend, the higher Capital Gain for Brutus allows it to be placed above Costcut.

A similar process operates for the other shares that are tied on share price.

It is now an easy matter to change the sort settings to focus on a different field variable as the primary basis of the sort. Simply select Sort from the menu and change the 'Sort by:' field settings to the order required. For example, Table 3.1 shows the first seven rows (six records) that result from sorting the data set in ascending order of dividend, with any tied ranks then sorted in ascending order of share price, and then in ascending order of capital gain. Confirm this now in your own worksheet but do not save the new ordering.

*Now attempt Exercise 3.1.*

**Table 3.1**

| Share Name | Share Price (£) | Dividend (£) | Capital gain % |
|---|---|---|---|
| Agricola | 0.65 | 0.12 | 10.50% |
| MBI | 0.99 | 0.18 | 1.30% |
| Pandora | 0.95 | 0.19 | 5.60% |
| IFI | 0.95 | 0.19 | 7.10% |
| Spoolers | 0.95 | 0.19 | 9.70% |
| Commercial Plus | 1.67 | 0.21 | 9.10% |

## 3.2 Filtering data

Filtering data is the process of selecting those records from a list that meet certain requirements (**criteria**) defined by the user. It might, for instance, be all female records or all married individuals or even all females who are **also** married.

The ultimate objective of filtering is to get Excel to interrogate the data list in terms of questions to which answers are required and clearly these answers will themselves be a list of records that meet the requirements of our questions.

*To follow the argument open Workbook 3.2 (W3_2.xls) now.*

You should have the sorted list of financial data for the portfolio of shares on screen. If not, load W3_2A.xls

To initiate the filtering process, the first thing to do is identify all of the **field names** to Excel.

*Do this now by clicking on A1 and dragging along to D1.*

The cells containing all of the field headers are now selected.

*Next, choose Data and then Filter and then AutoFilter from the Menu bar.*

When you have done this, it should be found that four arrow tabs have been inserted to the cells containing the field names (A1:D1).

*To interrogate this data list simply click on the arrow tab in the field that relates to the question that you want to ask.*

For example, in the current illustration, suppose that we want to create a list of all shares with a Capital Gain that was more than 10%.

*To do this, click on the arrow tab in the D1 cell (since this is the top of the capital gain field) and from the prompt that appears select {Custom . . .}. The dialogue box shown in Figure 3.2 will appear.*

*Now click on the top left-hand tab to obtain a list of arithmetic operators and from this list select 'greater than'.*

*Next, click on the adjacent box and enter the criterion (10% in this case).*

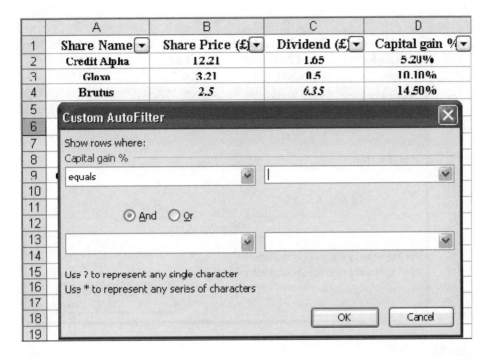

**Figure 3.2**

The dialogue box should now resemble Figure 3.3.

*If it does, click on OK and the list will be filtered.*

The effect should be the same as indicated in Workbook 3.3.

Notice that the arrow tab in D1 has turned from black to blue, indicating that this is a **filtered** list and the row numbers of the filtered records are now also blue.

To restore the original list simply click on the (blue) arrow tab and select {All} from the prompt that follows.

All of the original records will be restored on screen and the arrow tab will return to its normal black colour.

*Do this now.*

Now suppose we wanted a list of all shares whose Capital Gain was greater than 10% **but did not exceed** 13%.

The Custom AutoFilter dialogue box also has a second set of tabs towards the bottom of the box, that allow more complex questions to be asked.

*To do this, click on the arrow tab in the Capital Gain field (D1) and then select {Custom...}. Then select 'greater than' and enter 10% in the top right box. Next, making sure that And is checked in the middle of the screen select 'less than' and enter 13% in the bottom box.*

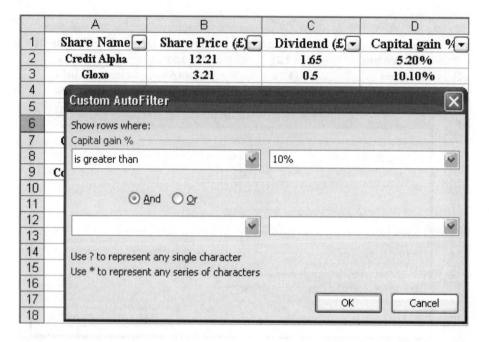

|   | A | B | C | D |
|---|---|---|---|---|
| 1 | Share Name ▾ | Share Price (£) ▾ | Dividend (£) ▾ | Capital gain % ▾ |
| 2 | Credit Alpha | 12.21 | 1.65 | 5.20% |
| 3 | Gloxo | 3.21 | 0.5 | 10.10% |
| 4 | | | | |
| 5 | | | | |
| 6 | | | | |

**Custom AutoFilter** ✕

Show rows where:

Capital gain %

| is greater than ▾ | 10% ▾ |

⦿ And  ○ Or

| ▾ | ▾ |

Use ? to represent any single character
Use * to represent any series of characters

[ OK ]  [ Cancel ]

**Figure 3.3**

|   | A | B | C | D | E |
|---|---|---|---|---|---|
| 1 | Share Name ▾ | Share Price (£) ▾ | Dividend (£) ▾ | Capital gain % ▾ | |
| 3 | Gloxo | 3.21 | 0.5 | 10.10% | |
| 4 | Brutus | 2.5 | 0.35 | 14.50% | |
| 5 | Costcut | 2.5 | 0.35 | 12.40% | |
| 6 | Pan-europe | 2.5 | 0.26 | 15.60% | |
| 17 | Agricola | 0.65 | 0.12 | 10.50% | |

**Workbook 3.3**

*Click OK and the records satisfying both of these requirements will be selected from the list.*[2]

*To follow the next stage of the discussion, restore all of the original records by clicking on the arrow tab in D1 and selecting All from the prompt that follows.*

We should now note that the previous filtering only took place on the basis of **one** field (Capital Gain), but it is a simple matter to interrogate the list on the basis of questions relating to **more than** one field.

For example, suppose that we wanted a list of all shares with more than 10% Capital Gain **and** with a Dividend payment of more than £ 0.3.

*To do this, click on the arrow tab in the Capital Gain field (D1) and use the same procedure as before to select all records with a Capital Gain of more than 10%.*

*Once the list has been reduced to include only these records, click on the arrow tab in the Dividend field (C1) and use the same procedure to select those records with a Dividend payment of more than £ 0.3.*

You should find that only three records—Gloxo, Brutus and Costcut satisfy **both** of these requirements.

Now, when more than one field has been used for interrogation purposes, rather than clicking on each blue arrow tab **individually** and selecting All to restore the original list **field by field**, it is quicker to select **Data** and then **Filter** from the Menu bar and then click on **Show All**.

*Do this now.*

There are two further points to be noted about filtered lists.

First, when a list has been filtered, selecting Print will produce hard copy of the **filtered** rather than the original list. This is the easiest way of obtaining a copy of those records that satisfy the questions that you have asked.

*Practise this now by printing the list of all shares with more than 8% capital gain. Use File, and then Print from the main menu and select whatever printer your system supports (usually the default will be fine).*

Second, there will frequently be circumstances in which you require to total, or perform some other calculation, on the values in one or more fields of a filtered list.

For example, in the context of the current illustration we might want to obtain the total share price and the total dividend payment of those shares **that had more than 10% capital gain.**

At first sight it might seem simply to be a case of writing two SUM functions such as

$$=SUM(B2:B17) \quad and \quad =SUM(C2:C17)$$

**and hoping that once the list is filtered only the sum of the selected records will be produced.**

However, this conventional summing procedure will only work on an **unfiltered** list and will **not** produce the correct results when the list is filtered.

For filtered lists Excel has a special totalling function known as SUBTOTAL.

*To follow the discussion, ensure that all of the original records are restored and read on.*

To see the difference between using a simple SUM function and the equivalent SUBTOTAL function make the following entries: in E1: =SUM(B2:B17) and in F1: =SUM(C2:C17); then in G1 and H1 make the entries

$$=SUBTOTAL(9,B2:B17) \quad and \quad =SUBTOTAL(9,C2:C17)$$

Notice that this function (SUBTOTAL) contains two arguments: a number (9 in this case) and the range of cells in the original list. The number tells Excel which of a variety of arithmetic operations is to be performed on the specified range—9 is the code for SUM; but if we had used code number 1 then the list would have been averaged instead. A full list of the meanings of each of the numerical codes will be supplied at a later date. For the moment it is sufficient to note that a value of 9 calculates the sum of the values and a value of 1 calculates the average of the values in the range defined.

Clearly the SUM and the SUBTOTAL functions return identical values for each of the fields, i.e.

38.1 for the total price of all the shares   and

6.04 for the total dividend supplied by all the shares.

**This is only to be expected since the list has not yet been filtered.**

But now suppose that we filter the list to include only those shares that have experienced more than 10% capital gain.

*Do this now by the method explained above.*

It should be found that while the two SUM functions remain unchanged the two SUBTOTAL functions have adjusted **automatically** to contain the totals of the filtered list. In other words, E1 and F1 will contain 38.1 and 6.04 as previously, but G1 and H1 will contain 11.36 and 1.58 respectively. These are the totals of the **filtered** list.

This automatic adjustment is **entirely** due to using the SUBTOTAL function with a first argument value of 9 (sum), rather than a simple =SUM function.

*Now restore all of the records and confirm that the values in G1 and H1 have returned to 38.1 and 6.04 respectively since the list is now in its original, complete form.*

*Now attempt Exercises 3.2 and 3.3.*

## 3.3 Parsing data

In the not too distant past, data were usually obtained from published sources and then transferred manually to a spreadsheet or statistical package. This manual transfer was not only tedious and time-consuming but was also prone to error as a result of typing mistakes.

Fortunately, with the advent of the Internet this is no longer needed to the same extent. Sophisticated search engines such as Lycos, AltaVista and Google, can allow the researcher to find data easily and quickly, and then transport them electronically into Excel, where they can then be manipulated and analysed as required.

A number of sites are worth mentioning in this respect.

SOSIG—data and learning resources from the Social Science Internet Gateway.

BizED—Business data resources.

LTSN—Economic data and learning resources from the Learning and Teaching Support Network.

CSO—Economic and Business data from the Central Statistical Office.

OECD—Economic and Business data from the Organisation for Economic Co-operation and Development.

IMF—Economic and Social data from the International Monetary Fund.

Usually when one of these sites is accessed downloading the required data is simply a matter of selecting and then copying and pasting into Excel, although it is usually best to use Paste Special and then either the HTML or the Unicode Text option.

In some cases however, the web data are not in a form that imports conveniently into Excel. If this is the case, then the data must be **Parsed** using the **Text to Columns** facility under Excel's Data menu.

For example, it is frequently found that when data containing several fields are pasted into Excel from a web location, the field columns of the original data are compressed into a single column.

In other words, what appears in the web site as say three separate columns containing numerical values, is imported as one single column containing each of the values separated by a space.

From a computational point of view this is clearly useless since each separate field should ideally be located in a single column so that if desired they can be added together etc.

When data are imported to Excel as a single column the Data, Text to Columns command should be used to redistribute the implied field values of each record into separate column fields.

This facility is a Wizard command and Excel will usually suggest the best method of performing the redistribution.

For example, suppose that the data in Figure 3.4 had been copied and pasted from a web-based data source.

*Load the* W3_3.xls *file now to follow the discussion.*

The first thing to do is select the column containing the compressed data. This is most easily done by clicking once on the letter identifying the column. The whole column will be selected.

Then choose Data from the main menu and then Text to Columns. A Wizard dialogue screen will appear.

| | A | B | C | D | E | F |
|---|---|---|---|---|---|---|
| 1 | Region Population Unemployment% Crimerateper1000 | | | | | |
| 2 | A 2453420 3.7 4.8 | | | | | |
| 3 | B 1987892 2.8 3.1 | | | | | |
| 4 | C 3456321 7.1 6.2 | | | | | |
| 5 | | | | | | |

**Figure 3.4**

| | A | B | C | D |
|---|---|---|---|---|
| 1 | Region | Population | Unemployment% | Crimerateper1000 |
| 2 | A | 2453420 | 3.7 | 4.8 |
| 3 | B | 1987892 | 2.8 | 3.1 |
| 4 | C | 3456321 | 7.1 | 6.2 |
| 5 | | | | |

**Figure 3.5**

In this case the fields in the original data happen to be separated by a space so at the Wizard prompt select Delimited and then Next.

A choice of separator options will appear and in this case 'space' should be chosen. The bottom section of the Wizard will show how Excel proposes to distribute the data among the available fields, and if it looks OK, select Finish and the results should resemble Figure 3.5

A solution file containing the results of this process is called W3_3A.xls and can be loaded if required.

Notice that in other cases the data may be separated by characters other than spaces—tab stops, semi-colons, etc. In this case select the appropriate option and see what it looks like.

Finally, in still other cases Excel may have determined that the data are of 'fixed width', in which case it will usually be all right to select Next and Finish straight away.

*Now attempt Exercise 3.4.*

## 3.4 Exercises

### Exercise 3.1

Prepare the model shown in Workbook 3.4 or load it from the online resource centre (W3_4.xls).

(a) Sort the list of products in ascending order of sales in Region 3. Separate any tied product ranks by performing a secondary sort in terms of sales in Region 4, also in ascending order. Separate any product sales ranks that are still tied by using a descending tertiary sort on Region 5.

(b) Sort the regions in ascending order from left to right in terms of their sales of Product 5. (Hint: at the Sort menu under Options look for sort left to right).

### Exercise 3.2

Prepare the model shown in Workbook 3.5 or load it from the online resource centre (W3_5.xls).

| B14 | ▼ | $f_x$ =SUM(B3:B13) | | | | |
|---|---|---|---|---|---|---|
| | A | B | C | D | E | F | G |

| | A | B | C | D | E | F | G |
|---|---|---|---|---|---|---|---|
| 1 | | Sales volume (units) | | | | | |
| 2 | | Region 1 | Region 2 | Region 3 | Region 4 | Region 5 | Total all regions |
| 3 | Product 1 | 2034 | 1056 | 8256 | 478 | 2045 | 13869 |
| 4 | Product 2 | 3012 | 2356 | 7145 | 721 | 2903 | 16137 |
| 5 | Product 3 | 1034 | 1691 | 6918 | 319 | 1402 | 11364 |
| 6 | Product 4 | 692 | 891 | 6918 | 201 | 1567 | 10269 |
| 7 | Product 5 | 1932 | 1267 | 6918 | 201 | 1956 | 12274 |
| 8 | Product 6 | 1587 | 1935 | 6918 | 567 | 1835 | 12842 |
| 9 | Product 7 | 1298 | 1732 | 7024 | 408 | 1382 | 11844 |
| 10 | Product 8 | 3678 | 4891 | 12579 | 800 | 3819 | 25767 |
| 11 | Product 9 | 5612 | 3215 | 9120 | 792 | 4956 | 23695 |
| 12 | Product 10 | 4301 | 3710 | 9818 | 653 | 4642 | 23124 |
| 13 | Product 11 | 2981 | 2198 | 8156 | 812 | 3001 | 17148 |
| 14 | Total all products | 28161 | 24942 | 89770 | 5952 | 29508 | 178333 |
| 15 | | | | | | | |

**Workbook 3.4**

| | A | B | C | D | E | F | G | H |
|---|---|---|---|---|---|---|---|---|
| 1 | MARSTAT = 1 = MARRIED, MARSTAT = 0 = SINGLE | | | | | | | |
| 2 | GENDER = F = FEMALE, SEX = M = MALE | | | | | | | |
| 3 | NAME | INITIAL | SALARY | MARSTAT | GENDER | TAX | SUPERANN | TAKEHOME |
| 4 | ALLAN | L | 7058.27 | 1 | M | 1764.57 | 705.83 | 4587.88 |
| 5 | ALLEN | D | 43966.55 | 0 | M | 14508.96 | 4396.66 | 25060.93 |
| 6 | BROWN | G | 53531.38 | 0 | M | 17665.36 | 5353.14 | 30512.89 |
| 7 | BROWN | I | 889.64 | 1 | M | 222.41 | 88.96 | 578.27 |
| 8 | BROWN | L | 37085.07 | 1 | M | 9271.27 | 3708.51 | 24105.29 |
| 9 | COOPER | F | 50799.24 | 0 | F | 16763.75 | 3809.94 | 30225.55 |
| 10 | DAVIES | R | 33501.75 | 1 | F | 8375.44 | 2512.63 | 22613.68 |
| 11 | REDMOND | K | 12323.86 | 0 | F | 4066.87 | 924.29 | 7332.69 |
| 12 | REILLY | G | 14764.91 | 1 | F | 3691.23 | 1107.37 | 9966.32 |
| 13 | ROBERTS | F | 35054.07 | 1 | F | 8763.52 | 2629.05 | 23661.49 |
| 14 | SMITH | G | 51378.43 | 1 | M | 12844.61 | 5137.84 | 33395.98 |
| 15 | SMITH | P | 47981.05 | 1 | F | 11995.26 | 3598.58 | 32387.21 |
| 16 | SMITH | R | 56824.75 | 0 | M | 18752.17 | 5682.48 | 32390.11 |
| 17 | STEWART | R | 41444.09 | 1 | F | 10361.02 | 3108.31 | 27974.76 |
| 18 | | | | | | | | |

**Workbook 3.5**

Produce the following selective lists from the main data set, remembering to restore the complete list between each interrogation.

(a) SALARY greater than £ 25000.

(b) SALARY greater than £ 25000 but less than £ 40000.

(c) TAKEHOME less than £ 10000.

(d) FEMALES with TAKEHOME between £ 10000 and £ 25000 inclusive.

(e)  SINGLE FEMALES with TAKEHOME between £ 10000 and £ 25000 inclusive.

(f)  SINGLE MALES with TAKEHOME more than £ 27000.

When you have finished save the file as W3_5.xls.

## Exercise 3.3

Using the model produced in Exercise 3.2 (Workbook 3.5), create formulae in H1:K2 to compute the totals and the averages of the SALARY, TAX, SUPERANN and TAKEHOME fields. These formulae should adjust automatically to accommodate any filtering that is done.

On the basis of these formulae compute the following amounts.[3]

(a)  The total and the average TAKEHOME of all FEMALES.

(b)  The total and the average SALARY of all MARRIED MALES.

(c)  The total and the average TAX of all SINGLE FEMALES.

(d)  The total and the average SUPERANN of all MARRIED MALES with a SALARY in excess of £ 20000.

(e)  The total and the average TAX of all MARRIED FEMALES with TAKEHOME between £ 10000 and £ 30000 inclusive.

## Exercise 3.4

Load Workbook 3.6 (W3_6.xls). These data have been copied and pasted from an Internet site directly into Excel and show the final team positions for the first division of the Spanish football league in season 2003–4.

Use the Text to Columns facility to parse the data into fields that can be used for further analysis.

## 3.5  Solutions to the exercises

### Solutions to Exercise 3.1

(a)  Select the area containing the raw data and the row and column labels. In other words, click and drag over the A2:F13 range.[4]
Now choose Data and then Sort.
The primary sort is on Region 3, Ascending, **Then By** Region 4, also Ascending, **Then By** Region 5, Descending this time. Make sure that the My List Has: Header Row is checked and then choose OK.
The results should resemble Workbook 3.7.

(b)  Sorting across columns rather than down rows is slightly trickier. First select the area containing the data—once again excluding the row and column totals, and

|  | A | B | C | D | E | F | G |
|---|---|---|---|---|---|---|---|
| 1 | | Sales volume (units) | | | | | |
| 2 | | Region 1 | Region 2 | Region 3 | Region 4 | Region 5 | Total all regions |
| 3 | Product 5 | 1932 | 1267 | 6918 | 201 | 1956 | 12274 |
| 4 | Product 4 | 692 | 891 | 6918 | 201 | 1567 | 10269 |
| 5 | Product 3 | 1034 | 1691 | 6918 | 319 | 1402 | 11364 |
| 6 | Product 6 | 1587 | 1935 | 6918 | 567 | 1835 | 12842 |
| 7 | Product 7 | 1298 | 1732 | 7024 | 408 | 1382 | 11844 |
| 8 | Product 2 | 3012 | 2356 | 7145 | 721 | 2903 | 16137 |
| 9 | Product 11 | 2981 | 2198 | 8156 | 812 | 3001 | 17148 |
| 10 | Product 1 | 2034 | 1056 | 8256 | 478 | 2045 | 13869 |
| 11 | Product 9 | 5612 | 3215 | 9120 | 792 | 4956 | 23695 |
| 12 | Product 10 | 4301 | 3710 | 9818 | 653 | 4642 | 23124 |
| 13 | Product 8 | 3678 | 4891 | 12579 | 800 | 3819 | 25767 |
| 14 | Total all products | 28161 | 24942 | 89770 | 5952 | 29508 | 178333 |
| 15 | | | | | | | |

**Workbook 3.7**

this time, also excluding the row labels in column A. The selected area should therefore be B2:F13.

Then select **Data** and **Sort** from the Menu bar as before. This time, however, select **Options** and then on the **Orientation** tab select **Sort Left to Right** instead of the default setting of **Sort Top to Bottom**. Click OK and select the row number containing Product 5 (it should be row 3 after the initial top to bottom sort) from the top tab on the Sort menu. Then click OK again and the result shown in Workbook 3.7A should be obtained.

|  | A | B | C | D | E | F | G |
|---|---|---|---|---|---|---|---|
| 1 | | Sales volume (units) | | | | | |
| 2 | | Region 4 | Region 2 | Region 1 | Region 5 | Region 3 | Total all regions |
| 3 | Product 5 | 201 | 1267 | 1932 | 1956 | 6918 | 12274 |
| 4 | Product 4 | 201 | 891 | 692 | 1567 | 6918 | 10269 |
| 5 | Product 3 | 319 | 1691 | 1034 | 1402 | 6918 | 11364 |
| 6 | Product 6 | 567 | 1935 | 1587 | 1835 | 6918 | 12842 |
| 7 | Product 7 | 408 | 1732 | 1298 | 1382 | 7024 | 11844 |
| 8 | Product 2 | 721 | 2356 | 3012 | 2903 | 7145 | 16137 |
| 9 | Product 11 | 812 | 2198 | 2981 | 3001 | 8156 | 17148 |
| 10 | Product 1 | 478 | 1056 | 2034 | 2045 | 8256 | 13869 |
| 11 | Product 9 | 792 | 3215 | 5612 | 4956 | 9120 | 23695 |
| 12 | Product 10 | 653 | 3710 | 4301 | 4642 | 9818 | 23124 |
| 13 | Product 8 | 800 | 4891 | 3678 | 3819 | 12579 | 25767 |
| 14 | Total all products | 5952 | 24942 | 28161 | 29508 | 89770 | 178333 |
| 15 | | | | | | | |

**Workbook 3.7A**

## Solutions to Exercise 3.2

Select A3:H3 as the range containing the field names and then choose **Data**, **Filter** and **AutoFilter** from the Menu bar. The black arrow tabs will appear in the cells containing the field name.

(a) Click on the arrow tab in the SALARY field, select {Custom...}, then select 'greater than' from the top left-hand tab and type 25000 into the adjacent box. Click OK and ten records will be selected, beginning with Allen, D. and ending with Stewart, R.

The procedures to produce the remainder of the selective lists are summarized below.

*Make sure that you select Data, Filter and Show All between each separate interrogation.*

*Now continue in the same way to produce the following summarized results.*

(b)  SALARY          >        25000       <        40000
3 records selected—Brown, Davies and Roberts.

(c)  TAKEHOME     <        10000
4 records selected—Allan, Brown, Redmond and Reilly.

(d)  TAKEHOME     >=       10000       <=       25000
SEX                  =        F
2 records extracted—Davies and Roberts.

(e)  TAKEHOME     >=       10000       <=       25000
SEX                  =        F
MARSTAT         =        0
0 records selected.

(f)  SEX                 =        M
MARSTAT         =        0
TAKEHOME     >        27000
2 records selected—Brown and Smith.


## Solution to Exercise 3.3

Assuming that A3:H3 is still selected as the field header range of the list and that the Autofilter is still turned on, in H1 enter:

$$=SUBTOTAL(9,C4:C17)$$

In I1 enter:

$$=SUBTOTAL(9,F4:F17)$$

and copy this into J1:K1 to give the totals.
Then, in H2 enter:

$$=SUBTOTAL(1,C4:C17)$$

and in I2 enter:

$$=SUBTOTAL(1,F4:F17)$$

and copy this into J2:K2 to give the averages.

Now perform the filters as instructed to obtain the following answers:

|     | TOTAL       | AVERAGE     |
|-----|-------------|-------------|
| (a) | £154161.71  | £ 22023.10  |
| (b) | £96411.41   | £ 24102.85  |
| (c) | £20830.62   | £ 10415.31  |
| (d) | £8846.35    | £ 4423.175  |
| (e) | £27499.98   | £ 9166.66   |

## Solution to Exercise 3.4

Select column A by clicking on the top of the column.

Then choose Data and Text to Columns.

In this case Excel reckons that the source data are in columns of fixed width and defaults to that option. This will not always be correct, but in this case it is, so click

| | A | B | C | D | E | F | G | H | I | J |
|---|---|---|---|---|---|---|---|---|---|---|
| 1 | 1 | Valencia | 38 | 23 | 8 | 7 | 71 | - | 27 | 77 |
| 2 | 2 | Barcelona | 38 | 21 | 9 | 8 | 63 | - | 39 | 72 |
| 3 | 3 | Deportivo | 38 | 21 | 8 | 9 | 60 | - | 34 | 71 |
| 4 | 4 | R.Madrid | 38 | 21 | 7 | 10 | 72 | - | 54 | 70 |
| 5 | --- | ------------ | --- | ---- | ---- | ----- | ----- | --- | ----- | ----- |
| 6 | 5 | Athletic | 38 | 15 | 11 | 12 | 53 | - | 49 | 56 |
| 7 | 6 | Sevilla | 38 | 15 | 10 | 13 | 56 | - | 45 | 55 |
| 8 | --- | ------------ | --- | ---- | ---- | ----- | ----- | --- | ----- | ----- |
| 9 | 7 | At.Madrid | 38 | 15 | 10 | 13 | 51 | - | 53 | 55 |
| 10 | 8 | Villarreal | 38 | 15 | 9 | 14 | 47 | - | 49 | 54 |
| 11 | 9 | Betis | 38 | 13 | 13 | 12 | 46 | - | 43 | 52 |
| 12 | 10 | Malaga | 38 | 15 | 6 | 17 | 50 | - | 55 | 51 |
| 13 | 11 | Mallorca | 38 | 15 | 6 | 17 | 54 | - | 66 | 51 |
| 14 | 12 | Zaragoza | 38 | 13 | 9 | 16 | 46 | - | 55 | 48 |
| 15 | 13 | Osasuna | 38 | 11 | 15 | 12 | 38 | - | 37 | 48 |
| 16 | 14 | Albacete | 38 | 13 | 8 | 17 | 40 | - | 48 | 47 |
| 17 | 15 | R.Sociedad | 38 | 11 | 13 | 14 | 49 | - | 53 | 46 |
| 18 | 16 | Espanyol | 38 | 13 | 4 | 21 | 48 | - | 64 | 43 |
| 19 | 17 | Racing | 38 | 11 | 10 | 17 | 48 | - | 63 | 42 |
| 20 | --- | ------------ | --- | ---- | ---- | ----- | ----- | --- | ----- | ----- |
| 21 | 18 | Valladolid | 38 | 10 | 11 | 17 | 46 | - | 56 | 41 |
| 22 | 19 | Celta | 38 | 9 | 12 | 17 | 48 | - | 68 | 39 |
| 23 | 20 | Murcia | 38 | 5 | 11 | 22 | 29 | - | 57 | 26 |

**Workbook 3.8**

Next to obtain a preview of how Excel is going to allocate the data to columns. If the preview looks fine click Finish and the required result should be obtained. This is shown in Workbook 3.8.

### ■ NOTES

1. Sorting is a very powerful procedure and can be highly destructive if not carried out properly. The Undo feature is indispensable if a mistake is made—click on it *immediately* if you suspect that the sorting has destroyed the structure of your worksheet.

2. You should find that the list has been reduced from five to three records—Gloxo, Costcut and Agricola.

3. Remember to restore all of the original records between each separate calculation.

4. It is neither necessary nor advisable to include the row and the column containing the totals in the area to be sorted. Since these entries are formula-based they will compute the totals automatically once the data have been sorted.

# 4 Charting data

The following files from the online resource centre should be loaded as instructed:

W4_1.xls     W4_2.xls     W4_3.xls

## 4.1 Principles of charting

Few essays, projects or dissertations will fail to be improved by judicious use of pictorial material. At the same time, however, if these graphs and charts are poorly prepared then the effect will be diminished and can even become confusing and counter-productive. For this reason, there are a number of principles and rules of thumb that should always be followed when constructing graphs and charts.

Since most graphs will have two axes—$y$ vertical and $x$ horizontal—the first question to answer is: which variables should be placed on which axes? Conventionally there will only ever be one variable on the horizontal axis, but there can be several on the vertical axis.[1]

Excel follows this convention in constructing its charts, meaning that for any graph range that is defined, the first column of this will be treated as the horizontal variable data, and the remaining columns as the data for the vertical axis variable(s). A further implication of this procedure is that when we say that we are plotting for example, Expenditure *versus* Income then the Expenditure data are placed on the vertical and the Income data on the horizontal axis. On the other hand, if we plot Income *versus*

Expenditure this procedure is reversed. Clearly the word 'versus' is used to indicate which variables are placed on which axes—as in 'vertical versus horizontal'.

When there are more then two variables to be graphed then the terminology used above remains valid. For example, to plot Expenditure and Savings versus Income we should place Expenditure and Savings on the vertical axis and Income on the horizontal. Consequently, Income should be the first column of our defined chart range, with Expenditure and Savings being defined as the next two columns. Once these conventions have been understood, the next issue relates to the type of chart to be employed. Excel supports a wide variety of types, so the guiding principle should be one of clarity.

The next issue relates to the choice of scale to employ for the axes. Excel automatically scans the data and by default chooses scale categories that it thinks are appropriate. It is not infallible, however. In particular, when there are one or two extreme observations then the need to accommodate these can often produce unsatisfactory results.

## 4.2 XY scatter graphs

Consider the data shown in Table 4.1.

The full data set is contained in the Data1 sheet of the W4_1.xls file *and should be loaded now.*

The task is to produce a simple XY graph of Savings and Expenditure versus Income, and the procedure is as follows. (Full solutions are contained in the Graph1 sheet of the file.)

**Table 4.1**

| Income (£000) | Expenditure (£000) | Savings (£000) |
|---|---|---|
| 250 | 250 | 0 |
| 500 | 490 | 10 |
| 750 | 720 | 30 |
| 1000 | 950 | 50 |
| 1250 | 1190 | 60 |
| 1500 | 1430 | 70 |
| 1750 | 1695 | 55 |
| 2000 | 1900 | 100 |
| 2250 | 2150 | 100 |
| 2500 | 2370 | 130 |
| 2750 | 2600 | 150 |
| 3000 | 2820 | 180 |
| 3250 | 3050 | 200 |
| 3500 | 3300 | 200 |
| 3750 | 3500 | 250 |
| 4000 | 3730 | 270 |

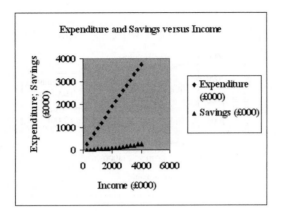

**Figure 4.1**

*Select the Chart Wizard option from the Tool bar and choose an XY scatter graph with the default subtype. Click Next and enter the range to graph as A1: C17. A sample graph will appear and, if it looks OK, click Next again. You now have the opportunity to enter titles for the graph as a whole and for each of the axes. Enter these and click Next again. Assuming that the graph is to be created in the existing worksheet, accept the default setting and click Finish.*

The results should resemble Figure 4.1.

Notice that the legends for each of the graph's series (Expenditure and Savings) have been inserted automatically. This was because the graph range was defined to include the labels in the first row of the raw data. Excel automatically picks these up as the legends to be used to distinguish the Expenditure series from the Savings series. This means that the legends employed can be altered if necessary, simply by changing the contents of the header rows in the data set. They will then be transferred automatically to the chart.

Also notice that although the data only have a maximum value for income of £4000, Excel has extended this to £6000 on the horizontal axis. This means that the area to the right of 4000 is blank. Clearly we should try to fix this and a few other things that are not immediately appealing.

To do this we note that once created this chart can be altered and customized in a variety of ways. It can be resized or moved by clicking on the chart and then either dragging the solid border (to move) or dragging one of the black markers (to resize). Other options are obtained by clicking on the graph area and then selecting the Chart option from the main menu.[2] We can then choose from a range of options.

Alternatively, we can double-click directly on any chart feature (such as scale, legend or title) to obtain the editing options available for that feature.

Using either of these devices it is now easy to alter the appearance of any chart from Excel's default provision. Follow the instructions and then check your progress against the Graph sheets in the W4_1.xls file. These suggested charts can be tracked and inspected in the file by using F5 (Goto) and then choosing the named figure from the list.

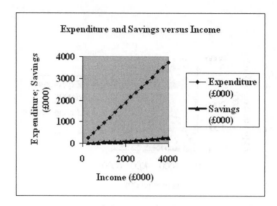

**Figure 4.2**

Also, if a particular alteration is particularly attractive, then select the graph and then copy and paste the chart into a vacant area of the worksheet. (To delete a chart, select it and then hit the Delete key.)

Consequently, to make Figure 4.1, ignore any values for income in excess of £4000 we should double-click on the horizontal axis scale and then select Scale from the menu that appears. Now change the maximum value for the $X$ values from the 6000 that is showing to 4000. The scale will be adjusted.

Figure 4.1 is known as a 'scatter diagram' because only the data coordinates have been plotted. But it is an easy matter to join them up with lines. To do this, select the original chart and then copy and paste it into D20. Now select the new chart, and from the Chart menu choose the fourth subtype option. With both of these adjustments made, the result should look like Figure 4.2.

## 4.3 Column and bar charts

The data in Table 4.1 can also be shown as a Column (vertical) or Bar (horizontal) chart.

This has been done in Figure 4.3 simply by clicking on Figure 4.2 so that black handles appear around the frame, selecting copy, and then pasting to a vacant area of the worksheet. Then, with this copy still selected, choose Chart from the main menu and then Chart Type from the next menu. Select the default chart subtype and the results shown in Figure 4.3 will be reproduced.

Figure 4.3 shows each of the vertical axis variables as separate columns for each value of the variable on the horizontal axis (Column subtype 1). However, the same information could also be conveyed in a stacked chart. This is shown in Figure 4.4.

Here Column subtype 2 has been chosen, while Figure 4.5 shows the same data portrayed as a percentage component chart in which the value of each variable is shown as a percentage of the total value (Column subtype 3).

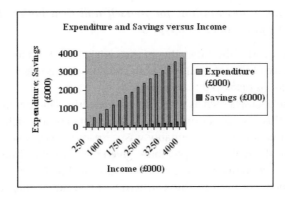

**Figure 4.3**

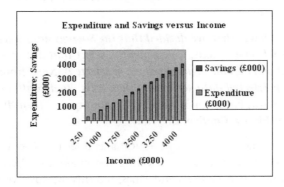

**Figure 4.4**

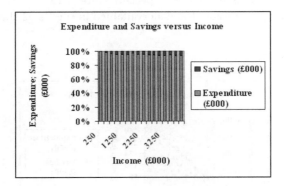

**Figure 4.5**

*Confirm each of these presentations for yourself and then notice the fundamental difference between types 1 and 2 and type 3.*

The former both show the absolute value of the variables on both axes, while the latter shows the percentage of the total value of both variables that is due to each category. No absolute information is displayed.

Even with simple data sets such as these, the nature of the data themselves can militate against clarity. In this case, for example, the Savings data are so much smaller than the Expenditure data that any graph inevitably wastes space in accommodating differences in magnitude. Indeed it is almost impossible—given our current techniques—to prepare a meaningful graph when one variable is only a very small percentage of the other(s).

When this happens we need to think in terms of two rather than one scale for the vertical axis.

We have done this in Figure 4.6 where Figure 4.1 has been copied and then amended to show the Expenditure data on the left-hand vertical scale and the Savings data on the right-hand vertical scale.

*This was done as follows. First, we decided that the Savings data were to be shown on the (new) right-hand vertical axis. Consequently, select that data series on the graph by clicking on it (it will become highlighted when selected). Next, from the main menu select Format, then Selected data series and then Axis. By default, only one axis (the primary one) is selected, but if you now select Secondary axis then the effect shown in Figure 4.6 will be achieved. Confirm this now.*

Also notice that we have changed the vertical axis titles to reflect the fact that there are now effectively two vertical axes. Selecting the graph and then Chart from the main menu, and then Chart Options and Titles, did this. Because we have created the secondary axis the Secondary Y axis title box is now available, so we have removed Savings from the primary axis title and added it as the secondary axis title.

Clearly this is a very useful device, especially since it can be used for more than one series. For example, consider the data contained in the Data2 sheet and shown in Table 4.2.

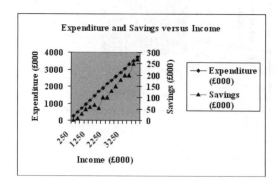

**Figure 4.6**

**Table 4.2**

| Time | Variable 1 | Variable 2 | Variable 3 | Variable 4 |
|------|-----------|-----------|-----------|-----------|
| 1 | 100 | 0.1 | 150 | 0.9 |
| 2 | 200 | 1.1 | 200 | 1.7 |
| 3 | 300 | 2.1 | 250 | 2.5 |
| 4 | 400 | 3.1 | 300 | 3.3 |
| 5 | 500 | 4.1 | 350 | 4.1 |
| 6 | 600 | 5.1 | 400 | 4.9 |
| 7 | 700 | 6.1 | 450 | 5.7 |
| 8 | 800 | 7.1 | 500 | 6.5 |
| 9 | 900 | 8.1 | 550 | 7.3 |
| 10 | 1000 | 9.1 | 600 | 8.1 |

Figure 4.7 shows the initial result of plotting the data contained in the A1:E11 range.

Since variables 2 and 4 are similar in magnitude to each other, but significantly smaller than variables 1 and 3, we have placed the smaller variables on the right-hand axis and the larger ones on the left-hand axis. The result now looks like Figure 4.8, and clearly improves the presentational features of the chart.

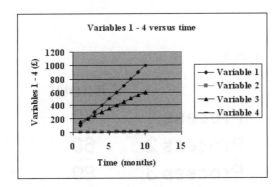

**Figure 4.7**

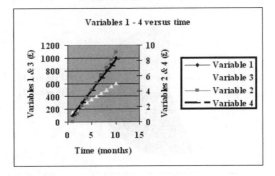

**Figure 4.8**

## 4.4 **Pie charts**

The charts considered to date have all had the ability to compare the variables chosen for the vertical axis against the one chosen for the horizontal axis. Sometimes, however, such comparison is not required, and in this case pie charts are a popular device.

The most important feature of any pie chart is that there are no axes and hence no axes scale. The chart itself is a circular object of any size, with the variable values being expressed as proportional or percentage slices of the pie.

For example, the data in Table 4.3 show the output of a particular product from three processes (1, 2 and 3).

The data and subsequent graphs are contained in the Data3 and Graph3 sheet of the current file.

Figure 4.9 is a basic pie chart created from the subtype 1 option.

It will be noticed that by default the values (either in absolute or percentage terms) are not shown.

This is rectified in Figure 4.10 where we have used the Chart/Chart options routine to choose Data Labels. From the list of options that appears, we then chose Show Percent.

Confirm this now.

**Table 4.3**

|  | Output |
|---|---|
| Process 1 | 40 |
| Process 2 | 60 |
| Process 3 | 80 |

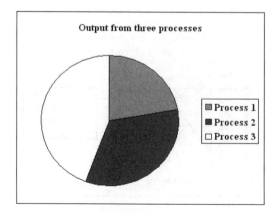

**Figure 4.9**

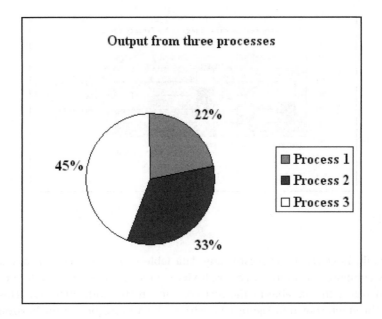

Figure 4.10

## 4.5 **Some practicalities in preparing graphs**

When the data sets are simple (only two or three variables in total) then graph construction is fairly straightforward. However, as the number of variables increases then complexities can emerge. For example, consider the data contained in the Data4 sheet and shown in Table 4.4. Suggested graphs are contained in the Graph4 sheet.

The data show the various categories of cost experienced by three classes of factory (A, B and C).

The first issue is to decide which variables are to be placed on which axes. In other words, do we want to show how all costs behave at each factory, or how each cost category behaves at all factories? Each would be equally valid representations of the data, and so the outcome revolves around which of the categories Excel places on the horizontal axis—and it can do either.

Table 4.4

| Cost category (£000) | Factory A | Factory B | Factory C |
|---|---|---|---|
| Overheads | 10.1 | 14.9 | 17.6 |
| Fuel costs | 8.3 | 7.1 | 6.4 |
| Labour costs | 15.9 | 19.2 | 13.4 |
| Interest Charges | 3.6 | 2.7 | 4.5 |
| Raw material costs | 9.5 | 10.6 | 11.9 |

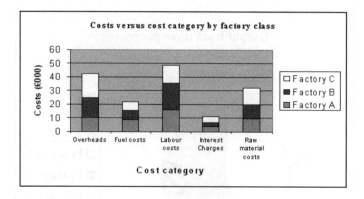

**Figure 4.11**

By default, however, Excel regards any data table such as the current one as being primarily composed of columns. That is, it views these data as six rows of four columns, and then places the variable in the first column on the horizontal axis. This would produce the graph shown in Figure 4.11, with each cost category on the horizontal axis and the costs at each factory on the vertical axis.

However, it is an easy matter to get Excel to view the data primarily in rows—that is, four columns of six rows.

*Confirm this now.*

This is done at the second stage of the Graph Wizard (where you are asked to define the data range or where the data range that you previously selected is displayed).

*Simply alter the lower check box from columns to rows after using the Chart and Source data options from the menu.*

*Alternatively, you can alter an existing configuration by selecting the graph and then choosing Chart and Source Data from the main menu and change from columns to rows.*

This has been done in Figure 4.12 and clearly shows how the graph has been transposed—and we also remembered to edit the label on the horizontal axis to reflect this transposition.

We have also produced a new type of chart—called an 'area chart', in Figures 4.13 and 4.14. The first of these uses the second subtype of the Area chart and shows the absolute cost amounts for each cost category.

*Reproduce these now by copying one of the original charts and then using Chart from the main menu, and then Chart Type to alter the forms to the ones shown.*

Remember Chart is only available as a main menu option if an existing chart has been selected.)

Figure 4.14 transposes the axes and then uses Area chart subtype 3 to show the percentage of total costs accounted for by each cost category at each factory. Notice

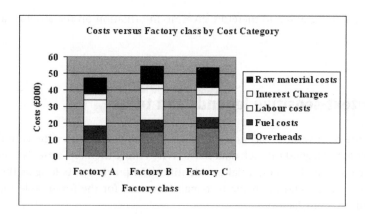

**Figure 4.12**

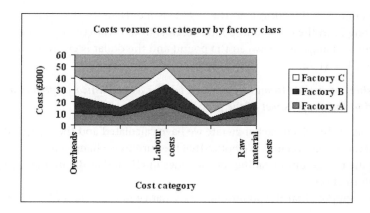

**Figure 4.13**

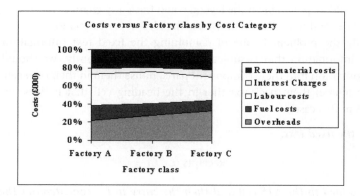

**Figure 4.14**

that it is a relative graph and therefore gives no information on the absolute amount of these costs.

## 4.6 Context-sensitive legends and titles

Earlier in the discussion it was noted that Excel automatically uses the column header text entries as the legend for each data series. When more then one series is being plotted on the vertical axis this is essential for identification purposes. As long as these entries are constant values, and are liable to remain constant for the foreseeable future, then this procedure is satisfactory.

However, suppose that there are circumstances in which the column heading is not only composed of fixed text elements, but also of numerical values that can change over time.

As an example of this idea, load the W4_2.xls file. Here, in the Data sheet we have data showing both the dollar and pound receipts from a variety of projects (A, B, etc.). The current exchange rate between the pound and the dollar is given in C1, and at the moment is £1 = $1.72.

*Use this sheet of the file to make your own entries as explained (a prepared version is contained in the Graph sheet of the file).*

On the basis of this given exchange rate we have calculated and then graphed both the dollar and the pound receipts. We notice that the current exchange rate has been entered as part of the text column heading for the series in C5, and at the moment displays the correct information.

However, suppose that the pound–dollar exchange rate becomes £1 = $1.49.

*Enter this new value to the C1 cell and observe that although the calculations for the graph have changed the legend still shows the old exchange rate.*

Clearly it would be preferable if the legend could track any changes in the exchange rate that take place, and to do this we must use the idea of concatenation.

Essentially the problem is one of combining the fixed text information with the numerical information that is subject to change. Consequently, we should split any legend information into these component parts, house them in their own cells and then join (concatenate) them back together in the heading cell that is to be used for the legend (C5 in this case).

*To do this the fixed text:*

Receipts (£): £1 =

*should be added to the A18 cell and then the entry in C5 concatenates the A18 and the C1 cells from:*

=A18&C1   (the ampersand (&) is the concatenation operator)

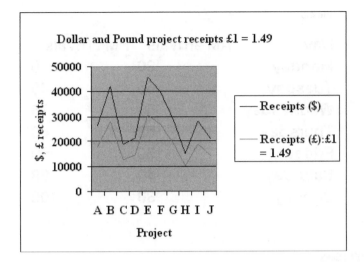

**Figure 4.15**

(Remember that C5 is the header row for the chart range and will automatically appear as the legend in any graph that includes this row in the defined range.)

*Make these entries now.*

We now have a legend that is context-sensitive to the entry in the C1 cell—sometimes known as a 'hot legend'. The effect is shown in the Graph sheet of the file and in Figure 4.15.

A similar procedure can also be used to create 'hot' chart titles—for the graph title or for the axis titles. For example:

*First, enter the label:*

*Dollar and Pound project Receipts to the C2 cell*

*Then concatenate C2, B1 and C1 in the C3 cell from:*

$$=C2\&B1\&C1$$

*Now click on the existing graph title, which is clearly a fixed text item. The title will become available for editing, so click on the formula bar, type an equals sign and then click on C3.*

The title will become sensitive to the exchange rate that is located in C1 and will update accordingly whenever this should change. Both effects are shown in Figure 4.15.

Notice that Excel will not allow you to refer to a cell for the title when creating the title for the first time. It needs a standard text entry. However, once this has been done you should simply proceed as explained above.

**Table 4.5**

| Day | AM arrivals | PM arrivals |
|---|---|---|
| Monday | 80 | 40 |
| Tuesday | 65 | 45 |
| Wednesday | 50 | 75 |
| Thursday | 58 | 60 |
| Friday | 150 | 80 |
| Saturday | 40 | 68 |
| Sunday | 30 | 100 |

## 4.7 Exercises

### Exercise 4.1

The data in Table 4.5 show, for each day of the week, the number of planes arriving at an airport, in the morning (AM) and in the afternoon (PM).

(a) Prepare a chart showing both the absolute numbers of AM and PM arrivals versus the day of the week.

(b) Prepare two pie charts showing the relative distribution of arrivals in the morning and the afternoon.

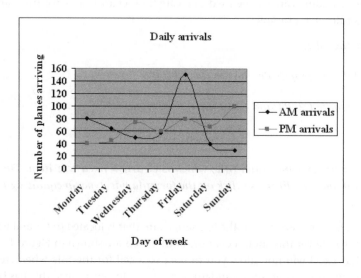

**Figure 4.16**

(c) Prepare a component bar chart showing the AM and PM arrivals versus the day of the week.

## 4.8 Solutions to the exercises

### Solutions to Exercise 4.1

Full solutions are contained in the W4_3.xls file

(a) The suggested solution is shown in Figure 4.16 where a line graph was chosen from the option list (since the horizontal axis data—week day—is categorical).

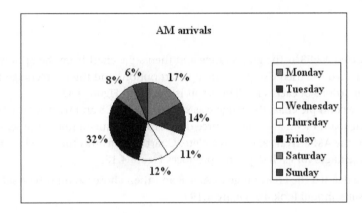

**Figure 4.17**

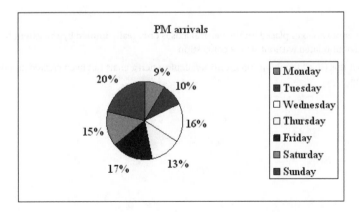

**Figure 4.18**

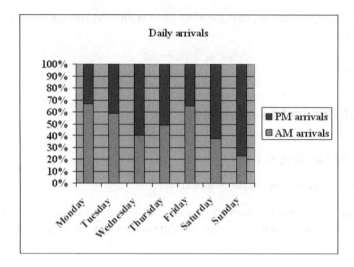

**Figure 4.19**

(b) We selected A2:B8 as the graph range and then a pie chart from the option list. Once created, we used Chart and then Chart options and then Percentage to show the proportions of each slice. The result is shown in Figure 4.17.
For the second pie chart the range was selected as A2:C8 and then we used Chart from the main menu and then Source data. From this menu under the series box we selected the AM arrivals and then Delete. Chart options was then used to include the percentages for each day. This produces Figure 4.18.

(c) Here we defined the chart range as A2:C8 and then chose Column type sub type 3. The results should look like Figure 4.19.

■ **NOTES**

1. The number of variables placed on the vertical axis is only really limited by the extent to which they can be accommodated without severe congestion.

2. Notice that this Chart menu option is only available when a chart has been created and then selected by clicking.

# Elementary modelling (1)

## 5.1  Symbols, expressions and simple models

If the exceptional mathematical modelling power of the Excel spreadsheet is to be used to its full potential, then several fundamental principles need to be understood. In the first instance, most modelling problems will be phrased in terms of a series of verbal and arithmetic statements that define the nature and structure of the problem to be solved. Usually, however, it will be necessary to rephrase these statements in **symbolic** rather than **verbal** form and when this is carried out the result is an **algebraic expression**. For example, the verbal question: 'What is the sum of any two numbers?' has its symbolic algebraic equivalent as $x + y =?$, where $x$ and $y$ represent *any* two numbers.

Once the algebraic form of the problem has been obtained the next task will be to translate it into the equivalent **spreadsheet** symbolic form. Thus, continuing with the example, if we choose *any* two values for $x$ and $y$ and enter them into cells A1 and A2 of the worksheet, then the required symbolic form can be written in A3, say, as:

$$=A1+A2$$

In this form, the statement in A3 is instructing Excel to take *whatever* value is contained in A1 and add it to *whatever* value is contained in A2. The result of this process will be returned to the A3 cell and will change **automatically** if any of the values in A1 and/or

A2 are changed. In this sense, the spreadsheet expression in A3 is completely equivalent to the abstract algebraic form $x + y$.

Thus, if A1 and A2 are used to contain the values of $x$ and $y$ respectively, then the algebraic statement $x + y$ has its spreadsheet **symbolic equivalent** as =A1+A2.

By a similar logic (and continuing to store the values of $x$ and $y$ in A1 and A2) the following further equivalencies can be observed.

| algebraic expression | spreadsheet equivalent |
|---|---|
| $x - y$ | =A1-A2 |
| $x$ times $y$ | =A1*A2 |
| $x$ divided by $y$ | =A1/A2 |
| $x$ to the power of $y$ | =A1^A2 |

With these ideas in mind we can now proceed to consider the modelling process in the context of a less abstract example.

Suppose that a firm selling kitchen units charges its customers a price of £80 per unit. However, also suppose that it offers a discount of 5% of the value of any order if payment is made in cash. Calculate the invoice to be sent to a customer who orders 50 units and pays in cash.

We can proceed by identifying the following relationships:

Order value = the number of units ordered times the price per unit

= 50 times £80 = £4000.

Discount offered = 5% of the order value = 5%of £4000 = 5/100 times £4000 = £200.

Invoice = Order Value − Discount offered = £4000 − £200 = £3800.

This is clearly the answer to the **specific** problem that was posed, but it will be noted that a different answer would be obtained if any of the given arithmetic values were to change.

Yet, although this need to recompute when specific data values change will always exist, the ease and efficiency with which this recalculation is carried out will be much greater if we can specify the model in **general algebraic** terms rather than in specific arithmetic ones.

To see this, consider the following reformulation of the problem.

Suppose that the firm selling kitchen units charges its customers a price of £$P$ per unit. Also suppose that it offers a discount of $d$% of the value of any order if payment is made in cash. Calculate the invoice to be sent to a customer who orders $x$ units and pays in cash.

Proceeding as before, we can write:

Order value = the number of units ordered times the price per unit

= $x$ times £$P$ = £$Px$.

Discount offered = $d$% of the order value = $d$% of £$Px$ = $d/100$ times £$Px$ = £$dPx/100$

Invoice = Order Value − Discount offered = £$Px$ − £$dPx/100$.

Invoice = £$Px(1 - d/100)$ when the £$Px$ common term is factored out.

| | B4 | | ▼ | $f_x$ | =B1*B3*(1-B2/100) | | | |
|---|---|---|---|---|---|---|---|---|
| | A | B | C | D | E | F | G | H |
| 1 | Price £P= | 80 | | | | | | |
| 2 | discount rate d= | 5 | | | | | | |
| 3 | units ordered x= | 50 | The formula in B4 is equivalent to the algebraic expression: | | | | | |
| 4 | Invoice= | 3800 | | | Px(1-d/100) | | | |
| 5 | | | when it is noticed that B1 represents P, | | | | | |
| 6 | | | B2 represents d and B3 represents x. | | | | | |
| 7 | | | | | | | | |
| 8 | | | | | | | | |

**Workbook 5.1**

This expression for the invoice is seen to be a completely **general** statement that will only adopt a **specific** numerical value once values are given for $P$, $x$ and $d$.

Consequently, if we can rewrite it in its spreadsheet symbolic equivalent we will create an expression that will always produce the correct answer when we supply specific values for the price, the discount rate and the number of units ordered. To do this rewriting, we must first choose three cells to contain the three unknowns ($P$, $x$ and $d$). This has been done in Workbook 5.1, where B1 contains the value of £$P$, B3 contains the value of $x$ and B2 contains the value of $d$.

*Open a new workbook and make up this worksheet now. After entering the illustrated values for £P, d and x to B1:B3, enter the following formula in the B4 cell:*

$$=B1*B3*(1-B2/100)$$

*Then confirm that it computes the invoice accurately for any changes to the values in B1:B3*

*Save this model now as* W5_1.xls.

## 5.2 Creating general algebraic models

Now although we have satisfactorily achieved our objective of creating an operational model of the problem, it might still be regarded as deficient because it can only produce the correct invoice for **one** chosen value of the order size. Yet there may well be circumstances in which we would want to observe the invoices that result from a *range* of different order sizes. In other words, we need to consider **several** values of x and their associated invoice values. (This is exactly what is meant by $x$ being variable and the value of the invoice depending upon the value of that variable.)

To do this we can take Workbook 5.1 and modify it as indicated in Workbook 5.2, where values of $x$ between 1 and 10 have been entered in the cells A5 to A14.

| | B5 | ▼ | $f_x$ | =A5*B1*(1-B2/100) | | | | |
|---|---|---|---|---|---|---|---|---|
| | A | B | C | D | E | F | G | H |
| 1 | Price £P= | 80 | | | | | | |
| 2 | discount rate d= | 5 | | | | | | |
| 3 | | | | | | | | |
| 4 | units ordered x | Invoice | | | | | | |
| 5 | 1 | 76 | The formula in B5 is equivalent to Px(1-d/100) when | | | | | |
| 6 | 2 | 10 | it is noted that A5 now contains the first value of x, | | | | | |
| 7 | 3 | #VALUE! | while B1 and B2 represent P and d as before. | | | | | |
| 8 | 4 | #VALUE! | | | | | | |
| 9 | 5 | 342 | However, we have copied this formula into B6:B14 | | | | | |
| 10 | 6 | #VALUE! | and this has clearly created a problem as the | | | | | |
| 11 | 7 | #VALUE! | #VALUE returns indicate. | | | | | |
| 12 | 8 | #VALUE! | | | | | | |
| 13 | 9 | #VALUE! | | | | | | |
| 14 | 10 | #VALUE! | | | | | | |
| 15 | | | | | | | | |

**Workbook 5.2**

*Study this worksheet now and then make it up for yourself. Enter the labels and values shown in A1:B4. Then enter the values 1 to 10 in A5:A14. Finally, in B5 enter:*

$$=A5*B1*(1-B2/100)$$

*and copy this into B6:B14.*

The reason for the difficulty noted in the worksheet (#VALUE!) is that, as was seen in Chapter 1, Excel automatically carries out all copying of formula in a **fully** relative manner.[1] This means that when the entry in B5 of

$$=A5*B1*(1-B2/100)$$

is copied in to B6 it becomes

$$=A6*B2*(1-B3/100)$$

and when it is copied into B7 it becomes

$$=A7*B3*(1-B4/100)$$

and so on, for the copies made into B8 and below.

Now, while this relative updating of the column A cell references is **exactly** what we require to refer to each of the 10 values of $x$ (i.e. the column A references), it is **not** what we require for the B1 and B2 cell references. They must **always** remain as B1 and B2 and must **not** update in the copying process.

Consequently, both of these cell addresses will need to be 'dollar-fixed' with regard to their row numbers (since we are copying down the sheet). That is, instead of writing B1 and B2 as the cell references for the price and the discount rate, we write B$1 and

B\$2. The row numbers of these cell references are now dollar-fixed for the purposes of copying down the sheet.

This adjustment to the formula in B5 is made in Workbook 5.3 and is seen to rectify the problem perfectly since the formulae in B5 to B14 now read as:

$$B5: \quad =A5*B\$1*(1-B\$2/100)$$

$$B6: \quad =A6*B\$1*(1-B\$2/100)$$

$$B7: \quad =A7*B\$1*(1-B\$2/100)$$

$$\ldots$$

$$B14: \quad =A14*B\$1*(1-B\$2/100)$$

*Make this adjustment to your own model now by entering, in B5:*

$$=A5*B\$1*(1-B\$2/100)$$

*and copying this down into B6:B14.*

*Now name the B1 and B2 cells as P and d respectively and replace the formula in B5 with the equivalent formulae in terms of the named cells. That is:*

$$=P*A5*(1-d/100)$$

*and copy this down into B6:B14.*

The same results should be obtained and indicate another advantage of using named cells in formulae: namely that, when named, a cell is **automatically** treated by Excel as row and column dollar-fixed (\$B\$1 and \$B\$2 in this case).

In this form, the model has a high degree of generality, since if either the price charged or the discount rate offered, or both, should change, all that is required is to enter the

| | B5 | | $f_x$ | =A5*B$1*(1-B$2/100) | | | | | |
|---|---|---|---|---|---|---|---|---|---|
| | A | B | C | D | E | F | G | H |
| 1 | Price £P= | 80 | | | | | | |
| 2 | discount rate d= | 5 | | | | | | |
| 3 | | | | | | | | |
| 4 | units ordered x | Invoice | | | | | | |
| 5 | | 1 | 76 | The dollar signs attached to B1 and B2 now | | | | |
| 6 | | 2 | 152 | ensure that they will not update when copied | | | | |
| 7 | | 3 | 228 | down the sheet. | | | | |
| 8 | | 4 | 304 | However, A5 will become A6, A7 and so on | | | | |
| 9 | | 5 | 380 | when copied, which is what is required. | | | | |
| 10 | | 6 | 456 | Alternatively, if B1 and B2 had been named as P and d | | | | |
| 11 | | 7 | 532 | repectively, then the formula in B5 could be rewritten as: | | | | |
| 12 | | 8 | 608 | =P*A5*(1-d/100) | | | | |
| 13 | | 9 | 684 | and copied down consistently. | | | | |
| 14 | | 10 | 760 | | | | | |

**Workbook 5.3**

new values in B1 and/or B2 and the new invoices will be computed automatically. It will also be noted that the generality of this approach to worksheet design derives from the fact that all operational formulae are entirely composed of cell references or named cells (as opposed to specific numbers).

This suggests a simple design rule that should **always** be followed: namely that the **only** numbers which should appear in a formula should be those that identify the row address of the cell: 3 in B3, 6 in G6, 12 in P12, etc. Any other numbers appearing in a formula must therefore represent the given or calculated data elements of the problem, and should really be located in their own cells and then referred to by their cell addresses or names in any formulae that require to make use of these values. In this way formulae will never need to be edited to accommodate changing arithmetic values and the risk of forgetting to edit a formula that needs to be altered as a result of such changes is eliminated.

In short, if a formula appears as something like

$$=2*A1-6*B1+9*C1$$

then the cells D1, E1 and F1 (say) should be made to contain 2, −6 and 9 respectively and the formula re written as

$$=D1*A1+E1*B1+F1*C1$$

Now, returning to the model illustrated in Workbook 5.3, it should be noted that its flexibility can in fact be improved in relation to the *range* of x values for which the invoices are to be calculated. In the first instance these were simply entered in the normal manner (i.e. manually).

However, if the range of x values for which the invoices were to be computed needed to change (from 1 to 10 to 5 to 14 say) then at the moment manual re-entry would be the only method of doing this. With a small number of x values this is little more than a minor inconvenience, but when a large number of x values are involved it will become a major source of inefficiency.

To address this issue we can proceed as illustrated in Workbook 5.4.

*Use Workbook 5.3 as a template to make the additions as suggested below.*

*In C1 enter the label: Start value for x and in C2 the label: Step value for x.*

Then use D1 and D2 to contain actual numerical values that we choose for these terms.

Thus, assuming that we want x to start at a value of 9 and to increase in steps of 3:

*Enter 9 in D1 and 3 in D2.*

With these values established we now require to 'hook up' this information with the values of x that are actually to be created in A5 to A14. This will be done by two formulae and in two stages.

| | B5 | ▼ | fx | =A5*B$1*(1-B$2/100) | | |
|---|---|---|---|---|---|---|
| | A | B | C | D | E |
| 1 | Price £P= | 80 | Start value for x = | 9 | |
| 2 | discount rate d= | 5 | Step value for x = | 3 | |
| 3 | | | | | |
| 4 | units ordered x | Invoice | | | |
| 5 | 9 | 684 | the formulae in A5 and A6 are: | | |
| 6 | 12 | 912 | =D1 | | |
| 7 | 15 | 1140 | =A5+C$2 | | |
| 8 | 18 | 1368 | | | |
| 9 | 21 | 1596 | | | |
| 10 | 24 | 1824 | | | |
| 11 | 27 | 2052 | | | |
| 12 | 30 | 2280 | | | |
| 13 | 33 | 2508 | | | |
| 14 | 36 | 2736 | | | |
| 15 | 39 | 2964 | | | |
| 16 | 42 | 3192 | | | |
| 17 | 45 | 3420 | | | |
| 18 | 48 | 3648 | | | |
| 19 | 51 | 3876 | | | |
| 20 | | | | | |

**Workbook 5.4**

*First, in A5 enter:*

$$=D1$$

This will transfer the chosen start value for $x$ that we have entered in D1 to the A5 cell that represents the start of the range of $x$ values to be evaluated.

*Next, in A6 write:*

$$=A5+D\$2$$

This will add the chosen step increase in the value of $x$ that we have located in D2 to the start value in A5. Furthermore, the \$ symbol in the D\$2 term ensures that when we copy A5+D\$2 from A6 into A7 to A14, the cell containing the step (D2) remains absolutely fixed, but the A5 reference becomes A6, A7, A8, etc.

In other words, we get:

| Cell location | Cell contents | Result |
|:---:|:---:|:---:|
| A5 | =D1 | 9 |
| A6 | =A5+D$2 | 12 |
| A7 | =A6+D$2 | 15 |
| A8 | =A7+D$2 | 18 |
| ... | | |
| A14 | =A13+D$2 | 36 |

*To produce this effect, copy the contents of A6 into A7:A14.*

The net effect is clearly to add the constant step amount in D2 to the *previous value of x*, and represents a highly efficient way of altering the range of x values for which the invoice is to be evaluated. (Note: the formulae in column B are the same as before.) With these formulae established the range of x values in A5 to A14 is easily altered, simply by changing the start and/or step values contained in D1 and D2.

*Practise doing this now.*

Furthermore, in this illustration only ten separate values of x have been computed, but with the formulae in A5 and A6 established it is an easy matter to copy the crucial one in A6, into as many cells below as are required. (Clearly the associated formula in Column B will also have to be copied down to match any extension in the range of x values.) This will increase the **number** of x values to be evaluated and then, by changing the values in D1 and/or D2, the **range** of x values to be evaluated will also be changed.

For example, with A6 copied into A7 to A19, fifteen values for x will be created, and if the start value for x is 9 (D1 contains 9), while if the step value for x is 3 (D2 contains 3), then the range of x values becomes:

9, 12, 15, 18, 21, 24, 27, 30, 33, 36, 39, 42, 45, 48 and 51.

*Do this now in your own worksheet by copying A14:B14 into A15:B19. Then save the workbook as* W5_4.xls *for future use.*

*Now attempt Exercises 5.1 and 5.2.*

## 5.3 Expressions involving logical tests

Recall that in the illustration we have been using it was stipulated that the discount was **only** to be applied if the client paid **in cash**. The task that we will now address is that of incorporating this stipulation into the operational worksheet model.

To do this we will make use of what is known as a **logical function**. This is a pre-programmed Excel statement that can make logical decisions of the yes/no variety (higher or lower than 10, odd or even, for example). There are a number of logical functions available in Excel, but the one we will use most frequently is called the IF function.

Conceptually, and in *verbal terms* it can be understood as follows:

=IF(Test of condition,Result if condition test is true,Result if condition test is false)[2]

The term outside the brackets, =IF, is known as the **function** and the three terms inside the brackets separated by commas are known as the function's **arguments**, with *either* one of the last two being the result returned to the cell containing the function *depending* upon whether the result of the test is true or false.

In the context of our example we can therefore modify this general logic (again in verbal terms) as follows:

=IF(Pay in cash, Discount offered, No discount offered)

*Now open Workbook 5.4 and use it as a template to follow the discussion.*

As such, the ideas involved should be fairly clear, but to put this **verbal** logic into action in the worksheet we need to rephrase it in numerical terms that the function can address more easily.

*Consequently in the cell A3 of Workbook 5.4 add the label:*

Payment form 1 = cash, 0 = other

*Then, in B3 enter 1 to indicate that payment is in cash.*

*Next, in C3 enter the label:*

Actual discount rate

Set up like this we can now use the D3 cell to house our conditional test, and build it up as follows:

=IF(B3=1,   i.e. if payment is in cash, THEN

B2,   i.e. use the discount rate contained in B2, OTHERWISE

0)   i.e. use a zero discount rate

*Putting each of the parts together gives the D3 entry as:*

=IF(B3=1,B2,0)

Clearly this allows the D3 cell to contain *either* of two values—the discount rate fed in from B2 if payment is in cash, or zero if it is not.

Finally, we must remember to adjust the formula that is currently located in B5 since it looks to B2 for the discount rate, whereas **now** it should look to D3 (and discover **either** zero or the actual discount rate to be applied).

*Consequently, edit the contents of B5 from*

=A5*B$1*(1-B$2/100)   to   =A5*B$1*(1-D$3/100)

*and copy this into B6 to B19.*

*Finally, construct an XY scatter graph showing the invoice versus the order quantity.*

The result should resemble Workbook 5.5.

You can now experiment with this worksheet and observe the effects upon the invoice of changes in the price charged, the discount rate offered and whether payment is made in cash or not.

For example, if the price of the kitchen units increased to £90 and the discount offered for cash increased to 7.5% then we should simply change the contents of B1 and B2 to 90 and 7.5 respectively and the new invoices will be calculated and graphed automatically. These will include the discount if a value of 1 has been entered in B3, but will not include the discount if B3 has been forced to contain 0.

*Experiment with this now on your own sheet and when you have finished restore the values in B1, B2 and B3 to 80, 5 and 1 respectively.*

*Now save this file as W5_5.xls for future use.*

*Exercise 5.3 can now be attempted.*

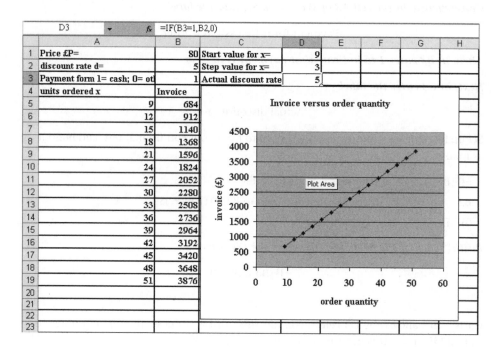

**Workbook 5.5**

## 5.4 **Linear functions in business**

As another illustration of the process of modelling business relationships in Excel, we can discuss the following example.

Consider the types of cost that typically are endured by a business enterprise in carrying out its line of activity. On the one hand, there are costs such as rent on premises, local taxes and insurance premiums, that **do not vary** regardless of the **level of activity**. These costs must be suffered if the enterprise is to remain operational and *cannot be avoided* except by closing down.

They are frequently referred to as **overheads** or **fixed costs** and are characterized by their **invariance** with regard to the **scale** of operations.

On the other hand, there are also categories of cost that depend upon the **level** of operational activity and that (usually) increase with that level. Wage, delivery, raw material and energy costs typically come into this category and are regarded as **variable costs** in the sense that they vary with the level of activity. Clearly they must be viewed in a different way from fixed costs in the modelling process.

We can make this distinction more formal if we argue as follows:

Total Costs (TC) = Fixed Costs (FC) + Variable Costs (VC)

Now consider an enterprise that has an activity level that is denoted by $x$. The units in which $x$ is measured could be units of output per day, number of clients seen per day, or any other of a large range of measures of activity. The point is that $x$ represents the variable and it is this value of $x$ that will determine the variable costs since these are the only ones that change with the level of activity.

With this idea in mind we can now reason as follows:

**TC = FC + VC times $x$**

This is a mathematical statement of the composition of total costs between their two constituent parts. However, letting $y$, $a$ and $b$ represent Total Costs, Fixed Costs and Variable Costs respectively, we can rewrite the last expression as:

$$y = a + bx$$

This is known as a **linear** equation, since when y is plotted against x the resulting graph shows a straight line starting at the value of 'a' on the vertical axis and rising upwards by '$b$' units on the vertical scale for every 1 unit along the horizontal scale. Thus:

$$y = a + bx$$

is the general mathematical form of any of the countless number of straight lines that could be drawn.

However, to define a *specific* straight line requires that numerical values be assigned to the '$a$' and '$b$' terms.

Thus:

$$y = 10 + 2x$$

defines a straight line that starts at a value of 10 on the vertical axis, and which rises by 2 units on the y axis for every 1 unit increase in the value on the horizontal axis. We can see this in Workbook 5.6 which uses the principles outlined in the previous worksheets to create a model that can calculate and graph any linear function for various values of x if the values for 'a' and 'b' are supplied.

**Open a new workbook and make up the model in line with the subsequent instructions.**

This worksheet has been constructed using the same principles as previous ones, with the exception that the formula in B5 reflects the new nature of the problem.

Hence, if x represents the number of units produced, total costs (y) are given generally by:

$$y = a + bx$$

and if the B1 and B2 cells contain 'a' and 'b' respectively, then with the first value of x located in A5:

$$a + bx$$

has

$$=B\$1+B\$2*A5$$

| | B5 | | $f_x$ =B$1+B$2*A5 | | | | | |
|---|---|---|---|---|---|---|---|---|
| | A | B | C | D | E | F | G | H |
| 1 | Fixed costs (a)= | 100 | Start value for x = | 0 | | Total cost = | | |
| 2 | Variable costs (b)= | 12 | Step value for x = | 10 | | + | | |
| 3 | | | Total cost = 100 + 12 times x | | | times x | | |
| 4 | units produced (x) | Total cost (y) | | | | | | |
| 5 | 0 | 100 | | | | | | |
| 6 | 10 | 220 | | | | | | |
| 7 | 20 | 340 | | | | | | |
| 8 | 30 | 460 | | | | | | |
| 9 | 40 | 580 | | | | | | |
| 10 | 50 | 700 | | | | | | |
| 11 | 60 | 820 | | | | | | |
| 12 | 70 | 940 | | | | | | |
| 13 | 80 | 1060 | | | | | | |
| 14 | 90 | 1180 | | | | | | |
| 15 | | | | | | | | |
| 16 | | | | | | | | |
| 17 | | | | | | | | |
| 18 | | | | | | | | |
| 19 | | | | | | | | |
| 20 | | | | | | | | |
| 21 | | | | | | | | |
| 22 | | | | | | | | |
| 23 | | | | | | | | |

Chart: Total cost = 100 + 12 times x — total cost (£) on vertical axis (0 to 1400), units produced on horizontal axis (0 to 100).

**Workbook 5.6**

as its spreadsheet equivalent in B5.

*Enter this now to the B5 cell.*

*Then copy this formula into the B6 to B14 cells, again noticing the use of the dollar symbols to allow consistent copying.*

The chart was prepared as an XY scatter graph with a data range defined as A5:B14.

*Create this chart now in the indicated area, and for the moment enter your name to the chart title box.*

Now make the following entries:

In F1: Total costx=    In F2:+   In F3: times x

*Finally, concatenate the F1, B1, F2, B2 and F3 cells in C3 from*

=F1&B1&F2&B2&F3

*Now, to create the 'hot' title, click on the chart to edit it and then click on the title box.*

*With the title available for editing, click on the Formula bar type an equals sign and then click on the C3 cell and press enter.*

*Now make some changes to the contents of B1 and B2 and observe the effects upon the graph and the 'hot' title.*

*When you have finished, restore the values in B1 and B2 to 100 and 12 respectively and save this workbook as W5_6.xls.*

*Now attempt Exercise 5.4.*

## 5.5 Exercises

### Exercise 5.1

A firm's profits ($y$) are known to be $r$% of the value of its capital assets ($x$). Set up a worksheet that will calculate the value of the firm's profits for any value of $r$ and for each of 50 specified values of $x$.

These 50 values of $x$ should be able to include any required numerical range simply by changing the values contained in two chosen cells that are used to house the start and step values for the range of $x$ values.

### Exercise 5.2

Using the data created in Exercise 5.1 prepare a suitably labelled and titled graph indicating how the firm's profits vary with the value of its capital assets.

## Exercise 5.3

The fire insurance premium on factories is £10 per square metre of floor space if that space is 500m² or less, but £15 per m² for all larger areas.

(a) Prepare a worksheet that can calculate the total insurance due when the floor space of the factory is entered.

(b) Prepare a suitably labelled and titled graph showing how the total insurance due varies with the floor space of the factory for any range of floor spaces that are entered. (Use the principles established in Exercises 5.1 and 5.2.)

## Exercise 5.4

In foreign currency transactions a bank charges customers a fixed amount of £ 15 per transaction, plus a commission of 1% of the value of the transaction for deals of £ 5000 or less. For larger deals the fixed charge is still £ 15, but the commission rate reduces to 0.75% of the value of the entire transaction.

Prepare a worksheet that will compute, and a graph that will display, the transaction costs associated with foreign currency purchases by clients between values of £1000 and £20000 in steps of £1000.

The worksheet should allow easy alteration of any of the fixed data elements and also the range of transaction values to be computed.

| | C7 | ▾ | _fx_ =B$1*B7 | | | |
|---|---|---|---|---|---|---|
| | A | B | C | D | E | F |
| 1 | Value of r (%) | 15% | | | | |
| 2 | Start value for x | 100 | | | | |
| 3 | Step value for x | 1000 | | | | |
| 4 | | | | | | |
| 5 | FORMULAE IN | | | FORMULAE IN | | |
| 6 | COLUMN B | Capital asset value (x) | Profits (y) | COLUMN C | | |
| 7 | =B2 | 100 | 15 | =B$1*B7 | | |
| 8 | =B$3+B7 | 1100 | 165 | =B$1*B8 | | |
| 9 | =B$3+B8 | 2100 | 315 | =B$1*B9 | | |
| 10 | =B$3+B9 | 3100 | 465 | =B$1*B10 | | |
| 11 | AND SO ON | 4100 | 615 | AND SO ON | | |
| 12 | AFTER COPYING | 5100 | 765 | AFTER COPYING | | |
| 13 | B8 INTO B9:B56 | 6100 | 915 | C7 INTO C8:C56 | | |
| 14 | | 7100 | 1065 | | | |
| 15 | | 8100 | 1215 | | | |

**Workbook 5.7**

## 5.6 **Solutions to the exercises**

### Solution to Exercise 5.1

A section of the solution worksheet along with explanation of the formulae used is shown in Workbook 5.7.

### Solution to Exercise 5.2

Using Workbook 5.7 define the data range as B7:C56 and use the first column for the *x* axis labels. Then add a title and text for the *x* and *y* axes to produce the chart shown in Figure 5.1.

### Solutions to Exercise 5.3

(a) The solution is shown in Workbook 5.8A.

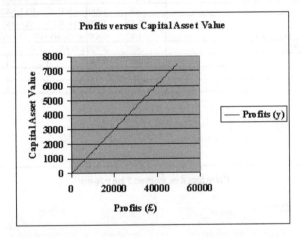

**Figure 5.1**

| | B7 | ▼ | *fx* | =IF(B6<=B3,B2*B6,B4*B6) | | | |
|---|---|---|---|---|---|---|---|
| | A | B | C | D | E | F | G |
| 1 | | | FORMULAE IN COLUMN B | | | | |
| 2 | Insurance premium 1 | 10 | NONE | | | | |
| 3 | Maximum floor space for insurance premium 1 | 500 | NONE | | | | |
| 4 | Insurance premium 2 | 15 | NONE | | | | |
| 5 | | | | | | | |
| 6 | Floor space (square metres) | 700 | NONE | | | | |
| 7 | Insurance premium due | 10500 | =IF(B6<=B3,B2*B6,B4*B6) | | | | |
| 8 | | | | | | | |
| 9 | | | | | | | |
| 10 | | | | | | | |

**Workbook 5.8A**

(b) The data for the graph are calculated as shown in Workbook 5.8B and the graph constructed in Figure 5.2 from a data range of B14:C27. Notice the 'step' that is created in the graph at a floor space value of 500m$^2$.

| | C14 | ▼ | $f_x$ =IF(B14<=B$3,B$2*B14,B$4*B14) | | | | | |
|---|---|---|---|---|---|---|---|---|
| | A | | B | C | D | E | F | G |
| 1 | | | | FORMULAE IN COLUMN B | | | | |
| 2 | Insurance premium 1 | | 10 | NONE | | | | |
| 3 | Maximum floor space for insurance premium 1 | | 500 | NONE | | | | |
| 4 | Insurance premium 2 | | 15 | NONE | | | | |
| 5 | | | | | | | | |
| 6 | Floor space (square metres) | | 700 | NONE | | | | |
| 7 | Insurance premium due | | 10500 | =IF(B6<=B3,B2*B6,B4*B6) | | | | |
| 8 | | | | | | | | |
| 9 | Start value for floor space | | 0 | | | | | |
| 10 | Step value for floor space | | 100 | | | | | |
| 11 | | | | | | | | |
| 12 | | | Floor | Premium | | | | |
| 13 | FORMULAE IN COLUMN B | | Space | Due | FORMULAE IN COLUMN C | | | |
| 14 | =B9 | | 0 | 0 | =IF(B14<=B$3,B$2*B14,B$4*B14) | | | |
| 15 | =B14+B$10 | | 100 | 1000 | =IF(B15<=B$3,B$2*B15,B$4*B15) | | | |
| 16 | =B15+B$10 | | 200 | 2000 | =IF(B16<=B$3,B$2*B16,B$4*B16) | | | |
| 17 | =B16+B$10 | | 300 | 3000 | =IF(B17<=B$3,B$2*B17,B$4*B17) | | | |
| 18 | AND SO ON AFTER COPYING | | 400 | 4000 | AND SO ON AFTER COPYING | | | |
| 19 | DOWN TO ROW 27 | | 500 | 5000 | DOWN TO ROW 27 | | | |
| 20 | | | 600 | 9000 | | | | |
| 21 | | | 700 | 10500 | | | | |
| 22 | | | 800 | 12000 | | | | |

**Workbook 5.8B**

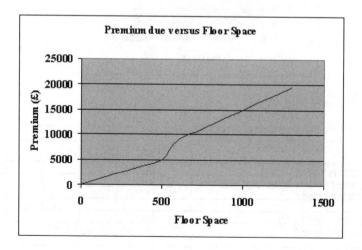

**Figure 5.2**

| | C9 | ▾ | *fx* | =IF(B9<=B$4,B$2*B9,B$3*B9)+B$1 | | | | | |
|---|---|---|---|---|---|---|---|---|---|
| | A | B | C | D | E | F | G | H |
| 1 | Fixed commission charge | 15 | | | | | | |
| 2 | Commission rate 1 | 1.00% | | | | | | |
| 3 | Commission rate 2 | 0.75% | | | | | | |
| 4 | Minimum purchase for commission rate 2 | 5000 | | | | | | |
| 5 | Start value for transaction amount | 1000 | | | | | | |
| 6 | Step value for transaction amount | 1000 | | | | | | |
| 7 | | Transaction | Transaction | | | | | |
| 8 | FORMULAE IN COLUMN B | Amount | Cost | FORMULAE IN COLUMN C | | | | |
| 9 | =B5 | 1000 | 25 | =IF(B9<=B$4,B$2*B9,B$3*B9)+B$1 | | | | |
| 10 | =B9+B$6 | 2000 | 35 | =IF(B10<=B$4,B$2*B10,B$3*B10)+B$1 | | | | |
| 11 | =B10+B$6 | 3000 | 45 | =IF(B11<=B$4,B$2*B11,B$3*B11)+B$1 | | | | |
| 12 | =B11+B$6 | 4000 | 55 | =IF(B12<=B$4,B$2*B12,B$3*B12)+B$1 | | | | |
| 13 | AND SO ON AFTER COPYING | 5000 | 65 | AND SO ON AFTER COPYING | | | | |
| 14 | DOWN TO ROW 28 | 6000 | 60 | DOWN TO ROW 28 | | | | |
| 15 | | 7000 | 67.5 | | | | | |
| 16 | | 8000 | 75 | | | | | |
| 17 | | 9000 | 82.5 | | | | | |

**Workbook 5.9**

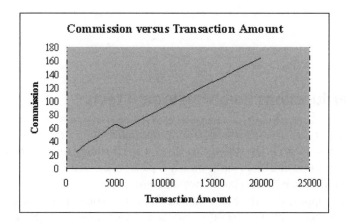

**Figure 5.3**

## Solution to Exercise 5.4

Workbook 5.9 illustrates the formulae used for the calculations and the graph shown in Figure 5.3 can be obtained by defining the data range as B9:C28. Once again it has a step in it where the lower commission rate cuts in.

### ■ NOTES

1. For a reminder of how to copy a formula see Section 1.5 of Chapter 1.
2. This is only a verbal indication of the syntax used by the IF function. *It will not work* as an actual operational formula until it has been translated into cell references or named cells.

# 6 Elementary modelling (2)

## 6.1 Linear functions involving logical tests

As a further application of the use and natural appearance of linear functions in business, consider a simple income tax system in which a fixed allowance of £4000 is awarded against gross income. In other words, no tax is paid on the first £4000 of gross income. Thereafter, all income is *taxable* but at two different rates.

To be exact: suppose that the first £16000 of taxable income is taxed at a rate of 20%, but any taxable income above £16000 is taxed at a higher rate of 25%. (Note: it is only the amount of taxable income **above £16000 that is taxed at the higher rate.**)

The task set is to calculate the tax due and hence the net income of an individual who earns a gross income of £30000.

For this *arithmetic* problem we can proceed as follows.

$$\text{Taxable income (TI)} = £30000 - £4000 = £26000$$

The first £16000 of this £26000 is taxed at 20%, giving

$$\text{Tax due(1)} = 20/100(£16000) = 0.2(£16000) = £3200$$

The remaining £10000 (£26000 − £16000) of taxable income is taxed at 25%, giving

$$\text{Tax due(2)} = 25/100(£10000) = 0.25(£10000) = £2500$$

Consequently,

Total tax bill = Tax due(1) + Tax due(2) =  £3200 + £2500 = £5700

Net income is therefore

$$£30000 - £5700 = £24300$$

Now consider the following more general formulation of the problem.

An income tax system contains a fixed allowance of £$A$ which is awarded against gross income. Thereafter, all income is taxable but at two different rates. The first £$M$ of taxable income is taxed at a rate of $t_l$%, and any taxable income above £$M$ is taxed at a higher rate of $t_h$%.

Calculate the tax due and hence the net income of an individual who earns a gross income of £$G$.

We can proceed in the same way as with the arithmetic example, only using symbols instead of numbers this time. Hence:

$$\text{Taxable Income (TI)} = G - A$$

However, although this appears to be a reasonable enough statement, the difficulties that can arise when moving from the **specific** to the **general** are immediately encountered. This is because the possibility exists that $G$ could be less than $A$, in which case TI would be negative. Algebraically, this would imply a negative amount of tax due (i.e. a rebate to the tax payer) yet few tax systems allow for this eventuality. In general practice, if an individual's gross income is less than their fixed allowance then their taxable income is regarded as zero rather than some negative amount. Consequently, with a view to modelling the problem on a spreadsheet, we require some form of *test* to be applied to the expression for taxable income that will prevent negative values being returned for low gross incomes. In other words, we need something like:

$$=IF(G\text{-}A{<}0,0,G\text{-}A)$$

This will test the difference between $G$ and $A$ and return 0 if that difference is less than 0, but return the actual (positive or zero) difference otherwise.

Now, turning to the tax due on *positive* taxable incomes, we again note that this will *depend* upon the magnitude of that taxable income. To be exact, if TI is less than or equal to £$M$ then the tax due is simply given by:

Tax due = $t_l \times$TI     (i.e. the lower tax rate times the taxable income).

However, if TI exceeds $M$ then the tax due is composed of two parts:

$$t_l \times M + t_h * (\text{TI} - M).$$

That is, the lower tax rate times the threshold value of taxable income for the higher tax rate to apply ($M$), plus the higher tax rate times the difference between taxable income and the threshold.

Translating these ideas into an IF statement, gives

$$=IF(G\text{-}A{<}{=}M,tl{*}(G\text{-}A),tl{*}M{+}th{*}(G\text{-}A\text{-}M))$$

or, in terms of TI,

| | B10 | ▼ | $f_x$ | =IF(TI<=M,tl*TI,tl*M+th*(TI-M)) | | | |
|---|---|---|---|---|---|---|---|
| | A | | B | C | D | E | F |
| 1 | | TAX CALCULATOR | | | | | |
| 2 | | | | FORMULAE IN COLUMN B | | | |
| 3 | Fixed allowance (A) = | | 4000 | NONE | | | |
| 4 | Lower tax rate (tl) = | | 0.2 | NONE | | | |
| 5 | Higher tax rate (th) = | | 0.25 | NONE | | | |
| 6 | Threshold for higher tax rate (M) = | | 16000 | NONE | | | |
| 7 | | | | | | | |
| 8 | Gross income (G) | | 30000 | NONE | | | |
| 9 | Taxable income (TI) | | 26000 | =IF(G-A<0,0,G-A) | | | |
| 10 | tax due (TD) | | 5700 | =IF(TI<=M,tl*TI,tl*M+th*(TI-M)) | | | |
| 11 | Net income (NI) | | 24300 | =G-B10 | | | |
| 12 | | | | | | | |

**Workbook 6.1**

$$=IF(TI<=M,tl*TI,tl*M+th*(TI-M))$$

Now consider Workbook 6.1 where the verbal logic above has been translated into spreadsheet form and then applied.

*Open a new workbook and proceed as instructed.*

*First, enter the indicated labels in A3:A11 and then the shown values to B3:B8. Leave B9:B11 empty for the moment.*

Note that the two tax rates have been entered in their decimal form (i.e. 20% = 20/100 = 0.2). If these tax rates were to change then they must be entered in this form, otherwise the calculations will be in error by a factor of 100. In other words, in this model a tax rate of 18% must be entered as 0.18 or 18% and **not** as 18.

*Now name the following cells:*

B3 as A   B4 as tl   B5 as th   B6 as M   B8 as G   B9 as TI

The IF statements in B9 and B10 correspond exactly to those outlined in the discussion above when the cells have been named as suggested.

*Consequently, in B9 enter:*

$$=IF(G-A<0,0,G-A)$$

This expression ensures that the value of taxable income (TI) is always non-negative, and allows us to address the B9 cell as the value for TI in the knowledge that negative values cannot occur.

*Then in B10 enter:*

$$=IF(TI<=M,tl*TI,tl*M+th*(TI-M))$$

*Finally, to compute net income use B11 to contain:*

$$=G-B10$$

The tax calculator is therefore completely general and will accurately compute the tax due and the net income for any value of gross income that is entered to B8.

Furthermore, it can clearly accommodate changes in the tax regime and/or gross income simply by making the relevant changes to any or all of the B3 to B8 cells. For example, use the model to compute the tax due for an individual who earns a gross income of £45000 if the fixed allowance has been increased to £6000, the lower tax increased to 23%, the higher tax rate increased to 35% and the threshold for the higher tax rate to apply increased to £19000.

If the model has been prepared correctly then figures of £11370 and £33630 should be obtained for the tax due and the net income respectively.

*Save the model as* **W6_1.xls**

Now consider how to obtain a chart of tax due versus gross income for a range of gross income values.

*Open a new workbook to follow the argument*

The first step will be to create our flexible scale adjuster for the variable to be placed on the horizontal axis (gross income). The procedure is the same as before—define start and step values for gross income and then link these to the range that is to contain these values with a formula that adds the defined step on to each previous value. This has been done in Workbook 6.2 for a tax system in which $A = £5000$, $t_l = 0.25$, $t_h = 0.5$ and $M = £19000$.

*Enter these new labels and values now as indicated in the A1:E5 range of Workbook 6.2.*

*Then in A6, enter:*

$$=E1$$

*and in A7 enter:*

$$=A6+E\$2$$

*and copy this into A8 to A19.*

*Finally, name the B1:B4 cells as A, tl, th and M respectively.*

The rest of the worksheet has been constructed as follows.

In B6 the taxable income is computed and then forced to become zero if the result turns out to be negative.

*To do this use B6 to contain:*

$$=IF(A6-A<0,0,A6-A)$$

*and then copy this into the B7 to B19 cells.*

*Then, in C6 write:*

$$=IF(B6<=M,tl*B6,tl*M+th*(B6-M))$$

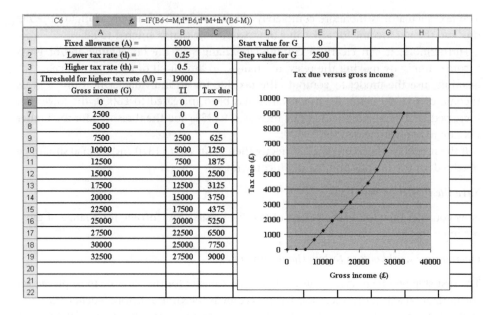

| | C6 | ▾ | | $f_x$ | =IF(B6<=M,tl*B6,tl*M+th*(B6-M)) | | | | | | |
|---|---|---|---|---|---|---|---|---|---|---|---|

| | A | B | C | D | E | F | G | H | I |
|---|---|---|---|---|---|---|---|---|---|
| 1 | Fixed allowance (A) = | 5000 | | Start value for G | 0 | | | | |
| 2 | Lower tax rate (tl) = | 0.25 | | Step value for G | 2500 | | | | |
| 3 | Higher tax rate (th) = | 0.5 | | | | | | | |
| 4 | Threshold for higher tax rate (M) = | 19000 | | | | | | | |
| 5 | Gross income (G) | TI | Tax due | | | | | | |
| 6 | 0 | 0 | 0 | | | | | | |
| 7 | 2500 | 0 | 0 | | | | | | |
| 8 | 5000 | 0 | 0 | | | | | | |
| 9 | 7500 | 2500 | 625 | | | | | | |
| 10 | 10000 | 5000 | 1250 | | | | | | |
| 11 | 12500 | 7500 | 1875 | | | | | | |
| 12 | 15000 | 10000 | 2500 | | | | | | |
| 13 | 17500 | 12500 | 3125 | | | | | | |
| 14 | 20000 | 15000 | 3750 | | | | | | |
| 15 | 22500 | 17500 | 4375 | | | | | | |
| 16 | 25000 | 20000 | 5250 | | | | | | |
| 17 | 27500 | 22500 | 6500 | | | | | | |
| 18 | 30000 | 25000 | 7750 | | | | | | |
| 19 | 32500 | 27500 | 9000 | | | | | | |
| 20 | | | | | | | | | |
| 21 | | | | | | | | | |
| 22 | | | | | | | | | |

**Workbook 6.2**

This tests whether the taxable income figure in B6 is less than the threshold for the upper rate of tax. If it is, then the tax due is simply the lower rate of tax times the taxable income. However, as with the model in Workbook 6.1, if taxable income exceeds the threshold then the higher rate of tax is applied to the amount by which taxable income **exceeds** the threshold and added to the (fixed) amount of the lower tax rate times the threshold.

*Now copy the contents of C6 into C7:C19*

*To produce the illustrated graph, define the data range as:*

$$A6:A19,C6:C19$$

(i.e. missing out the column B data).

As can be seen from the chart in Workbook 6.2, the tax due goes through three distinct phases. First, as long as gross income is less than the fixed allowance there is no tax due. This is shown by the line coinciding with the horizontal axis. Second, once taxable income becomes positive, but still less than the threshold, the tax due rises by £25 for every extra £100 of taxable income. This continues until the threshold for the higher rate of tax is reached, whereupon the tax due is the constant 25% of £19000 (£4750) plus £50 for every **extra** £100 of taxable income.

These three phases are clearly indicated on the chart and illustrate the power of the worksheet in giving a clear visual impression of what is by no means a trivial problem.

*Save this model now as W6_2.xls.*

Finally, it might well be asked:

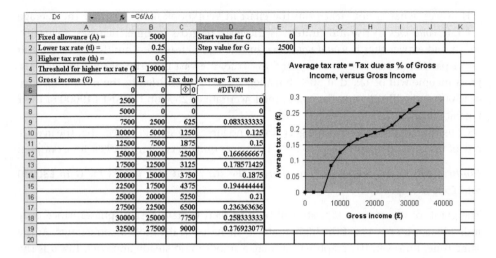

| | D6 | ▾ | *fx* | =C6/A6 | | | | | | | |
|---|---|---|---|---|---|---|---|---|---|---|---|
| | A | B | C | D | E | F | G | H | I | J | K |
| 1 | Fixed allowance (A) = | 5000 | | Start value for G | 0 | | | | | | |
| 2 | Lower tax rate (tl) = | 0.25 | | Step value for G | 2500 | | | | | | |
| 3 | Higher tax rate (th) = | 0.5 | | | | | | | | | |
| 4 | Threshold for higher tax rate (N | 19000 | | | | | | | | | |
| 5 | Gross income (G) | TI | | Tax due | Average Tax rate | | | | | | |
| 6 | 0 | 0 | ◈ 0 | #DIV/0! | | | | | | | |
| 7 | 2500 | 0 | 0 | 0 | | | | | | | |
| 8 | 5000 | 0 | 0 | 0 | | | | | | | |
| 9 | 7500 | 2500 | 625 | 0.083333333 | | | | | | | |
| 10 | 10000 | 5000 | 1250 | 0.125 | | | | | | | |
| 11 | 12500 | 7500 | 1875 | 0.15 | | | | | | | |
| 12 | 15000 | 10000 | 2500 | 0.166666667 | | | | | | | |
| 13 | 17500 | 12500 | 3125 | 0.178571429 | | | | | | | |
| 14 | 20000 | 15000 | 3750 | 0.1875 | | | | | | | |
| 15 | 22500 | 17500 | 4375 | 0.194444444 | | | | | | | |
| 16 | 25000 | 20000 | 5250 | 0.21 | | | | | | | |
| 17 | 27500 | 22500 | 6500 | 0.236363636 | | | | | | | |
| 18 | 30000 | 25000 | 7750 | 0.258333333 | | | | | | | |
| 19 | 32500 | 27500 | 9000 | 0.276923077 | | | | | | | |
| 20 | | | | | | | | | | | |

**Workbook 6.3**

What proportion of various amounts of gross income is taken by the tax authorities?

In other words what is the *average* rate of tax paid at different gross income levels?

To answer this, we simply have to note that the average rate of tax will be **the total tax due as a percentage of gross income.**

Workbook 6.2 contains all the data required to perform these calculations and then graph the results when modified as shown in Workbook 6.3.

*Use Workbook 6.2 as a template to produce the results indicated in Workbook 6.3.*

Workbook 6.3 was easily obtained from Workbook 6.2 by using column D to contain the ratio between tax due and gross income. The entry in D6 is therefore:

$$=C6/A6.$$

*Make this addition now and then copy from D6 to D19. Pay no attention to the first result in D6 which will be #DIV0!*

*Lastly, change the label for the data in column D to:*

Average tax rate

*and edit the title and vertical axis labels in the chart to reflect the changed nature of the problem.*

Clearly the average tax rate, although always rising with gross income, goes through a series of 'phases' that are determined by the levels of taxable income at which each of the three tax rates (0%, 25% and 50%) come into play. These correspond to the three phases of the chart in Workbook 6.2, although the movement between the phases is no longer linear.

However, what is not clear from the chart in Workbook 6.3 is whether the average tax rate *continues* to rise indefinitely as the level of gross income increases. Logically, we should expect that it *would not*, since in this tax regime even multi-billionaires will never pay tax at any rate in excess of 50%. True, the vast majority of such individuals' gross income will be taxed at 50%, but they will still be entitled to the fixed allowance of £5000 and will still only pay tax at the lower rate of 25% on the first £19000 of their taxable income.

Consequently, as gross income gets larger and larger we should expect that the *average* rate of tax gets closer and closer to 50%, but never quite gets there (49.99% for example).

*Confirm this in Workbook 6.3 by altering the start and step values for G to £30000 and £50000 respectively.*

The graph of the average tax rate will now be seen to have lost its phases, since only individuals who pay tax at the higher rate are included in the gross income range. At the same time, however, the graph will display a smooth and steady approach towards the limit of 50% as the level of gross income increases.

In general, then, if an income tax system consists of a fixed allowance and several increasing tax rates, the average rate of tax will increase steadily with increases in gross income, but will reach a definite limit that is determined by the **highest** rate of tax in the system.

The various tax rates that apply at different levels of taxable income are known as **marginal** tax rates since they represent the tax rate to be applied to each **extra** (marginal) unit of income above each of the defined income thresholds. Therefore, it will always be the case that the *average* rate of tax approaches the **highest** marginal rate of tax as the limiting case when gross incomes become very large.

*Save this model now as* W6_3.xls.

*Now attempt Exercises 6.1 and 6.2.*

## 6.2 Vertical lookup functions

The previous discussion has indicated how the logical IF function can be used to address problems in which there are two or three possible outcomes depending upon the circumstances (for example, no tax paid, all tax paid at the lower rate, tax paid at both the lower and the higher rates). However, the question arises of how to deal with situations in which there are considerably **more** than two or three possible outcomes. In theory, the necessary series of IF statements could be composed and entered to the worksheet, but in practice the effort and complexity of doing this means that a more efficient mechanism should be sought.

To discover this mechanism consider the following reformulation of the 'discount rate' problem encountered in Chapter 5. To be exact, imagine that the firm selling kitchen units offers a **range** of discount rates depending upon the **size** of the order quantity.

| | B2 | ▾ | $f_x$ | =VLOOKUP(B3,D3:E8,2) | | |
|---|---|---|---|---|---|---|
| | A | B | C | D | E | F |
| 1 | price (£P) | 80 | VERTICAL LOOKUP TABLE | | | |
| 2 | discount rate applied (d%) | 0.07 | | order size (x) | discount rate | |
| 3 | order size (x) | 70 | | 0 | 0 | |
| 4 | discount obtained (£) | 392 | | 10 | 0.04 | |
| 5 | Invoice (£) | 5208 | | 25 | 0.06 | |
| 6 | | | | 45 | 0.07 | |
| 7 | | | | 75 | 0.075 | |
| 8 | | | | 100 | 0.09 | |
| 9 | | | | | | |

**Workbook 6.4**

Thus, for orders of less than 10 units no discount is offered.

For orders of at least 10 units but less than 25 units a 4% discount is offered.

For orders of at least 25 units but less than 45 units a 6% discount is offered.

For orders of at least 45 units but less than 75 units a 7% discount is offered.

For orders at least 75 units but less than 100 units a 7.5% discount is offered.

For orders of 100 units or more a 9% discount is offered.

Clearly in this scenario there are six different discount rates that can be applied, depending upon the order size, and the task is to get Excel to select the correct one and then apply it to the order quantity so that the correct invoice can be calculated. Notice, however, that unlike the previous income tax example, these discount rates are **not** assumed to be applied **marginally**. In other words, each appropriate discount rate is applied to *all* units in the order.

The mechanism for dealing with this situation is indicated in Workbook 6.4.

*Open a new workbook and proceed as instructed.*

*First enter the indicated labels to A1:A5, and D1:E2.*

*Then enter the illustrated values to B1 and B3.*

*Leave B2, B4 and B5 blank for the moment.*

*Next enter the six different order threshold values and their associated discount rates into a table located in the range D3:E8.*

Notice that the labels in the rows directly above are for information only; the range of values eventually to be addressed are in D3 to E8. Also notice that the discount rates have been entered as decimals, e.g. 4% = 4/100 = 0.04.

This has been called a 'vertical lookup' table–'vertical' because there are more rows than columns, and 'lookup' because we are going to get Excel to look up in this table any value of *x* that we care to enter and return the discount rate that lies immediately to the right of that *x* value.

The function that will do this is called =VLOOKUP and takes three arguments (separated, as usual, by commas).[1]

The first argument is *what* is to be looked up in the table. This can be an actual value (2, 6, etc.) or an actual label (A, X, etc.) or, more usually, a cell reference containing either of these. In our illustration we need to find the discount rate associated with any *order quantity*, so it is the latter that we use as the first argument. Furthermore, since the order quantity has been housed in the B3 cell we can use this cell reference as the first argument.

Thus, building the function up step by step, we have:

$$=VLOOKUP(B3, \ldots$$

The next argument is the location of the table where the looking up is to be done. In our illustration we have previously noted that this range is D3:E8. However, notice that although we only have two columns in our illustrated table there is nothing to stop us having more if necessary—the third argument of the VLOOKUP function will tell us which of the columns of the table contains the data that are to be returned.

Continuing with building up the function we now have:

$$=VLOOKUP(B3,D3:E8, \ldots$$

Finally, the third required argument is known as the **column offset.** This defines which one of the columns in the table is the one to be associated with the value being looked up. The offset starts at 1 (i.e. the first column of the table) and increases in steps of 1 for every subsequent column of data.

Notice, however, that since in our illustration we have defined the lookup table to be the range D3:E8, this means that there are only two columns in use as far as the illustration is concerned. Hence, the column offset for our illustration *can only* be 1 or 2. However, with three columns defined in a table (D to F for example) the legal offset values become 1, 2 or 3.

Consequently, since in this example it is the discount rate associated with the requested order size that we want to be returned to whatever cell contains our VLOOKUP function, the required offset in this case is 2.

The completed function is therefore:

$$=VLOOKUP(B3,D3:E8,2)$$

*Enter this now to the B2 cell.*

Once this has been done, the lookup capability is completely operational.

Notice that this particular lookup function can be read to mean the following.

Look up the value contained in the B3 cell in the first column of the table contained in D3:D8 and return the associated value contained in the second column of that table.

*Now enter any order quantity in B3 and confirm that B2 will contain the associated discount rate.*

Once again notice that *any* order quantity can be entered to B3, not just one of the six contained in the first column of the lookup table.

The worksheet is completed in a similar way to our previous illustration by writing formulae to compute the monetary value of the discount and the net invoice.

*Hence, in B4 enter:*

$$=B1*B3*B2$$

*and in B5 write:*

$$=B1*B3-B4$$

*Now confirm that the correct invoice is computed for any entered value of the order, and then save this model as* W6_4.xls.

Two final points should be noted about the VLOOKUP function.

First, the values in the first column of any lookup table (containing *what* is to be looked up), *must* be arranged in *ascending* numerical order if they are values, or in *ascending* alphabetical order if they are text.

(This is not strictly true, if we add FALSE as the last (optional) argument to a lookup function. In other words,

$$=VLOOKUP(B3,D3:E8,2,FALSE)$$

would not require that the values in the first column of the lookup table were in ascending order, whereas

$$=VLOOKUP(B3,D3:E8,2)$$

would.)

The second point is the following. Although in the example only six values have been entered in the first column on the lookup table, Excel regards the values to be looked up as continuous within this range. In other words, the first value (0) is effectively regarded as 0 to 9.99999 inclusive, and the second value (10) as 10 to 24.99999 inclusive.

This continues for the rest of the values in the first column of the lookup table and explains why **any** value—**not just those six contained in the first column of the lookup table**—can be entered to the B3 cell.


# 6.3 **Combining conditional statements with lookup functions**

Now suppose that the discounts used in the illustration were in fact *only* for cash payments, and that for non-cash payments the equivalent discounts were:

0%, 1.5%, 2.5%, 3.5%, 4% *and* 4.5%.

The task to be undertaken now is to modify the worksheet to take account of this added distinction.

This has been done in Workbook 6.5

*Use Workbook 6.4 as a template then resave to produce Workbook 6.5.*

*First, add the labels shown in A6:A7.*

| | B2 | ▼ | *fx* | =VLOOKUP(B3,D3:F8,B7) | | |
|---|---|---|---|---|---|---|
| | A | B | C | D | E | F |
| 1 | Price (£P) | 80 | | VERTICAL LOOKUP TABLE | | |
| 2 | Discount rate applied (d%) | 0.07 | | order size (x) | discount (cash) | discount (other) |
| 3 | Order size (x) | 70 | | 0 | 0 | 0 |
| 4 | Discount obtained (£) | 392 | | 10 | 0.04 | 0.015 |
| 5 | Invoice (£) | 5208 | | 25 | 0.06 | 0.025 |
| 6 | Payment form: 1= cash; 0= other | 1 | | 45 | 0.07 | 0.035 |
| 7 | Column offset for lookup table | 2 | | 75 | 0.075 | 0.04 |
| 8 | | | | 100 | 0.09 | 0.045 |

**Workbook 6.5**

*Second, enter the non-cash discount rates alongside those that apply for cash.*

Notice that the first implication of this is that the lookup table will have to be *redefined* as D3:F8 to accommodate this extra column of information.

Next, as in previous versions of this problem we have used a cell (B6 in this case) to contain a code that tells whether (1) or not (0) payment is in cash.

*So enter 1 to B6.*

Now notice that the heart of the problem created by the introduction of another set of discount rates lies in getting the VLOOKUP function to apply the proper column offset in the lookup table. This is because if payment **is** in cash, the column offset in the VLOOKUP function should be 2, whereas if it is **not** in cash the offset value should be 3.

Consequently, we require a cell that will contain a value of 2 if payment is in cash (i.e. B6 = 1) or a value of 3 if payment is not in cash (i.e. B6 = 0).

*Do this in the B7 cell with the following IF statement:*

$$=IF(B6=1,2,3)$$

Clearly B7 will now always contain the correct lookup offset and so the final step is to include B7 *in cell address form* as the third argument of the VLOOKUP function.

*That is, change the formula in B2 to:*

$$=VLOOKUP(B3,D3:F8,B7)$$

Note carefully how the inclusion of B7 in the formula means that the lookup function can be forced to refer to either the second or the third column of the lookup table depending upon the value that B7 adopts, which in turn depends upon whether or not payment is in cash (i.e. whether B6 contains 1 or 0).

*After making these alterations confirm that the correct invoice is obtained for any order amount and any payment form (i.e. cash or other).*

*Now save this model as* W6_5.xls.

*Exercise 6.3 can now be attempted.*

| | B5 | ▾ | $f_x$ =B$1*A5*(1-VLOOKUP(A5,D$3:F$8,2)) | | | | | |
|---|---|---|---|---|---|---|---|---|
| | A | B | C | D | E | F | G | H |
| 1 | Price (£P) | 80 | | order size (x) | discount rate applicable (d) | | | |
| 2 | | | | | cash | non-cash | | |
| 3 | | | | 0 | 0 | 0 | | |
| 4 | Order size (x) | Cash invoice | Non-cash invoice | 10 | 0.04 | 0.015 | | |
| 5 | 0 | 0 | 0 | 25 | 0.06 | 0.025 | | |
| 6 | 9 | 720 | 720 | 45 | 0.07 | 0.035 | | |
| 7 | 10 | 768 | 788 | 75 | 0.075 | 0.04 | | |
| 8 | 24 | 1843.2 | 1891.2 | 100 | 0.09 | 0.045 | | |
| 9 | 25 | 1880 | 1950 | | | | | |
| 10 | 44 | 3308.8 | 3432 | | | | | |
| 11 | 45 | 3348 | 3474 | | | | | |
| 12 | 74 | 5505.6 | 5712.8 | | | | | |
| 13 | 75 | 5550 | 5760 | | | | | |
| 14 | 99 | 7326 | 7603.2 | | | | | |
| 15 | 100 | 7280 | 7640 | | | | | |
| 16 | 110 | 8008 | 8404 | | | | | |

**Workbook 6.6**

Finally, by using the same methods as in previous illustrations we can extend Workbook 6.5 to provide a chart that will indicate how the invoice **varies** with the order size—for both cash **and** non-cash payment forms.

*Open a new workbook and make up Workbook 6.6 as explained in the text following the illustration*

*First, fill all of the indicated cells with the illustrated labels and data values except for those in B5:C16. These will be created by formulae.*

Now we can use the lookup function as a replacement for the cell that contained the discount rate in previous illustrations.

In other words with $P$, $x$ and $d$ representing the price, order quantity and discount rate (as a decimal) respectively, the entry in B5 should represent:

$$Px - Pxd = px(1 - d).$$

*Therefore in B5 enter:*

=B$1*A5*(1-VLOOKUP(A5,D$3:F$8,2))

Notice that the address of the lookup table (D3:F8) has had its row numbers dollar-fixed. This is **essential** to prevent the address of the table updating erroneously when the formula in B5 is copied into B6 to B16.[2] Also observe that since this column is **for payment in cash** the column offset in the lookup function can be **fixed** at 2.

*Now, in C5, make the equivalent entry:*

=B$1*A5*(1-VLOOKUP(A5,D$3:F$8,3))

Notice that the only change from the entry in B5 is that the column offset has become 3 instead of 2.

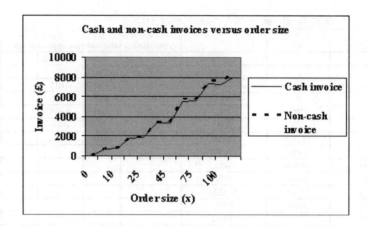

**Figure 6.1**

*Now copy B5:C5 into B6:C16.*

*Next, plot these three data series (A3:C16) with appropriate titles and legends. This time select a line graph instead of an XY and then at the next Wizard prompt choose the Series tab at the top of the screen.*

*From this screen remove the order quantity series and then click on the*

*'Category (X) axis labels' box.*

*Drag over A5:A16 then click next and add titles as before. The result should resemble the chart shown in Figure 6.1.*

As can clearly be seen, the data create a 'step-like' graph that shows both the cash and the non-cash invoices rising in steps until the maximum discount of 9% for cash or 4.5% for non-cash is reached. Thereafter, the graph for both payment forms would rise steadily and without any steps.

*Now save this worksheet with its embedded chart as W6_6.xls.*

Finally, the invoice *per unit ordered* could also be calculated and plotted simply by reforming the B5 and C5 entries.

*Use Workbook 6.6 (W6_6.xls) as a template and then make the following alterations.*

*Rewrite the formula in B5 as:*

$$=B\$1*A5*(1-VLOOKUP(A5,D\$3:F\$8,2))/A5$$

Or, after cancelling the A5 term from top and bottom, as:

$$=B\$1*(1-VLOOKUP(A5,D\$3:F\$8,2))$$

*Then rewrite the formula in C5 as:*

| | C13 | ▼ | $f_x$ | =B\$1*(1-VLOOKUP(A13,D\$3:F\$8,3)) | | | |
|---|---|---|---|---|---|---|---|
| | A | B | C | D | E | F | G |
| 1 | Price (£P) | 80 | | order size (x) | discount rate applicable (d) | | |
| 2 | | | | | cash | non-cash | |
| 3 | | Cash invoice | Non-cash invoice | 0 | 0 | 0 | |
| 4 | Order size (x) | per unit ordered | per unit ordered | 10 | 0.04 | 0.015 | |
| 5 | 0 | 80 | 80 | 25 | 0.06 | 0.025 | |
| 6 | 9 | 80 | 80 | 45 | 0.07 | 0.035 | |
| 7 | 10 | 76.8 | 78.8 | 75 | 0.075 | 0.04 | |
| 8 | 24 | 76.8 | 78.8 | 100 | 0.09 | 0.045 | |
| 9 | 25 | 75.2 | 78 | | | | |
| 10 | 44 | 75.2 | 78 | | | | |
| 11 | 45 | 74.4 | 77.2 | | | | |
| 12 | 74 | 74.4 | 77.2 | | | | |
| 13 | 75 | 74 | 76.8 | | | | |
| 14 | 99 | 74 | 76.8 | | | | |
| 15 | 100 | 72.8 | 76.4 | | | | |
| 16 | 110 | 72.8 | 76.4 | | | | |

**Workbook 6.7**

$$=B\$1*A5*(1-VLOOKUP(A5,D\$3:F\$8,3))/A5$$

or, again after cancellation:

$$=B\$1*(1-VLOOKUP(A5,D\$3:F"\$8,3))$$

*Finally, copy B5 and C5 into B6 to C16.[3]*

When this is done (using the second versions of the formulae) the results shown in Workbook 6.7 should be obtained.

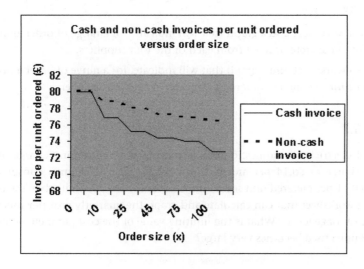

**Figure 6.2**

Notice that since we are using Workbook 6.6 as a template the graph will have adjusted automatically to reflect the new nature of the data, but the title, the axis labels and the legends for the data series still refer to the previous illustration.

*Use the editing facility to make the necessary changes so that your graph resembles the one shown in Figure 6.2 and then save the new version as W6_7.xls.*

Once again, as in the previous income tax example, these invoices per unit of order size reach a limit that is determined by the highest discount rate that the firm offers. To be exact, *once an order size of 100 units has been achieved* then the invoice per unit is simply the price less 9% of the price if payment is in cash, or the price less 4.5% of the price if the payment form is non-cash.

This is the same as (100%− 9%) = 91% of the price for cash payments or (100%− 4.5%) = 95.5% of the price for non-cash payments.

## 6.4 Exercises

### Exercise 6.1

A builder can obtain concrete from any of four suppliers.

Supplier W charges £12 per ton for the concrete and a fixed delivery charge of £50 regardless of the quantity ordered.

Supplier X charges £14 per ton including delivery.

Supplier Y charges £11.5 per ton for the concrete and a fixed delivery charge of £100. However, for orders in excess of 40 tons delivery is free from supplier Y.

Supplier Z charges £11 per ton for the concrete, £2 per ton delivery charge and a fixed delivery charge of £20.

(a) Prepare a worksheet and a graph that will indicate, for a range of order amounts, the *total cost* of concrete ordered from each of the four suppliers.

(b) Prepare a worksheet and a graph that will indicate, for a range of order amounts, the ***cost per unit*** of concrete ordered from each of the four suppliers.

### Exercise 6.2

The cost of electricity to domestic users is composed of a standing charge of £10 per quarter, a charge of £0.14 per metered unit for the first 2000 units consumed and a charge of £0.11 per metered unit for all units in excess of 2000 units that are used.

Prepare a worksheet that can calculate and graph the quarterly **cost per metered unit** for a range of usage levels. What is the limiting value of the cost per metered unit as the number of units used becomes very large?

**Table 6.1**

| SIZE | S | M | L | XL |
|---|---|---|---|---|
| TYPE | | | | |
| A | 15 | 17 | 18 | 19.5 |
| B | 21 | 26 | 29 | 32 |
| C | 43 | 52 | 67 | 78 |
| D | 3 | 5 | 8 | 9 |
| E | 29 | 34 | 38 | 49 |
| F | 63 | 69 | 73 | 81 |

## Exercise 6.3

A firm sells six different products (A, B, C, D, E and F) each of which is available in four different sizes (S, M, L, XL). Table 6.1 indicates the prices charged (in £s) for the products.

Prepare a worksheet that will compute the invoice to be sent to a customer when any product type, any size and any order quantity are entered to three cells of the sheet.

## 6.5 Solutions to the exercises

### Solution to Exercise 6.1

(a) A section of the calculations required to produce the total cost are shown in Workbook 6.8 and these data are then graphed in Figure 6.3 from the data range A8:E24 (i.e. including the column headers to provide the data series legends).

(b) Workbook 6.8 is easily modified to compute the **unit** as opposed to the total cost of concrete from each of the suppliers. All that needs to be done is divide the previous expressions for total cost by the number of tons ordered.

After cancelling any common terms from the top and the bottom this produces the formulae shown in Workbook 6.9.

Thus:

$$B9 \text{ becomes} := (B\$2 * A9 + B\$5)/A9 = B\$2 + B\$5/A9$$
$$C9 \text{ becomes} = (C\$2 * A9)/A9 = C\$2$$
$$D9 \text{ becomes} = IF(A9 > D\$4, D\$2 * A9/A9, (D\$2 * A9 + D\$5)/A9)$$

which is equivalent to:

$$= IF(A9 > D\$4, D\$2, D\$2 + D\$5/A9)$$
$$E9 \text{ becomes} := ((E\$2 + E\$3) * A9 + E\$5)/A9 = (E\$2 + E\$3) + E\$5/A9$$

| | D9 | ▾ | | $f_x$ | =IF(A9>D$4,D$2*A9,D$2*A9+D$5) | | | | |
|---|---|---|---|---|---|---|---|---|---|
| | A | B | C | D | E | F | G | H | I |
| 1 | Supplier | W | X | Y | Z | | | | |
| 2 | Cost per ton | 12 | 14 | 11.5 | 11 | | | | |
| 3 | Delivery charge per ton | 0 | 0 | 0 | 2 | | | | |
| 4 | Threshold for free delivery | 0 | 0 | 40 | 0 | | | | |
| 5 | Fixed delivery charge | 50 | 0 | 100 | 20 | | | | |
| 6 | Start value for order amount | 6 | | | | | | | |
| 7 | Step value for order amount | 3 | | | | | | | |
| 8 | Amount ordered | Cost W | Cost X | Cost Y | Cost Z | FORMULAE: | | | |
| 9 | 6 | 122 | 84 | 169 | 98 | B9: =B$2*A9+B$5 | | | |
| 10 | 9 | 158 | 126 | 203.5 | 137 | COPIED DOWN TO ROW 24 | | | |
| 11 | 12 | 194 | 168 | 238 | 176 | | | | |
| 12 | 15 | 230 | 210 | 272.5 | 215 | C9: =C$2*A9 | | | |
| 13 | 18 | 266 | 252 | 307 | 254 | COPIED DOWN TO ROW 24 | | | |
| 14 | 21 | 302 | 294 | 341.5 | 293 | | | | |
| 15 | 24 | 338 | 336 | 376 | 332 | D9: =IF(A9>D$4,D$2*A9,D$2*A9+D$5) | | | |
| 16 | 27 | 374 | 378 | 410.5 | 371 | COPIED DOWN TO ROW 24 | | | |
| 17 | 30 | 410 | 420 | 445 | 410 | | | | |
| 18 | 33 | 446 | 462 | 479.5 | 449 | E9: =(E$2+E$3)*A9+E$5 | | | |
| 19 | 36 | 482 | 504 | 514 | 488 | COPIED DOWN TO ROW 24 | | | |
| 20 | 39 | 518 | 546 | 548.5 | 527 | | | | |
| 21 | 42 | 554 | 588 | 483 | 566 | | | | |
| 22 | 45 | 590 | 630 | 517.5 | 605 | | | | |
| 23 | 48 | 626 | 672 | 552 | 644 | | | | |
| 24 | 51 | 662 | 714 | 586.5 | 683 | | | | |

**Workbook 6.8**

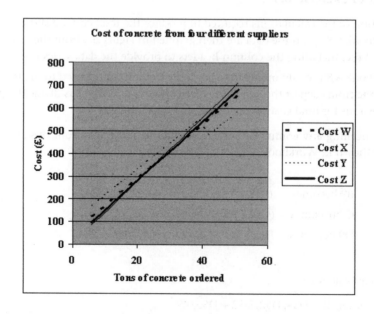

**Figure 6.3**

| | A | B | C | D | E | F |
|---|---|---|---|---|---|---|
| 1 | Supplier | W | X | Y | Z | |
| 2 | Cost per ton | 12.00 | 14.00 | 11.50 | 11.00 | |
| 3 | Delivery charge per ton | 0.00 | 0.00 | 0.00 | 2.00 | |
| 4 | Threshold for free delivery | 0.00 | 0.00 | 40.00 | 0.00 | |
| 5 | Fixed delivery charge | 50.00 | 0.00 | 100.00 | 20.00 | |
| 6 | Start value for order amount | 6.00 | | | | |
| 7 | Step value for order amount | 3.00 | | | | |
| 8 | Amount ordered | Cost/unit W | Cost/unit X | Cost/unit Y | Cost/unit Z | FORMULAE: |
| 9 | 6.00 | 20.33 | 14.00 | 28.17 | 16.33 | B9: =B$2+B$5/A9 |
| 10 | 9.00 | 17.56 | 14.00 | 22.61 | 15.22 | COPIED DOWN TO ROW 24 |
| 11 | 12.00 | 16.17 | 14.00 | 19.83 | 14.67 | |
| 12 | 15.00 | 15.33 | 14.00 | 18.17 | 14.33 | C9: =C$2 |
| 13 | 18.00 | 14.78 | 14.00 | 17.06 | 14.11 | COPIED DOWN TO ROW 24 |
| 14 | 21.00 | 14.38 | 14.00 | 16.26 | 13.95 | |
| 15 | 24.00 | 14.08 | 14.00 | 15.67 | 13.83 | D9: =IF(A9>D$4,D$2,D$2+D$5/A9) |
| 16 | 27.00 | 13.85 | 14.00 | 15.20 | 13.74 | COPIED DOWN TO ROW 24 |
| 17 | 30.00 | 13.67 | 14.00 | 14.83 | 13.67 | |
| 18 | 33.00 | 13.52 | 14.00 | 14.53 | 13.61 | E9: =(E$2+E$3)+E$5/A9 |
| 19 | 36.00 | 13.39 | 14.00 | 14.28 | 13.56 | COPIED DOWN TO ROW 24 |
| 20 | 39.00 | 13.28 | 14.00 | 14.06 | 13.51 | |
| 21 | 42.00 | 13.19 | 14.00 | 11.50 | 13.48 | |
| 22 | 45.00 | 13.11 | 14.00 | 11.50 | 13.44 | |
| 23 | 48.00 | 13.04 | 14.00 | 11.50 | 13.42 | |
| 24 | 51.00 | 12.98 | 14.00 | 11.50 | 13.39 | |

**Workbook 6.9**

When the data produced by these calculations are graphed the chart shown in Figure 6.4 is obtained.

The data range is the same as in Exercise 6.1 but the titles and column headers have been changed to reflect the changed nature of the calculations.

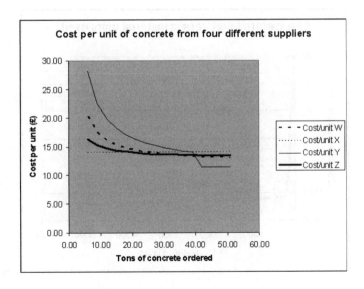

**Figure 6.4**

| | B9 | ▼ | *fx* | =IF(A9<=TQ,S+ch*A9,S+ch*TQ+cl*(A9-TQ)) | | | |
|---|---|---|---|---|---|---|---|

| | A | B | C | D | E | F | G |
|---|---|---|---|---|---|---|---|
| 1 | Standing charge | 10 | | | | | |
| 2 | Charge per metered unit 1 | 0.14 | | | | | |
| 3 | Charge per metered unit 2 | 0.11 | | | | | |
| 4 | Minimum consumption for charge 2 | 2000 | | | | | |
| 5 | Start value for usage | 10 | | | | | |
| 6 | Step value for usage | 200 | | | | | |
| 7 | | | | | | | |
| 8 | Usage (metered units) | Total cost | Unit Cost | FORMULAE: | | | |
| 9 | 10 | 11.4 | 1.14 | IN B9: | | | |
| 10 | 210 | 39.4 | 0.19 | =IF(A9<=TQ,S+ch*A9,S+ch*TQ+cl*(A9-TQ)) | | | |
| 11 | 410 | 67.4 | 0.16 | COPIED DOWN TO ROW 37 | | | |
| 12 | 610 | 95.4 | 0.16 | | | | |
| 13 | 810 | 123.4 | 0.15 | IN C9: | | | |
| 14 | 1010 | 151.4 | 0.15 | =B9/A9 | | | |
| 15 | 1210 | 179.4 | 0.15 | COPIED DOWN TO ROW 37 | | | |
| 16 | 1410 | 207.4 | 0.15 | | | | |
| 17 | 1610 | 235.4 | 0.15 | | | | |

**Workbook 6.10**

## Solution to Exercise 6.2

The B1:B4 cells were named as S, ch, cl and TQ respectively.

The calculations and formulae used are shown in Workbook 6.10 and then graphed in Figure 6.5 where a data range of A9:A37,C9:C37 has been used.

Clearly as the number of metered units increases the cost per unit approaches a limit of £0.122.

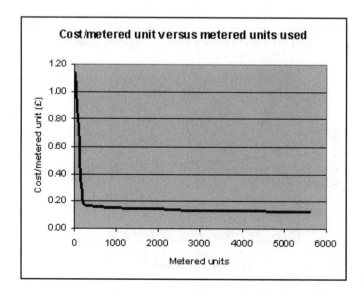

**Figure 6.5**

| | B6 | ▾ | *fx* | =B4*VLOOKUP(B2,B9:F14,B5) | | | | |
|---|---|---|---|---|---|---|---|---|
| | A | B | C | D | E | F | G | H |
| 1 | | FORMULAE IN COLUMN B | | | | | | |
| 2 | Product type | B | NONE | | | | | |
| 3 | Product size | S | NONE | | | | | |
| 4 | Number of units | 20 | NONE | | | | | |
| 5 | Column offset | 2 | =VLOOKUP(B3,B16:C19,2) | | | | | |
| 6 | Value of order | 420 | =B4*VLOOKUP(B2,B9:F14,B5) | | | | | |
| 7 | | Size | S | M | L | XL | | |
| 8 | | Product | | | | | | |
| 9 | | A | 15 | 17 | 18 | 19.5 | | |
| 10 | | B | 21 | 26 | 29 | 32 | | |
| 11 | | C | 43 | 52 | 67 | 78 | | |
| 12 | | D | 3 | 5 | 8 | 9 | | |
| 13 | | E | 29 | 34 | 38 | 49 | | |
| 14 | | F | 63 | 69 | 73 | 81 | | |
| 15 | | LOOKUP TABLE FOR COLUMN OFFSET VALUE | | | | | | |
| 16 | | L | 4 | | | | | |
| 17 | | M | 3 | | | | | |
| 18 | | S | 2 | | | | | |
| 19 | | XL | 5 | | | | | |
| 20 | | | | | | | | |

**Workbook 6.11**

## Solution to Exercise 6.3

The solution is shown in Workbook 6.11. The main lookup table has been located in B9: F14. However, notice how we have created a second lookup table in B16:C19 containing the sizes of the items (in ascending alphabetical order) in the first column and the appropriate column offsets in the main table in the second column.

The formula in B5 then uses this second table to look up the appropriate offset for the main table and this allows the contents of B5 to be used as the **offset argument** in the lookup formula that has been located in B6.

■ NOTES

1. There is also an equivalent horizontal lookup function (=HLOOKUP) if the data has been entered with more columns than rows.

2. You could get round this need to dollar-fix by naming the lookup table. That is, select D3:F8 and then choose Insert, Name and Define from the Menu bar. Then supply a name such as TABLEA and refer to this named range thereafter in any lookup functions that are written.

3. If you use the first versions of these formulae then B5 and C5 will show #DIV/0 since this is exactly what is being done in row 5. You can fix this by making the first value for order size = 0.001 rather than zero.

# 7 Collating and categorizing data

The following files from the online resource centre should be loaded as instructed:

W7_1.xls    W7_5.xls

W7_7.xls    W7_8.xls

## 7.1 Preliminaries

Whether you realize it or not, at some time or another you will almost certainly have performed some kind of elementary statistical analysis. This is because, at base, statistics is concerned with the process of making sense from, and bringing order to, collections of data observations.

Your monthly bank statement, your end of term assessment marks and your quarterly telephone bill are all examples of data observations that can be collected together (over several months, terms or quarters) to form what is known as a **data set**, thereby creating the basic unit of statistical analysis.

Once collected (from whatever source), data will have to be brought together and presented in some manageable form. This is known as **collation** and will frequently involve summarizing and/or tabulating the information so that it can be interpreted and analysed more efficiently.

One of the most useful devices for performing this collation is known as a **frequency distribution**.

## 7.2 Frequency distributions

One of the most effective ways of collating data is to create what is known as a frequency distribution. To see how this works consider the data contained in Workbook 7.1.

*Load the file called* **W7_1.xls** *now*

The data in column A are the number of occupants observed to be in each of 100 cars that arrived at a motorway service station over a period of 30 minutes on a particular day.

Clearly the data are in 'raw' form and as such are not easy to interpret until it is noticed that the number of occupants observed was always between 1 and 5 inclusive.

To collate these data without using Excel would require that a **manual** count of the number of cars containing one person was made, then a manual count of the number of cars containing two persons, and so on for the number of cars with three, four and five persons.[1]

If you can be bothered to do this manual count then you will find that in this data set there were: 22 cars with 1 occupant, 32 cars with 2 occupants, 27 cars with 3 occupants, 12 cars with 4 occupants and 7 cars with 5 occupants.

Now, if we regard the number of occupants as a **statistical variable** (since in this case its value can **vary** between 1 and 5 inclusive), and denote it by the symbol $x$, then each value of $x$ can be associated with the number of times that it was observed—its frequency (denoted by $f$). Thus, a value of $x = 2$ (cars) has an associated frequency of 32 (occurrences) in the illustrative data set.

Finally, if we consider each value of $x$ that *could* be observed and attach alongside the associated frequency of that value of $x$, then we obtain what is known as the **frequency distribution** of the $x$ variable. For the illustrative data this would be written as:

| Variable ($x$) | 1 | 2 | 3 | 4 | 5 |
|---|---|---|---|---|---|
| Frequency ($f$) | 22 | 32 | 27 | 12 | 7 |

This is the frequency distribution of the statistical variable $x$, and simply indicates the number of times that a particular value of $x$ was observed.

However, if you actually went through the manual counts for this data set you should appreciate that it is a extremely tedious process—even with only 100 observations. With ten or twenty thousand observations it would become a Herculean task.

This is where Excel can help.

*Make sure that you have Workbook 7.1 on-screen then proceed as follows*

*First, in B1 reproduce the header contained in A1 (number of occupants). Then, in B2:B6 enter the five distinct values that the variable can adopt (i.e. 1, 2, 3, 4 and 5)*

In Excel parlance this will be known as the 'bin' and simply provides information to the program as to which values of the variable it is to use in calculating the frequencies of the raw data.

For example, if you only supplied a bin range of 2, 4 and 5 then Excel would compute the combined frequencies of 1 and 2, 3 and 4, and then 5 alone.

However, with the bin established in this case as 1, 2, 3, 4 and 5, all that remains is to access Tools from the Menu bar and then Data Analysis.

### Do this now

If you are unable to find Data Analysis on the list of Tools options then this routine may not have been 'added in'.

**To do this, click on Tools and then Add-Ins. From the list that appears select Analysis ToolPak and Analysis ToolPak—VBA by checking their boxes**

The Data Analysis Add-In will now be available under the Tools menu.

**From the list of options that appears select Histogram**

The dialogue box shown in Figure 7.1 should now appear.
Excel must now be appraised of the range containing the raw data, as well as the range containing the bin values to be used, so that it can perform the classification.

**Consequently, click on the Input Range box and then click on the A1 cell and drag down to A101. Alternatively, enter the range directly to the box as A1:A101**

This will define the range containing the data observations

**Next, click on the Bin Range box and then click on B1 and drag down to B6**

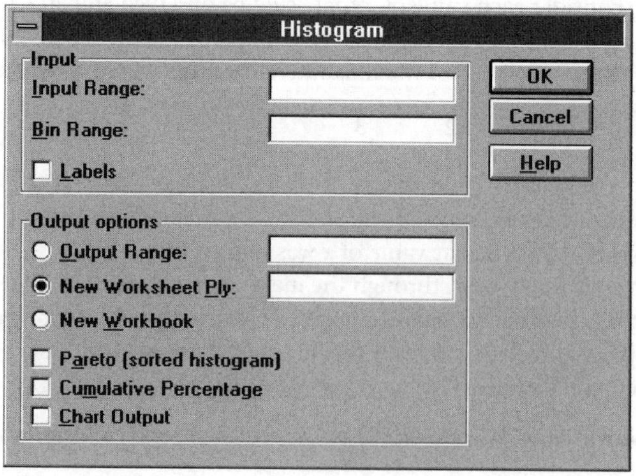

**Figure 7.1**

This will define the values that we have entered to B1:B6 as the range of *x* values to be used in the classification.

***Next, since we have included the column headers in both the Input and Bin ranges, click on the Labels tab so that a tick or a cross appears***

This tells Excel to expect labels as well as numerical values in the data range. Only the latter can be used in the classification process and so with this tab checked Excel will ignore any text entries used as labels.

***Finally, click on the Output Range tab and then on the adjacent box, and enter C1.***

This tells Excel where to put frequency distribution that it is about to compute. (If you do not specify an output range Excel will create a new sheet and place the results there.)
  The worksheet and Histogram dialogue box should now resemble Workbook 7.1.
  After a few seconds the frequency distribution will be computed and your worksheet should resemble Workbook 7.2.
  Notice that these are exactly the results that were obtained from the manual procedure explained above.

***Now save this file as* W7_2.xls**

Also notice that Excel has added an extra category—'*More*'—to the bin. In this case the associated frequency is zero, but in other cases it will indicate the number of observations that cannot be classified in terms of the bin that was defined.
  For example, had there in fact been 4 cars with 6 occupants, with the bin still being defined as 1 to 5 inclusive then the frequency associated with *More* would have been 4 (with one or more of the other frequencies being reduced by a total of 4).

| | A | B | C | D | E | F | G | H | I |
|---|---|---|---|---|---|---|---|---|---|
| 1 | No. of occupants | No. of occupants | | | | Histogram | | | |
| 2 | 1 | 1 | Input | | | | | | |
| 3 | 2 | 2 | Input Range: | | | $A$1:$A$101 | | OK | |
| 4 | 1 | 3 | | | | | | Cancel | |
| 5 | 3 | 4 | Bin Range: | | | $B$1:$B$6 | | | |
| 6 | 2 | 5 | X Labels | | | | | Help | |
| 7 | 1 | | | | | | | | |
| 8 | 3 | | Output options | | | | | | |
| 9 | 4 | | Output Range: | | | $C$1 | | | |
| 10 | 2 | | New Worksheet Ply: | | | | | | |
| 11 | 5 | | New Workbook | | | | | | |
| 12 | 3 | | | | | | | | |
| 13 | 2 | | Pareto (sorted histogram) | | | | | | |
| 14 | 1 | | Cumulative Percentage | | | | | | |
| 15 | 3 | | Chart Output | | | | | | |
| 16 | 5 | | | | | | | | |
| 17 | 2 | | | | | | | | |
| 18 | 3 | | | | | | | | |

Sheet1 / Sheet2 / Sheet3 / Sheet4 / Sheet5 / Sheet

**Workbook 7.1**

| | A | B | C | D | E | F | G | H | I | J |
|---|---|---|---|---|---|---|---|---|---|---|
| 1 | No. of occupants | No. of occupants | No. of occupants | Frequency | | | | | | |
| 2 | 1 | 1 | 1 | 22 | | | | | | |
| 3 | 2 | 2 | 2 | 32 | | | | | | |
| 4 | 1 | 3 | 3 | 27 | | | | | | |
| 5 | 3 | 4 | 4 | 12 | | | | | | |
| 6 | 2 | 5 | 5 | 7 | | | | | | |
| 7 | 1 | | More | 0 | | | | | | |
| 8 | 3 | | | | | | | | | |

K ◄ ► M \ Sheet1 / Sheet2 / Sheet3 / Sheet4 / Sheet5 / Sheet6 / Sheet7 / Sheet8 / Sheet9 / Sl ◄

**Workbook 7.2**

The frequencies that this Excel routine produces are known as **absolute** frequencies in the sense that they indicate the **actual** number of occurrences of $x$ values of 1, 2, 3, 4 or 5.

However, it will sometimes be useful to convert these absolute frequencies into what are known as **relative** frequencies.

Quite simply, a relative frequency is simply each absolute frequency expressed as a proportion or percentage of the total number of frequencies.

The Excel Data Analysis routine does not compute relative frequencies automatically, but it is an easy matter to write formulae in the worksheet that perform this task.

*To see how, use the most recent version of* **W7_2.xls** *as a template and read on*

The first thing to do is compute the total number of frequencies in the data set.

*Do this now in the D8 cell by entering the formula:*

$$=SUM(D2:D7)$$

For the illustration, a value of 100 should be returned.

*Now name D8 as FT (for frequency total)*

*Next, in E1 enter the label:*

Frequency %

*and then, in E2 the formula:*

$$=D2/FT$$

*Now copy the contents of E2 into E3:E7.*

The results show each of the frequencies as a proportion of the total number of frequencies, and at the moment these are expressed in decimal form.

| | A | B | C | D | E | F | G | H | I | J |
|---|---|---|---|---|---|---|---|---|---|---|
| 1 | No. of occupant | No. of occupants | No. of occupants | Frequency | Frequency % | | | | | |
| 2 | 1 | 1 | 1 | 22 | 22.00% | | | | | |
| 3 | 2 | 2 | 2 | 32 | 32.00% | | | | | |
| 4 | 1 | 3 | 3 | 27 | 27.00% | | | | | |
| 5 | 3 | 4 | 4 | 12 | 12.00% | | | | | |
| 6 | 2 | 5 | 5 | 7 | 7.00% | | | | | |
| 7 | 1 | | More | 0 | 0.00% | | | | | |
| 8 | 3 | | | 100 | | | | | | |
| 9 | 4 | | | | | | | | | |

H ◀ ▶ H \Sheet1 / Sheet2 / Sheet3 / Sheet4 / Sheet5 / Sheet6 / Sheet7 / Sheet8 / Sheet9 / Sl| ◀|         ▶|

**Workbook 7.3**

*To make them display as percentages, select the E2:E7 area with the mouse and then Format from the Menu bar. Then choose Cells and then Percentage and use two decimal places.*

The results should resemble Workbook 7.3.

*Now save this file as W7_3.xls.*

*Now attempt Exercise 7.1.*

## 7.3 Cumulative frequency distributions

Absolute and relative frequencies tell us about the number and proportion of times each particular value of $x$ occurs. However, suppose we were concerned with the frequency of occurrence of more than one particular value of $x$.

Simple inspection of the data suggests that a total of 54 (= 22 + 32) cars had 1 or 2 occupants. Similarly, a total of 81 (= 22 + 32 + 27) cars had 1 or 2 or 3 occupants.

Continuing with this logic reveals that 93 cars had 1 or 2 or 3 or 4 occupants, and 100 had 1 or 2 or 3 or 4 or 5 occupants.

Another way of phrasing this argument is to work in terms of '$x$ occupants or less'. Thus, 22 cars had 1 occupant or less, 54 cars had 2 occupants or less, 81 cars had 3 occupants or less, 93 cars had 4 occupants or less and 100 cars (all of them) had 5 occupants or less.

When the variable is regarded as '$x$ or less' as opposed to 'exactly equal to $x$' then what is known as a **cumulative frequency distribution** is produced.

Furthermore, these absolute cumulative frequencies could also be translated into percentage terms to obtain a **relative** cumulative frequency distribution.

Both of these are produced below from the data obtained in the discussion above.[2]

| Exactly x occupants | 1 | 2 | 3 | 4 | 5 |
|---|---|---|---|---|---|
| Absolute frequency | 22 | 32 | 27 | 12 | 7 |
| x occupants or less | 1 | 2 | 3 | 4 | 5 |
| Cumulative frequency | 22 | 54 | 81 | 93 | 100 |
| Cumulative frequency % | 22% | 54% | 81% | 93% | 100% |

However, now that we understand how cumulative frequencies are derived, we can get Excel to calculate them for us.

*Use Workbook 7.3 as a template to follow the discussion*

*The first thing to do is run the Histogram routine again and define the Input, Bin and Output ranges as in the previous illustration.*[3]

*Now click on the Cumulative Percentage tab in the bottom half of the dialogue box, and while you are there also click on the Chart output tab. Then click OK*

Excel knows that since you have not changed the output range, some of the previous information contained there will be overwritten, and it warns you of this fact.

*In this case this is all right so click OK* [4]

The calculations will now be performed and the sheet should resemble Workbook 7.4.

As you can see from the worksheet, the cumulative percentage frequencies have been calculated in addition to the individual absolute frequencies and the former are identical to the ones that were calculated manually.

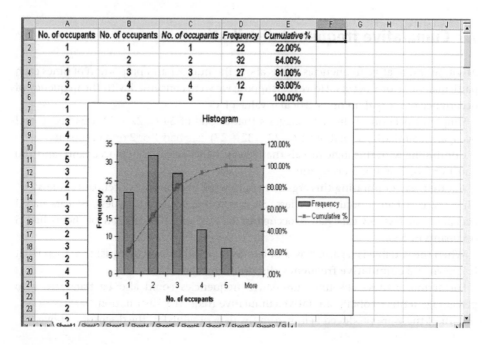

**Workbook 7.4**

Furthermore, checking the Chart Output tab has caused Excel to graph both sets of frequencies automatically.[5]

Notice that the heights of the columns represent **absolute** individual frequencies as measured on the left-hand scale, whereas the line graph represents the **cumulative** percentage frequencies as measured on the right-hand scale.

It should now be an easy matter to answer questions such as:

 (i) How many cars contained **exactly** 3 occupants? (Answer = 27.)

 (ii) What proportion of cars contained 4 occupants **or less**? (Answer = 93%).

(iii) What is the most frequently observed number of car occupants? (Answer = 2 with a frequency of 32 observations.)

(iv) What proportion of cars contained 3 occupants **or more**? (Answer = 100% minus the 54% with 2 occupants or less = 46%.)

*Now save this file as* W7_4.xls.

*Now attempt Exercise 7.2.*

## 7.4 Discrete and continuous data sets

It should now be pointed out that in this illustration the data (number of occupants) is to be regarded as discrete. That is, only whole numbers can be observed.

Not all data are discrete, however; sometimes they are continuous (i.e. capable of being measured to a large number of decimal places). When this is the case we must modify the approach that is used in the creation of frequency distributions.

*To understand the issues involved load the file called* W7_5.xls.

Here, we have created a second data set in column B from the 100 car observations, by assuming that each of the occupants was asked to reveal their age (correct to two decimal places). With 100 cars containing 250 occupants this means that we have 250 observations on age and unlike the number of occupants this new variable must be regarded as continuous.

The difficulties that continuous as opposed to discrete data sets create for the collation process can be appreciated by noting that the ages range from close to zero to over eighty and that they are measured to two decimal places.

This means that to include **every possible** age that *could* be observed, our bin would have to start at 0.01 and increase in steps of 0.01 until a value of 99.99 (say) was reached.

This would give almost 10000 values for the bin and so, with only 250 actual observations, approximately 97.5% of these bin values would have a **zero** frequency.

Far from **summarizing** the data set, such a procedure for defining the bin would actually **increase** the amount of information that would have to be considered.

The answer to this difficulty is to think of the bin in terms of a series of **class intervals** rather than in terms of **individual** values. Thus, we could define the bin in terms of 9 intervals of 10 years and then classify the data into each of these intervals.

*Consequently, in C1 enter the label:*

Age

*and then enter:*

10, 20, 30, 40, 50, 60, 70, 80 and 90

*to the C2:C10 range*

This will be the bin range for the new problem.

Before performing the classification, however, notice how Excel treats these intervals. The first bin value (10) will include all occupants whose age is less than or equal to 10.

The second bin value (20) will include all occupants who are more than 10 but less than or equal to 20.

This logic then continues for the remainder of the defined intervals.

*Now access Tools from the Menu bar and then Data Analysis and Histogram. Define the Input, Bin and Output ranges as B1:B251, C1:C10 and D1 respectively. Then click on the Cumulative Percentage and the Chart Output tabs and click OK*

The results should resemble Workbook 7.5A.

It is now an easy matter to answer questions such as:

(i) What proportion of occupants are 40 years old or less? (Answer = 50.00%.)

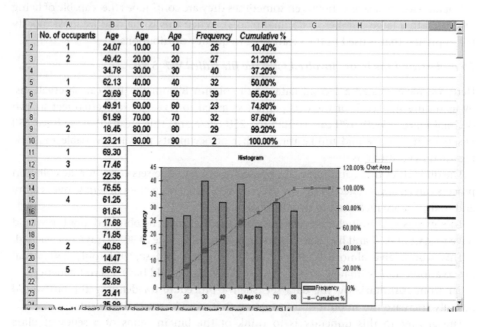

**Workbook 7.5A**

(ii)  What proportion of occupants are over 60 years old? (Answer = 100% minus the 74.8% who are 60 years old or less = 25.2%.).

(iii)  What proportion of occupants are over 20 but not over 60? (Answer = the 74.8% who are 60 or less minus the 21.2% who are 20 or less = 53.6%).

*Now save this file as* W7_5A.xls.

*Now attempt Exercise 7.3.*

## 7.5 **Principles of selecting class intervals**

In the two previous illustrations the user selected the bin values to be employed, and in both cases the nature of the data was such that the choice of values or intervals was fairly straightforward. However, particularly when large uneven data sets are involved, the process of choosing appropriate class intervals is not always so easy.

The problem derives from the inevitable trade-off between the process of **summarizing** data and the **information loss** that inevitably results from summary procedures.

By this we mean that the smaller is the width of each class interval then the more of them there will need to be to span a given data range. Consequently, the frequencies associated with each interval will tend to be lower than with a fewer number of intervals. There will therefore be relatively few frequencies in each class compared to a situation in which there were fewer intervals of larger width.

Now remember that any individual frequency simply tells us the number of observations that were observed in a particular interval, and tells us nothing about the actual values of the individual observations apart from the fact that they lie in that interval. Consequently, the wider is a class interval the greater is the scope for variation in the individual values and the greater is the potential loss of information.

To see this, consider an examination in which the mark can lie between 0% and 100% inclusive. Also assume that the marks are all rounded to the nearest whole number and that a pass mark is 50% or more.

Now suppose that a given number of students sat the examination and that the assessor chose a class interval of 100 percentage marks for classifying the marks. Clearly such an interval only allows the conclusion that 100% of examinees obtained between 0% and 100%—a classic example of a statistical statement of the obvious.

Now suppose that two intervals, each comprising 50 percentage marks, were used (i.e. 0% to 49% inclusive and 50% to 100% inclusive). Although not ideal, these intervals are significantly better since they would allow a conclusion such as $x$% of the examinees obtained 49% or less (and therefore failed) while the remainder passed by obtaining 50% or more.

Moving from one class interval to two has clearly improved our ability to draw conclusions from the data. At the same time, however, with such a wide interval we are unable to draw any conclusions about whether those who failed did so narrowly or abysmally, or whether those who passed did so marginally or with great ease.

To draw conclusions such as these requires that more intervals are employed, implying that each interval becomes narrower.[6] Consequently, the assessor might decide to use intervals of 10 percentage marks (10%, 20%, 30%, 40%, etc.).

Once again this will allow more detailed conclusions to be drawn but the cost is that the distribution is less **compact** than with only two intervals.

So far, the process of increasing the number of class intervals has increased the amount of information that the summarized data set can confer. Indeed, this will always be the case. However, suppose the assessor now decides to use intervals of 1 percentage mark (0%, 1%, 2%, etc.). You should be able to see that such a classification system simply reproduces the raw data set (with frequencies of zero for all marks that do not occur). There will be absolutely no loss of information, but at the same time there is very little summarizing taking place.

The upshot of this discussion is that there are no 'hard and fast' rules for choosing the ideal number of class intervals, or their ideal width. As a rough rule of thumb, however, there should rarely be fewer than 6 and rarely more than 16 class intervals. Within these limits the trade-off between information loss (too few intervals) and summarization (too many intervals) is usually at acceptable levels.

Also notice that in both of the illustrations, and in the most recent discussion, it has been implied that the intervals are of equal width. Thus, given the range of the data, if the number of intervals is chosen then their width is determined, or if the width is chosen then the number of intervals is determined. However, it is not hard to envisage data sets that might call for unequal class intervals.

For example, suppose that 80% of the values in a data set lie between 0 and 10 inclusive, but that the remaining 20% are spread out over a range of 11 to 5000.

Clearly we require a different set of class intervals for the 80% of observations in the narrow range from those to be applied to the 20% of observations in the wide range. Unequal class intervals are needed, and so we might try something like

$$2, 4, 6, 8, 10, 1000, 2000, 3000, 4000 \text{ and } 5000.$$

Once again, however, whether this produces satisfactory results will depend **entirely** on how the individual data observations are distributed within the proposed classification system. Trial and error until a 'reasonable' shape to the frequency distribution is obtained may well be the only answer.

Given the potential difficulties involved in choosing appropriate class intervals it is useful to know that Excel can choose them for us, although its methods are by no means perfect and it will never produce unequal class intervals.

To force Excel to make up its own class intervals simply erase the Bin Range box in the Histogram dialogue screen.

*To see this, re-load Workbook 7.5A (W7_5A.xls)*

*Keep the same Input Range as before (B1:B251), but erase the contents of the Bin Range box (if there is anything there)*

*Finally, to prevent overwriting specify the Output range as D24 and deselect the Chart Output tab.*

| | A | B | C | D | E | F | G | H | I |
|---|---|---|---|---|---|---|---|---|---|
| **23** | | 23.41 | | | | | | | |
| **24** | | 35.89 | | *Bin* | *Frequency* | *Cumulative %* | | | |
| **25** | | 43.81 | | 0.13 | 1 | .40% | | | |
| **26** | 3 | 30.99 | | 5.707333 | 15 | 6.40% | | | |
| **27** | | 69.21 | | 11.28467 | 13 | 11.60% | | | |
| **28** | | 76.81 | | 16.862 | 12 | 16.40% | | | |
| **29** | 2 | 15.11 | | 22.43933 | 25 | 26.40% | | | |
| **30** | | 46.81 | | 28.01667 | 15 | 32.40% | | | |
| **31** | 1 | 60.23 | | 33.594 | 25 | 42.40% | | | |
| **32** | 3 | 28.75 | | 39.17133 | 15 | 48.40% | | | |
| **33** | | 40.70 | | 44.74867 | 23 | 57.60% | | | |
| **34** | | 13.87 | | 50.326 | 22 | 66.40% | | | |
| **35** | 5 | 0.13 | | 55.90333 | 9 | 70.00% | | | |
| **36** | | 36.14 | | 61.48067 | 15 | 76.00% | | | |
| **37** | | 17.76 | | 67.058 | 21 | 84.40% | | | |
| **38** | | 43.87 | | 72.63533 | 18 | 91.60% | | | |
| **39** | | 0.52 | | 78.21267 | 13 | 96.80% | | | |
| **40** | 2 | 33.86 | | More | 8 | 100.00% | | | |
| **41** | | 50.12 | | | | | | | |

Sheet1 / Sheet2 / Sheet3 / Sheet4 / Sheet5 / Sheet

**Workbook 7.6**

The results should resemble Workbook 7.6

Whether this is an improvement on the set of intervals that we previously specified for this illustration (10, 20, 30,...90) is difficult to say. There are 15 equal intervals of approximately 5.57 years and a 'catch-all' of more than 78.21267 years. But the numbers themselves are a bit 'messy', especially computed as they are, to 5 or 6 decimal places.

However, you can rectify this last problem by formatting.

*Select the D25:D39 range and then Format and Cells from the Menu bar. Then select Number and choose 0 (decimal places)*

The bin values will now become whole numbers although the frequencies will still be **computed** on the basis of the six-decimal-place bin values, and this can create confusion.

For example, the first bin value as computed by Excel originally was 0.13004 years and there was one car occupant who was less than or equal to 0.13004 year old. This clearly must still be true after formatting the bin values to whole numbers, yet the 0.13004 becomes 0 and so it appears as if there is one occupant whose age is less than or equal to zero.

*Consequently to remove this confusion re-format the D26:D40 range to two decimal places (the 0.00 option)*

The bin values are now specified to the same number of decimal places as the raw data and this is probably the best we can do *when we let Excel choose the values for the bin*. Notice, however, that if you run the Histogram routine again, with the same specifications, then the two-decimal-place formatting that we have just established will **not** be retained. Excel will revert to the five or six decimal-place format.

*Now save this file as W7_6.xls*

*Now attempt Exercise 7.4.*


## 7.6 Categorizing data

The VLOOKUP function encountered in Chapter 6 can be very useful when we are required to classify a data set into two or more mutually exclusive categories (e.g. large, medium or small).

For example, suppose for the data in Table 7.1 we want to categorize each company as being large, medium or small employers, depending upon their number of employees.

Before we can begin we need some definitions for the categories, so suppose we create the following definitions.

Companies with less than 16 employees are defined as small (S).

Companies with 16 or more but less than 25 employees are defined as medium (M).

Companies with 25 or more employees are defined as large (L).

*For this small data set it is easy to perform this categorization by hand, as shown in Sheet1 of the W7_7.xls file, and also in Table 7.2*

*Load this file now and notice that in Sheet1 we have categorized each company simply by manual inspection.*

With larger data sets, however, it would clearly be more efficient to get Excel to do the categorization for us.

To do this we clearly need to inform Excel of the defined thresholds and the associated categories. This has been done in the A6:B8 range of Sheet2 of the current workbook. Note that this VLOOKUP table uses threshold values of 0, 16 and 25.

*It should also be said that we have named this range (A6:B8) as TABLE. Do this now*

This table is to be thought of as giving in its second column, the correct category for any given number of employees in its first column. Hence a company with 12 employees would be categorized as Small since 12 is less than the first threshold value of 16.

**Table 7.1**

| Company No. | 1 | 2 | 3 | 4 | 5 | 6 | 7 | 8 | 9 | 10 | 11 | 12 | 13 |
|---|---|---|---|---|---|---|---|---|---|---|---|---|---|
| No. of employees | 15 | 35 | 21 | 60 | 15 | 23 | 26 | 35 | 15 | 12 | 19 | 25 | 50 |

**Table 7.2**

| Company No. | 1 | 2 | 3 | 4 | 5 | 6 | 7 | 8 | 9 | 10 | 11 | 12 | 13 |
|---|---|---|---|---|---|---|---|---|---|---|---|---|---|
| No. of employees | 15 | 35 | 21 | 60 | 15 | 23 | 26 | 35 | 15 | 12 | 19 | 25 | 50 |
| Category (S, M, L) | S | L | M | L | S | M | L | L | S | S | M | L | L |

However, a company with 16 employees would be classified as Medium, as would all those with less than 25 employees. Finally, all companies with 25 or more employees will be categorized as Large.

With the thresholds and associated categories defined like this, all we need to do now is get Excel to calculate the appropriate category for any given number of employees.

This is most easily done with the =VLOOKUP function explained in Chapter 5.

*The required VLOOKUP function should be written as:*

$$=VLOOKUP(B2,TABLE,2)$$

*Enter this formula to the B4 cell, and then copy along the row to N4 to reproduces the results that were obtained by inspection. Confirm this now*

A visual impression of what is taking place is shown in Figure 7.2.

There are two points to note about this procedure.

First, if any of the data observations should change (through rectifying a recording error for example) then the VLOOKUP function will automatically change the category to which the observation belongs if necessary. For example, suppose the 13th company in fact had 5 instead of 50 employees.

*Change the value in N13 from 50 to 5 and the category will automatically change from L to S*

*Now restore the original value of 50*

Second, if it is decided to change one or more of the threshold values then VLOOKUP again implements any implied category changes automatically. For example, if the thresholds became 18 and 29 respectively, then change the values in A7 and A8 appropriately and the re-categorization will be performed.

*Try it out and you will find that there is one category change—the 7th company, with 26 employees, previously categorized as L is now only classified as M*

This is in fact a very important point, since it raises the question of the logic behind the choice of thresholds. In other words, why did we decide that 19 was a medium number of employees whereas 29 was a large number? We will return to this issue at a later stage.

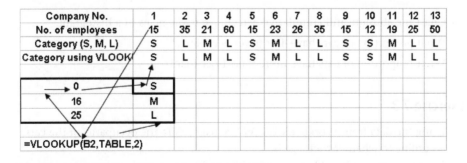

| Company No. | 1 | 2 | 3 | 4 | 5 | 6 | 7 | 8 | 9 | 10 | 11 | 12 | 13 |
|---|---|---|---|---|---|---|---|---|---|---|---|---|---|
| No. of employees | 15 | 35 | 21 | 60 | 15 | 23 | 26 | 35 | 15 | 12 | 19 | 25 | 50 |
| Category (S, M, L) | S | L | M | L | S | M | L | L | S | S | M | L | L |
| Category using VLOOK | S | L | M | L | S | M | L | L | S | S | M | L | L |

| 0 | S |
|---|---|
| 16 | M |
| 25 | L |

=VLOOKUP(B2,TABLE,2)

**Figure 7.2**

Third, the VLOOKUP function operates differently from the Histogram routine in the way that it treats the thresholds.

*To see this, look at Sheet3 of the current file (W7_7.xls)*

In D6:D8 we have used COUNTIF functions[7] to determine the number that were S, M or L, as computed from the VLOOKUP table. The values are seen to be 4, 3 and 6 respectively.

In B20:B22, however we have defined a bin range of 16 and 25 (the same values as were used in the VLOOKUP table). Then we ran the Histogram routine and obtained frequencies of 4, 4 and 5. Clearly one of the values that the VLOOKUP procedure regarded as large has become medium when subjected to the Histogram routine.

This is rectified by the bin range shown in G20:G22 which uses values of 15 and 24, i.e. one less than the VLOOKUP table's values. Using this second bin range solves the difficulty by returning the correct frequencies of 4, 3 and 6.

*Now save this file as* W7_7A.xls.

## 7.7 Exercises

### Exercise 7.1

Using the data from Workbook 7.1 (W7_1.xls) use Excel to classify the cars according to the numbers that respectively have:

only 1 occupant;   2 or 3 occupants;   4 or 5 occupants

### Exercise 7.2

(a) Using the data from Workbook 7.1 (W7_1.xls) use Excel to produce an **absolute** and a **cumulative percentage** frequency distribution of the number of cars that respectively have:

1, 2 or 3 occupants; 4 occupants; 5 occupants

(b) Chart the absolute and cumulative percentage frequencies in a histogram.

(c) What proportion of cars have 4 or fewer occupants?

(d) What proportion of cars have more than 1 occupant?

### Exercise 7.3

(a) Using the data from Workbook 7.5 (W7_5.xls) classify the occupants of the cars according to whether their age is:
15 or less; over 15 but 20 or less; over 20 but 40 or less; over 40 but 60 or less; over 60

(b)  What proportion of occupants are 40 or less?

(c)  What proportion of occupants are over 20?

(d)  What proportion of occupants are over 15 but not over 60?

## Exercise 7.4

Load Workbook 7.1 (W7_1.xls) and let Excel choose the bin values with which to classify the number of car occupants. Then create the frequency distribution and state whether you are satisfied with the results.

## Exercise 7.5

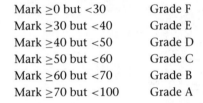

*Load the file* W7_8.xls.

The data are the percentage marks obtained by 250 candidates in an examination.

(a)  Use Excel to grade the data in line with the following regulations

| | |
|---|---|
| Mark $\geq 0$ but $<30$ | Grade F |
| Mark $\geq 30$ but $<40$ | Grade E |
| Mark $\geq 40$ but $<50$ | Grade D |
| Mark $\geq 50$ but $<60$ | Grade C |
| Mark $\geq 60$ but $<70$ | Grade B |
| Mark $\geq 70$ but $<100$ | Grade A |

(b)  Get Excel to prepare a table showing the number of candidates obtaining each of the grades.

## 7.8  Solutions to the exercises

### Solution to Exercise 7.1

Keep the Input Range as A1:A101 but redefine the bin values in B2:B4 as 1, 3 and 5.
   Make sure the Labels tab is checked.
   Output the results to C1 and do not check any of the tabs below the Output Range tab.
   Something resembling Workbook 7.9 should be obtained.

### Solutions to Exercise 7.2

(a)  Keep the Input Range as A1:A101 but redefine the bin values in B2:B4 as 1, 4 and 5.
     Make sure the Labels tab is checked.
     Output the results to C1 and check the Cumulative Percentage tab.

(b)  Check the Chart Output tab and repeat the previous Histogram routine.

|   | A | B | C | D | E | F | G | H | I |
|---|---|---|---|---|---|---|---|---|---|
| 1 | No. of occupants | No. of occupants | No. of occupants | Frequency | | | | | |
| 2 | 1 | 1 | 1 | 22 | | | | | |
| 3 | 2 | 3 | 3 | 59 | | | | | |
| 4 | 1 | 5 | 5 | 19 | | | | | |
| 5 | 3 | | More | 0 | | | | | |
| 6 | 2 | | | | | | | | |
| 7 | 1 | | | | | | | | |

**Workbook 7.9**

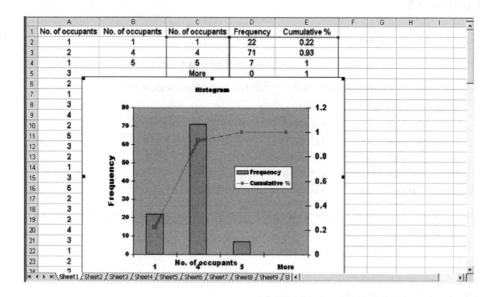

**Workbook 7.10**

The results should resemble Workbook 7.10.

(c) 93% of cars have 4 occupants or fewer.

(d) 100% − 22% = 78% of cars have more than 1 occupant.

## Solutions to Exercise 7.3

(a) Keep the Input Range as B1:B253 but redefine the bin values in C2:C5 as 15, 20, 40 and 60.

Output the results to D1 and check the Cumulative Percentage tab.

The results are shown in Workbook 7.11

| | A | B | C | D | E | [Formula Bar] | G | H | I | J | K | L | M |
|---|---|---|---|---|---|---|---|---|---|---|---|---|---|
| 1 | No. of occupants | Age | Age | Age | Frequency | Cumulative % | | | | | | | |
| 2 | 1 | 24.07 | 15 | 15 | 34 | 13.60% | | | | | | | |
| 3 | 2 | 49.42 | 20 | 20 | 19 | 21.20% | | | | | | | |
| 4 | | 34.78 | 40 | 40 | 72 | 50.00% | | | | | | | |
| 5 | 1 | 62.13 | 60 | 60 | 62 | 74.80% | | | | | | | |
| 6 | 3 | 29.69 | | More | 63 | 100.00% | | | | | | | |
| 7 | | 49.91 | | | | | | | | | | | |
| 8 | | 61.99 | | | | | | | | | | | |
| 9 | 2 | 18.45 | | | | | | | | | | | |
| 10 | | 23.21 | | | | | | | | | | | |

Sheet1 / Sheet2 / Sheet3 / Sheet4 / Sheet5 / Sheet6 / Sheet7 / Sheet8 / Sheet9 / Sl

Ready

**Workbook 7.11**

(b)  50% are aged 40 or less.

(c)  100% − 21.2% = 78.8% are aged 20 over 20.

(d)  74.8% are 60 or less (i.e. not over 60), and 13.6% are 15 or less. Therefore, 74.8% − 13.6% = 61.2% are over 15 but not over 60.

## Solution to Exercise 7.4

When Excel is allowed to choose the bin values for itself it does so as indicated in Workbook 7.12. This was done by selecting A1:A101 as the input range, leaving the Bin range blank and then selecting B1 as the start of the output range.

| | A | B | C | D | E | F | G | H |
|---|---|---|---|---|---|---|---|---|
| | [E20] | | | | | | | |
| 1 | No. of occupants | Bin | Frequency | Cumulative % | | | | |
| 2 | 1 | 1 | 22 | 22.00% | | | | |
| 3 | 2 | 1.4 | 0 | 22.00% | | | | |
| 4 | 1 | 1.8 | 0 | 22.00% | | | | |
| 5 | 3 | 2.2 | 32 | 54.00% | | | | |
| 6 | 2 | 2.6 | 0 | 54.00% | | | | |
| 7 | 1 | 3 | 27 | 81.00% | | | | |
| 8 | 3 | 3.4 | 0 | 81.00% | | | | |
| 9 | 4 | 3.8 | 0 | 81.00% | | | | |
| 10 | 2 | 4.2 | 12 | 93.00% | | | | |
| 11 | 5 | 4.6 | 0 | 93.00% | | | | |
| 12 | 3 | More | 7 | 100.00% | | | | |
| 13 | 2 | | | | | | | |
| 14 | 1 | | | | | | | |

Sheet1 / Sheet2 / Sheet3 / Sheet4 / Sheet5 / Sheet

**Workbook 7.12**

As you can see, the bin values are not whole numbers and so are rather unsatisfactory in the context of this data set where the number of occupants is clearly a discrete variable.

## Solutions to Exercise 7.5

(a) Use D1:E6 to contain the thresholds and grades as:

| | | | |
|---|---|---|---|
| D1: | 0 | E1: | F |
| D2: | 30 | E2: | E |
| D3: | 40 | E3: | D |
| D4: | 50 | E4: | C |
| D5: | 60 | E5: | B |
| D6: | 70 | E6: | A |

Next, name the D1:E6 range as GRADES, and then in B2 enter:

$$=VLOOKUP(A2,GRADES,2)$$

Now copy this into B3:B251 and each mark will have its correct grade placed alongside.

(b) To obtain a table of the number of candidates obtaining each grade use a COUNTIF function as follows:

| | |
|---|---|
| In F1: | =COUNTIF(B2:B251,"=F") |
| In F2 | =COUNTIF(B2:B251,"=E") |
| In F3: | =COUNTIF(B2:B251,"=D") |
| In F4: | =COUNTIF(B2:B251,"=C") |
| In F5: | =COUNTIF(B2:B251,"=B") |
| In F6: | =COUNTIF(B2:B251,"=A") |

A quicker way of doing this is to enter

$$=COUNTIF(B\$2:B\$251,"=F")$$

in F2 and then copy this into F3:F6.

Then edit each of the formula in F3:F6 to change E to D, C, B, A respectively.

The full solution is contained in the Solution sheet of the current file (W7_8.xls) and should resemble Workbook 7.13. Notice that we have also expressed the absolute frequencies for each grade as a percentage of the total number of examinees. This was done by writing:

$$=F1/SUM(F\$1:F\$6)$$

in G1, and copying into G2:G6.

| | A | B | C | D | E | F | G | H | I | J |
|---|---|---|---|---|---|---|---|---|---|---|
| B2 | | | fx | =VLOOKUP(A2,GRADES,2) | | | | | | |
| 1 | Mark | Grade | | 0 | F | 80 | 32.00% | | | |
| 2 | 9 | F | | 30 | E | 31 | 12.40% | | | |
| 3 | 57 | C | | 40 | D | 30 | 12.00% | | | |
| 4 | 71 | A | | 50 | C | 20 | 8.00% | | | |
| 5 | 0 | F | | 60 | B | 22 | 8.80% | | | |
| 6 | 54 | C | | 70 | A | 67 | 26.80% | | | |
| 7 | 27 | F | | | | | | | | |
| 8 | 86 | A | | | | | | | | |
| 9 | 69 | B | | | | | | | | |
| 10 | 18 | F | | | | | | | | |
| 11 | 57 | C | | | | | | | | |
| 12 | 40 | D | | | | | | | | |
| 13 | 88 | A | | | | | | | | |
| 14 | 54 | C | | | | | | | | |
| 15 | 19 | F | | | | | | | | |
| 16 | 31 | E | | | | | | | | |
| 17 | 11 | F | | | | | | | | |
| 18 | 11 | F | | | | | | | | |
| 19 | 33 | E | | | | | | | | |
| 20 | 47 | D | | | | | | | | |
| 21 | 52 | C | | | | | | | | |

Sheet1 \ Solution \ Sheet3

**Workbook 7.13**

## ■ NOTES

1. You are quite likely to have done something like this at some time or other with the 'five-bar gate' tallying device.

2. Because there were exactly 100 cars observed, the absolute and the relative frequencies are the same in this case. However, with any number of frequencies other than 100 this will not be the case.

3. Unless you have made any changes to the specification of the Histogram then these settings will have been retained by Excel and you can just accept them. Otherwise specify the settings again as A1:A101, B1:B6 and C1 respectively for the Input, Bin and Output ranges.

4. In other circumstances you may want to retain the original frequency distribution, in which case you specify a new Output range.

5. The Histogram chart will not be produced in **exactly** the same location nor with **exactly** the same dimensions as indicated in Workbook 7.4. However, it was an easy matter to move the chart and then resize it to obtain the illustrated effect.

6. Assuming, as we are at the moment, that each interval has the **same** width.

7. For a reminder of the COUNTIF function see Chapter 2.

# 8 Data description—central tendency

 The following files from the online resource centre should be loaded as instructed:

W8_1.xls    W8_2.xls    W8_3.xls
W8_4.xls    W8_5.xls

## 8.1 Introduction

Because there will usually be several values of the observed variable, it will frequently be instructive to calculate some **single** value that measures the **central** or 'average' value of the data set.

This measure of central tendency may well be the **same** as one of the observed data elements, but there is no necessity that this be the case, since the averaging process is capable of calculating a central value that is not the same as any one of the observed data items.

For example, if one car has two occupants and another has three, then the average number of occupants is $(2 + 3)/2 = 2.5$, clearly a value that could not be observed in practice.

Bearing these ideas in mind, we can proceed by explaining the three most commonly used measures of central tendency that statistics employs.

## 8.2 The arithmetic mean

The **arithmetic mean** is the name that statistics uses for what is more commonly referred to as the 'average'. To see how it can be calculated, consider the following example.

The following data are the daily number of clients placed by an employment agency over a period of 11 working days.

$x$ (number of clients placed) :  15,  28,  21,  13,  19,  23,  21,  16,  21,  17,  26

Calculate the arithmetic mean of the data set.

For any data set the arithmetic mean is calculated by obtaining the **total arithmetic worth** of all the observations and then dividing this total by the number of observations. For our data this would produce:

$$15 + 28 + 21 + 13 + 19 + 23 + 21 + 16 + 21 + 17 + 26)/11 = 220/11 = 20 \text{ client}$$

$$\text{placements per day.}$$

This means that 'on average' 20 clients were placed each day, and although this **happens** to be a whole number, you can see that there was **no** actual occasion over the 11-day period when 20 clients were **actually** placed. It should also be clear that there is no necessity for the arithmetic mean to be a whole number even when it is computed from a discrete data set such as the one being currently used. For example, with one less client being placed on any particular day the mean would become:

$$219/11 = 19.9090$$

More generally, we can use the following notational conventions to define the arithmetic mean.

Let $n =$ the total number of observations in the data set.

Let $x_i =$ the $i$th observation in the data set where $i$ can be any integer value in the range 1 to $n$ (we say: $i = 1 \ldots n$). Thus $x_1$ is the first recorded observation, $x_2$ the second, and so on until $x_n$, the last observation, is reached.

Let $\Sigma x_i$ represent the sum of the $n$ observations, i.e. $(x_1 + x_2 + \ldots + x_n)$

Let $\bar{x}$ represent the arithmetic mean of the data set.

Then:

$$\bar{x} = \Sigma x_i / n.$$

If you now apply this formula to the data in the illustration then you will find that

$$\Sigma x_i = 220 \quad \text{and} \quad n = 11.$$

Therefore,

$$\bar{x} = 220/11 = 20.00.$$

Excel can also perform these calculations with its AVERAGE function, which has the following **general** syntax:

**Table 8.1**

| Company No. | 1 | 2 | 3 | 4 | 5 | 6 | 7 | 8 | 9 | 10 | 11 | 12 | 13 | Count | 13 |
|---|---|---|---|---|---|---|---|---|---|---|---|---|---|---|---|
| No. of employe | 15 | 35 | 21 | 60 | 15 | 23 | 26 | 35 | 15 | 12 | 19 | 25 | 50 | Sum | 351 |

=AVERAGE(DATA RANGE).

*To see this function in operation consider the data shown in Table 8.1 and contained in the data sheet of the W8_1.xls file. Load this file now*

Simple arithmetic (or use of the sum function) confirms that $n = 13$, $\Sigma x = 351$ and so $\bar{x} = 351/13 = 27$.

*Confirm this by entering the appropriate AVERAGE function to a vacant cell (A4 say). The entry will be:*

=AVERAGE(B2:N2)

and will return a value of 27.

There are two things to note about how Excel computes the arithmetic mean with its AVERAGE function.

First, any *blank* cells or any cells that contain *text* are *ignored entirely* by Excel. This means that they add neither to the value of the total worth of the observations, nor to the number of observations used as the denominator. For this reason if we add an extra blank observation to the data range (or a text entry) the average value as calculated by Excel will be unchanged.

This is not the case if we add an extra value of zero, since although it will add nothing to the total worth of the observations, it will count as an extra observation and so the calculated arithmetic mean must fall.

The implication of these protocols is that any missing values in the data set should be entered either as blanks or as text labels if the AVERAGE function is to operate correctly.

Second, the appearance of any Excel error message such as #DIV0! or #N/A in the range addressed by the AVERAGE function will cause the latter to return the same error message. Consequently, it will be necessary to delete any entries that are error messages before computing the arithmetic mean.

The arithmetic mean measures central tendency in the sense that it will always be greater than the minimum observation value and less than the maximum observation value. It therefore lies between the extreme values of the data set. Exactly where it will lie, however, is not capable of being deduced, since it will depend upon the nature of the data values. However, it is true to say that the arithmetic mean is usually more sensitive to extreme observations than other measures of central tendency. This is because the addition of a single extremely large observation will pull the mean up significantly, while the addition of a single extremely small observation will pull it down significantly.

*All of these points are illustrated in the sheet called Arithmean of the current file (W8_1.xls), which should be consulted carefully now.*

## 8.3 **The median**

The median is defined as the value of the middle observation when the observations have been placed in ascending order. If the number of observations ($n$) is odd then there will be an observation at the middle position and the value of this observation is the median. If $n$ is even then there will be two observations in the middle position and the median is the mean of these two observation values.

*Access the Median sheet of the current file (W8_1.xls) now.*

As you can see the data from Table 8.1 have been ranked in ascending order in the top highlighted area. Then in the bottom highlighted area the data were expanded to contain an even as opposed to an odd number of observations and again ranked.

The Excel function =**MEDIAN** calculates the median from

=MEDIAN(Data Range)

Notice that there is actually no need to sort the data in ascending order before calculating the median from the Excel function—we have done so in this illustration simply to indicate the process.

Also note that the median as calculated by Excel obeys the same rules as the arithmetic mean—blanks and text are ignored, but zero values are included.

This is easily confirmed in the Median sheet by changing the value in O10 (65) to a blank (the median is unchanged), then to text (the median is unchanged) and then to zero (the median declines from 24 to 22).

Unlike the mean, however, the median is usually less sensitive to extreme observations. For example, change the value in O10 of the median sheet to 1 million, and it will be seen that the median is unchanged (24). Then change the O10 value to minus 1 million and note that the median only falls from 24 to 22 (exactly the same as if the value had changed to zero rather than minus 1 million). This confirms that, as we said earlier, the median is much less sensitive to changes in extreme observations than the mean.

## 8.4 **The mode**

The Mode is simply the observation value that occurs most frequently. For the data in Table 8.1 it is clear that the only observation value in the data set that occurs more than once is 15 (with a frequency of 3), so the mode for these data is 15.

The Excel function =**MODE** computes the mode from:

=MODE(Data Range)

and this has been used in the sheet called Mode of the current file (W8_1.xls).

*Consult this now.*

Notice that there may be no unique value for the mode if more than one value of $x$ occurs with equal frequency. In this case the distribution could be bi-modal, tri-modal or even multi-modal.

Like the median the mode is relatively insensitive to extreme observations (sometimes called **outliers**). This is because it considers the frequencies with which particular values occur rather than their actual arithmetic values (in the same way as the median concentrates on position in an ordered list rather than arithmetic worth).

Taken together, these observations about the relative properties of the mean, median and mode imply that if an outlying observation is having a marked effect upon the mean, then the median may well be a more appropriate measure of central tendency, since it avoids the effect of outliers. At the same time, however, neither the median nor the mode has the total arithmetic value property possessed by the mean.

If it is felt that this property (total value), is important to the investigation, and if at the same time there are significant outliers, then it may be necessary to exclude the outlier(s) from the data set to be averaged.

## 8.5 Comparison between the mean, the median and the mode

At this stage it is fair to ask which of the three measures of central tendency that have been explained is the 'best'. The answer is that 'best' is not really the correct word since we are more concerned with appropriateness. This means that the alternative measures should be viewed as being **complementary** rather than **competitive**, with the most appropriate being dependent upon the nature of the data to be investigated.

To see this, consider the following example.

The following data refer to the daily output of a particular component produced by each of five machines in a factory's production system:

$$x \text{ (daily output)} : 490, \ 510, \ 495, \ 490, \ 1000.$$

Calculate the most appropriate measure of central tendency that will allow you to advise the management on its proposed policy of scrapping the whole system if the 'average' machine output is less than 550 units per day, or if more than 50% of the machines have a daily output of less than 500 units.

*Enter the data to a new workbook and compute the arithmetic mean, the median and the mode as previously explained.*

The arithmetic mean output is 597 units per day so on the first criterion the system should **not** be scrapped (597 > 550), but since the median daily output is 495 units, on the second criterion it should be. (It should be clear, in fact, that 60% of the machines will have an output which is less than 500 units per day.) You would have to ask the management to give you more information on which of the two criteria is to be given more weight, since the single extreme observation of 1000 is exercising a **disproportionate** effect on the value of the arithmetic mean.

Finally, the mode is 490 units and indicates that an output that is less than 500 units occurs most frequently.

Having said all this, it should be clear that this is a very small data set, and as a result, can be highly sensitive to outlying observations.

***Now attempt Exercise 8.1.***

## 8.6 **Weighted averages**

Suppose that marks of 60% and 70% were obtained in two assignments (A and B).

It would seem reasonable to argue that the average mark overall would be (60% +70%)/2 = 65%.

However, this logic is only correct if it can be assumed that each of the assignments is of equal importance. For example, suppose that assignment B involved much more effort than assignment A. It might be decided to award it greater weight. Suppose this is the case and that assignment B is awarded a weight of 0.7. Since the weights must add up to 1 this means that assignment A is left with a weight of 1 minus 0.7 = 0.3.

The problem now faced is how to calculate the overall average of the two marks, and the answer is to multiply each mark by its weight and then add these weighted marks together. That is:

$$0.3 \times 60\% + 0.7 \times 70\% = 18\% + 49\% = 67\%$$

Clearly the weighted average overall mark is now 2% higher than the simple average calculated earlier.[1]

***To see how Excel can help to compute weighted averages load Sheet1 of the* W8_2.xls *file now.***

A section of the worksheet is shown in Figure 8.1.

The weights for each assignment have been entered to the A2 and B2 cells, then these cells named as **wa** and **wb** respectively.

Now calculate the first average mark in C4 from:

$$=wa*A4+wb*B4$$

and copy this down column C.

The results should be as shown in Sheet2 of the file.

With these overall average calculated in column C we can now get Excel to provide us with a verdict for each student if we supply an overall pass mark.

***This has been done in Sheet3 of the current file which should be consulted now.***

First, the pass mark was defined as 40 and entered to the D2 cell. This was then named as passmark.

***Next, in D4 write a conditional statement to test whether the actual overall mark is greater than or equal to the pass mark. This is done from:***

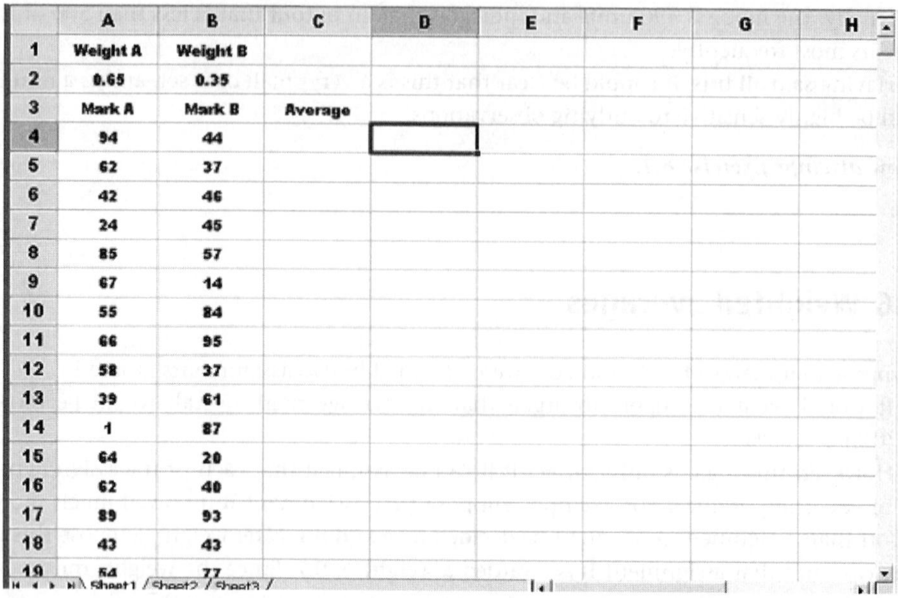

| | A | B | C | D | E | F | G | H |
|---|---|---|---|---|---|---|---|---|
| 1 | Weight A | Weight B | | | | | | |
| 2 | 0.65 | 0.35 | | | | | | |
| 3 | Mark A | Mark B | Average | | | | | |
| 4 | 94 | 44 | | | | | | |
| 5 | 62 | 37 | | | | | | |
| 6 | 42 | 46 | | | | | | |
| 7 | 24 | 45 | | | | | | |
| 8 | 85 | 57 | | | | | | |
| 9 | 67 | 14 | | | | | | |
| 10 | 55 | 84 | | | | | | |
| 11 | 66 | 95 | | | | | | |
| 12 | 58 | 37 | | | | | | |
| 13 | 39 | 61 | | | | | | |
| 14 | 1 | 87 | | | | | | |
| 15 | 64 | 20 | | | | | | |
| 16 | 62 | 40 | | | | | | |
| 17 | 89 | 93 | | | | | | |
| 18 | 43 | 43 | | | | | | |
| 19 | 54 | 77 | | | | | | |

H ◄ ► H\ Sheet1 / Sheet2 / Sheet3 /

**Figure 8.1**

$$=IF(C4 > =passmark,"Pass","Fail")$$

Notice that if we want an IF statement to return a text message rather than a number then the message is enclosed in double quotes.

Now copy the contents of D4 down column D and the correct verdicts for each of the 209 students will be returned.

Finally, in order to calculate the pass and fail rates use E2 to contain:

$$=COUNTIF(D4:D4000,"=Pass")$$

and in F2 enter:

$$=COUNTIF(D4:D4000,"=Fail")$$

Then calculate the total number of passes and fails in G2 from:

$$=E2 + F2$$

Finally calculate the pass and fail rates in E4 and F4 from:

$$=E2/G2 \quad and \quad =F2/G2$$

When completed the results should resemble Sheet 4 of the current file and the section shown in Figure 8.2. Note: E4 and F4 were both formatted to two decimal places.

| | A | B | C | D | E | F | G | H |
|---|---|---|---|---|---|---|---|---|
| 1 | Weight A | Weight B | | Pass Mark | Passes | Fails | Total | |
| 2 | 0.65 | 0.35 | | 40 | 134 | 75 | 209 | |
| 3 | Mark A | Mark B | Average | Verdict | Pass Rate | Fail Rate | | |
| 4 | 94 | 44 | 76.5 | Pass | 64.11% | 35.89% | | |
| 5 | 62 | 37 | 53.25 | Pass | | | | |
| 6 | 42 | 46 | 43.4 | Pass | | | | |
| 7 | 24 | 45 | 31.35 | Fail | | | | |
| 8 | 21 | 57 | 33.6 | Fail | | | | |
| 9 | 67 | 14 | 48.45 | Pass | | | | |
| 10 | 55 | 84 | 65.15 | Pass | | | | |
| 11 | 66 | 95 | 76.15 | Pass | | | | |
| 12 | 58 | 37 | 50.65 | Pass | | | | |
| 13 | 39 | 61 | 46.7 | Pass | | | | |
| 14 | 1 | 87 | 31.1 | Fail | | | | |
| 15 | 64 | 20 | 48.6 | Pass | | | | |
| 16 | 62 | 40 | 54.3 | Pass | | | | |
| 17 | 89 | 93 | 90.4 | Pass | | | | |
| 18 | 43 | 43 | 43 | Pass | | | | |
| 19 | 54 | 77 | 62.05 | Pass | | | | |

Sheet1 / Sheet2 / Sheet3 \ Sheet4 /

**Figure 8.2**

## 8.7 Exercises

### Exercise 8.1

Load the data contained in Workbook 8.3 (W8_3.xls). These are the numbers of car occupants and the ages of these occupants—data that we encountered in Chapter 7. Now use Excel statistical functions to calculate the mean, median and mode of both the number of car occupants and the age of those occupants.

### Exercise 8.2

Load the file called W8_4.xls.
   The Data sheet of this file contains the prices charged for a particular item at 10 retail outlets in each of two areas—urban (U) and rural (R).
   Calculate the mean, the median and the mode for each of the areas, and then compare these values.

### Exercise 8.3

Load the file called W8_5.xls.
The data are the annual incomes, measured in £ 000s of two countries—A and B.

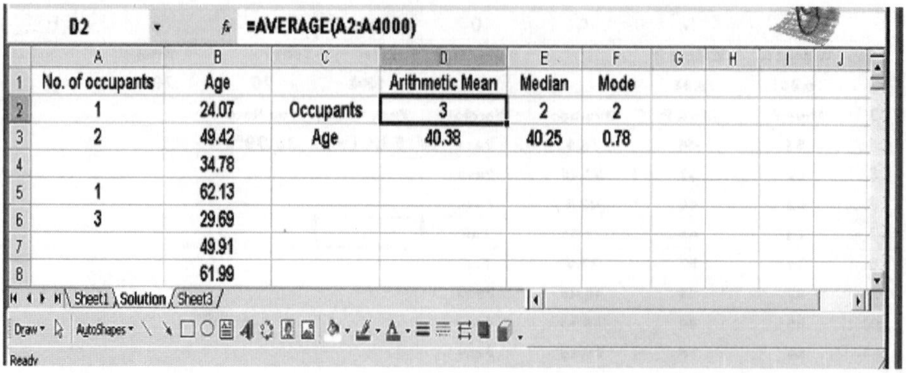

D2 =AVERAGE(A2:A4000)

| | A | B | C | D | E | F |
|---|---|---|---|---|---|---|
| 1 | No. of occupants | Age | | Arithmetic Mean | Median | Mode |
| 2 | 1 | 24.07 | Occupants | 3 | 2 | 2 |
| 3 | 2 | 49.42 | Age | 40.38 | 40.25 | 0.78 |
| 4 | | 34.78 | | | | |
| 5 | 1 | 62.13 | | | | |
| 6 | 3 | 29.69 | | | | |
| 7 | | 49.91 | | | | |
| 8 | | 61.99 | | | | |

**Figure 8.3**

(a) To what extent is it reasonable to argue that country A has a higher 'average' income than country B?

(b) Calculate the mean, median and modal incomes for both countries taken together.

## 8.8 Solutions to the exercises

### Solution to Exercise 8.1

The results are shown in Figure 8.3 and can also be found in the Solution sheet of the loaded file (W8_3.xls).

As you can see, the returned value for the modal age is 0.78. However, this would not be the case if the data were measured to the nearest year.

To see this, use the H2 cell of the worksheet to contain:

=ROUND(B2,0)

i.e. round the contents of B2 to 0 decimal places.

Then copy H2 into H3:H252.

Now use I1 to contain:

=MODE(H2:H251)

and confirm that for this data set the most frequently observed age, when measured to the nearest year is now 30.

### Solution to Exercise 8.2

The results are shown in Figure 8.4 and contained in the solution sheet of the file (W8_4.xls).

| Area U Outlet | Area U Price(£) | Area R Outlet | Area R Price(£) | Arithmetic Mean | Area U | Area R |
|---|---|---|---|---|---|---|
| | | | | | 1.48 | 1.79 |
| | | | | Median | 1.46 | 1.80 |
| 1 | 1.45 | 1 | 1.74 | Mode | 1.59 | 1.81 |
| 2 | 1.35 | 2 | 1.79 | | | |
| 3 | 1.59 | 3 | 1.84 | | | |
| 4 | 1.43 | 4 | 1.81 | | | |
| 5 | 1.36 | 5 | 1.7 | | | |
| 6 | 1.61 | 6 | 1.83 | | | |
| 7 | 1.5 | 7 | 1.77 | | | |
| 8 | 1.59 | 8 | 1.75 | | | |
| 9 | 1.42 | 9 | 1.82 | | | |
| 10 | 1.47 | 10 | 1.81 | | | |

**Figure 8.4**

As you can see, on every measure of central tendency prices at outlets in the rural area are higher than those in the urban area.

## Solution to Exercise 8.3

(a) As Figure 8.5 shows, it is clearly the case that country A has a higher mean income than country B (13.18 > 10.14).

However, the median value for country B is higher than for A, as is the mode. Essentially, the comparison between the two countries is made difficult by the fact that in A there is one large earner, whose exceptional income pulls the arithmetic mean up. For example, if you had to choose which country you would rather live in, then you would note that in country A you have a one in ten chance of earning 100 thousand, and a nine in ten chance of earning 5.6 thousand or less. On the

| | A | B | C | D | E | F | G |
|---|---|---|---|---|---|---|---|
| 1 | | | | Country A | Country B | | |
| 2 | Country A | Country B | Arithmetic Mean | 13.18 | 10.14 | | |
| 3 | Income (£000s) | Income (£000s) | Median | 4.10 | 9.95 | | |
| 4 | 100 | 9.6 | Mode | 1.20 | 10.30 | | |
| 5 | 4 | 9.5 | | | | | |
| 6 | 3 | 10.1 | | | | | |
| 7 | 5.1 | 10.3 | | | | | |
| 8 | 4.2 | 9.8 | | | | | |
| 9 | 6 | 8.9 | | | | | |

H ◂ ▸ H \ Data \ Solution /

**Figure 8.5**

|  | A | B | C | D | E | F | G |
|---|---|---|---|---|---|---|---|
| 1 |  |  |  | Country A | Country B |  |  |
| 2 | Country A | Country B | Arithmetic Mean | 13.18 | 10.14 |  |  |
| 3 | Income (£000s) | Income (£000s) | Median | 4.10 | 9.95 |  |  |
| 4 | 100 | 9.6 | Mode | 1.20 | 10.30 |  |  |
| 5 | 4 | 9.5 |  |  |  |  |  |
| 6 | 3 | 10.1 |  |  |  |  |  |
| 7 | 5.1 | 10.3 |  |  |  |  |  |
| 8 | 4.2 | 9.8 |  |  |  |  |  |
| 9 | 6 | 8.9 |  |  |  |  |  |
| 10 | 5.6 | 12 | Overall |  |  |  |  |
| 11 | 1.2 | 10.3 | Arithmetic Mean | 11.6585 |  |  |  |
| 12 | 1.2 | 9.7 | Median | 9.2 |  |  |  |
| 13 | 1.47 | 11.2 | Mode | 10.3 |  |  |  |
| 14 |  |  |  |  |  |  |  |

H ◀ ▶ H \ Data \ Solution /

**Figure 8.6**

other hand, in country B you would never earn less than 9.5 thousand and never earn more than 11.2 thousand. This discussion should give us a clue to the next area of descriptive statistics to be discussed—namely how the values in a data set are dispersed around their central values. We do this in the next chapter.

(b) To consider both countries together simply define the range for each of the Excel central tendency functions as A4:B13.

The results are shown in the C11:D13 range of the Solution sheet of the current file and in Figure 8.6.

■ NOTES

1. Notice that the simple average effectively implies that each of the weights is equal to $1/n$ where $n$ is the number of assignments.

<table>
<tr><td rowspan="2" style="border:1px solid;">**9**</td><td rowspan="2"># Data description— dispersion</td></tr>
</table>

| | | |
|---|---|---|

The following files from the online resource centre should be loaded as instructed:

W9_1.xls      W9_2.xls      W9_3.xls

## 9.1 Introduction

Data sets are like individuals or objects—they can be described in terms of a number of **characteristics**. The previous chapter has explained one of these characteristics—central tendency—but since the eventual purpose of descriptive statistics is to allow the investigator to observe the **differences** between two or more data sets, a **single** characteristic will rarely be sufficient. This would be like trying to distinguish between two individuals simply in terms of their height rather than in terms of their height **and** weight **and** hair colour and so on. Clearly a **full** description of any object usually requires that **more than one** characteristic be defined.

In descriptive statistics the most frequently used second characteristic is known as **dispersion** and it attempts to measure the extent to which the observations are **spread out**.

One of the simplest measures of dispersion is the **range** and is quite simply defined as the maximum observed value of the variable minus the minimum observed value.

## 9.2 The range

The range is defined as the difference between the maximum and minimum values in the data set. It is therefore a simple measure of the *spread* of the data.

In Excel the range is easily computed by combining the MAX and the MIN functions as follows:

$$=MAX(DATA\ RANGE) - MIN(DATA\ RANGE) = RANGE$$

However, although easy to calculate, the range suffers from the major deficiency that it only considers the two extreme observations in the data set. This means, for example, that two data sets could have identical ranges, yet be significantly different in terms of how the *intermediate* values are distributed. Furthermore, it is clear that the range is measured in the same units as the variable, and this means that a larger range could result simply from larger measurement units. (For example if the data are measured in grams then it is only to be expected that the range will be larger than if the *same data* were measured in kilograms.)

One way of partially dealing with this last deficiency would be to express the range as a proportion of the mean value, since this would introduce an element of *standardization* to the measure. However, even if this were done, there remains the deficiency that such a modification still ignores the distribution of observation values between the extreme values.

These limitations do not imply that the range has no real use in descriptive statistics. It can be an invaluable aid for choosing the number and width of the class intervals to be employed when creating a frequency distribution. For example, if a data set ranges between, say, 0 and 200, and if 10 class intervals are required, then dividing the range by the desired number of intervals (200/10 = 20) gives interval widths of 0, 20, 40, etc.

*The data from Table 8.1 (numbers of employees) have been reproduced in the W9_1.xls file which should now be loaded.*

The first sheet (Range) computes this simple measure of dispersion, while the range as a proportion of the arithmetic mean has also been calculated from the formula

$$=(MAX(B2:N2)-MIN(B2:N2))/AVERAGE(B2:N2)$$

*Study these entries now.*

The limitations in the range noted above have prompted statisticians to devise a more effective measure of dispersion known as the **variance**, and its square root—the **standard deviation**.

## 9.3 The variance and the standard deviation

The essence of these measures is that they consider how each individual observation in the data set differs (or deviates) from the central value as measured by the arithmetic mean.

*The argument is slightly more complicated than previously calculated measures, so the Variance sheet of the current file (W9_1.xls) should be loaded now.*

*Now follow the discussion along with the text and the in-file comments.*

Here we have the same data set as before and we have calculated the mean in the B7 cell. We then named the B7 cell as MEAN.

In row 3 we are now going to calculate the difference between each individual observation value and the calculated mean, and we will call these differences the mean deviations.

This implies that the entry in B3 should be:

=B2-MEAN   copied into C3:N3

If life were simple then all we would now do is add up these deviations to obtain an overall measure of the data set's dispersion relative to the mean.

Unfortunately, as should be clear from the calculations in row 3, some of these deviations are positive and some are negative, so there will be a tendency for them to cancel each other out when we add them up.

In fact, there is not just a *tendency* towards cancellation—they will always cancel out perfectly, as can be seen by summing the deviations in the O3 cell from =SUM(B3:N3).

This creates a serious problem, since it happens for *every possible data set*, and implies that the sum of deviations from the mean will always be the same (zero) *regardless* of how the data observations are distributed. As a measure of dispersion, therefore, the sum of mean deviations is never able to distinguish between data sets in terms of their degree of dispersion.

However, before rejecting the deviation idea entirely, we should ask whether we could retain the concept after some modification. The answer is that we can, if we square the deviations so that there are no longer any negative values. This will prevent the perfect cancellation that was causing the difficulty.

This is done in row 4 from the formula:

=B3^2   copied into C4:N4

As is clear from the total calculated in O4 of the worksheet, the sum of squared mean deviations for this data set is 2524, and importantly, this figure will vary from data set to data set in line with their dispersion patterns.

As a measure of dispersion this figure (the sum of squared deviations) is a clear improvement, but is still imperfect in the sense that it does not take account of the number of observations. In other words, the sum of squared deviations—other things being equal—will tend to be larger the greater is the number of observations. For this reason we divide the sum of squared deviations by the number of observations to obtain a statistic known as the **variance**.

This has been done in the B9 cell and returns a value of 194. Consequently, for these data, the variance number of employees is 194.

Finally, to compensate for having squared the mean deviations we take the square root of the variance, and obtain a statistic known as the **standard deviation**.

The result is shown in the B10 cell, and for these data returns a value of 13.93 employees.

Now that we are aware of the principles behind the calculation of the variance and the standard deviation, we can employ two Excel functions to perform the calculations for us.

The required functions are =VARP and =STDEVP and have the following syntax:

$$=VARP(Data\ Range)$$

$$=STDEVP(Data\ Range)$$

Appropriate versions of these functions have been entered to the B12 and B13 cells and clearly return the same values as obtained from first principles.

*Confirm this now.*

Broadly speaking, the higher is the variance or the standard deviation of the data set, the greater is the extent of its dispersion.

The variance and the standard deviation are by far the most frequently used measures of dispersion, and can be used to give an accurate idea of any differences in spread between two or more data sets.

For example, the worksheet called Variance(1) of the current file contains a second employee numbers data set (perhaps for a different region or country or time period).

*Access this sheet now.*

The task imposed is to compare the two data sets in terms of their central tendency and dispersion characteristics.

We notice immediately that the two data sets contain different numbers of observations (13 and 10), and that there appear to be no outlying observations in either data set.

The respective measures of central tendency and dispersion have been calculated for each region in columns B and C.

These allow us to make the following general observations.

(a) On all measures of central tendency companies in region B have a higher number of employees than those in region A.

(b) On all measures of dispersion companies in region B have a greater spread of employee numbers than those in region A.

On average, therefore, employee numbers are higher and more widely dispersed in region A than in region B.

The final point to note about this discussion is that, like the range, the variance and the standard deviation are measured in the same units as the data from which they were computed. In this sense they are what are known as *absolute* measures, since the measurement units employed directly determine their computed magnitudes.

If these measurement units are the same, then it is valid to argue that the higher is the variance (or standard deviation) then the greater is the degree of dispersion in the data set.

*Now attempt Exercise 9.1.*

If the measurement units are different then the last conclusion may have to be modified to take account of these differences.

For example, consider the Variance(2) sheet of the current file. Here we have two data sets measuring the weekly income of five individuals in each of the UK and the USA. The UK data are measured in pounds and the USA data are measured in dollars.

Suppose now that we compare the mean and the standard deviation of these weekly incomes for the two countries. The results apparently show that, as measured, mean weekly incomes in the USA are higher and more widely dispersed than in the UK (486.27 > 299.81; 74.95 > 65.01).

However, the validity of this conclusion must be tempered by the realization that we are not measuring income in the same units. This means that if there are approximately 1.65 dollars to the pound then this information should somehow be introduced in our calculations.

If the exact exchange rate between the pound and the dollar is known, and is fairly stable, then all we have to do is use this exchange rate to convert one currency into the other and then repeat the comparison. This has been done in the Variance(3) sheet of the W9_1.xls file, for an exchange rate of £1 = $1.65.

*Access this sheet now and follow the argument.*

Now that the UK incomes are expressed in dollars a different picture emerges, since it is now the case that mean weekly incomes in the UK are higher and more widely dispersed than in the USA[1] (486.27 < 494.68; 74.95 > 107.26).

Clearly, however, it was the knowledge of a given fixed exchange rate between the two currencies that allowed us to make a *consistent* comparison of weekly incomes, and resolve the difficulties created by different measurement units. But how should we proceed if no such conversion factor is conveniently available?

## 9.4 The coefficient of variation

The coefficient of variation is a statistic that measures relative as opposed to absolute variation in a data set, independently of the units of measurement and without having to make recourse to known exchange factors between different measurement units.

For example, suppose that a delivery company handles cargo with a mean weekly weight of 3.2 kg and a standard deviation of 2.1 kg. Also suppose that in the same week the cargo handled had a mean volume of 1.3 m$^3$ and a standard deviation of 0.54 m$^3$.

There is obviously no exchange rate between kilograms and cubic metres, so how can we decide whether there is more dispersion in the weight data than in the volume data? The answer is to form a statistic known as the coefficient of variation (CV), defined as the standard deviation divided by the mean. That is:

$$\text{Coefficient of variation} = \text{Standard deviation/Mean.}$$

**Table 9.1**

|  | UK(£s) | USA($s) |
|---|---|---|
| Arithmetic mean | 299.81 | 486.268 |
| Standard Deviation | 65.01 | 74.95 |
| Coefficient of Variation = St Dev/Mean | 0.216835 | 0.154124 |

Computing this statistic for the weight and volume data gives:

$$\text{CV Weight} = 2.1/3.2 = 0.677$$
$$\text{CV Volume} = 0.54/1.3 = 0.415$$

Notice that the coefficient of variation will always be less than or equal to one and greater than zero, so the calculated value can be regarded as a percentage (lying between 0 and 100%). Furthermore, since the coefficient of variation has been calculated by relating the standard deviation to the mean it is known as a *relative* measure of dispersion.

Consequently, without knowledge of any conversion factor, the calculated values for the coefficient of variation indicate that the weights of the cargo are relatively more dispersed than the cargo volumes (0.677 > 0.415).

It is now a simple matter to calculate the coefficients of variation for the weekly income data expressed in domestic currencies (i.e. without reference to an exchange rate).

This is done in the Coefficient of Variation sheet of the current file and the results are shown in Table 9.1.

From this it is clear that as far as relative dispersion is concerned weekly incomes in the UK are more widely distributed than in the USA (0.22 > 0.15). This is the same conclusion that was reached when using the exchange rate to convert pounds to dollars.

*Now attempt Exercise 9.2.*

## 9.5 The interquartile range

It was suggested earlier that there can be data sets for which the median is a more appropriate measure of central tendency than the mean. When this is the case then it follows that a measure of dispersion such as the standard deviation—which is based upon the mean—may no longer be the most appropriate measure of dispersion.

An alternative measure of dispersion is available, and is known as the **inter quartile range**, but before it can be fully appreciated the concept of a **quartile** must be explained.

We know that the median (roughly) splits a data set into two—about half the observations lie above the median and about half lie below. As might be imagined, therefore, quartiles split the data set into four parts that are equal in terms of their percentage frequencies. Consequently, the lower quartile (LQU) will have 25% of the total number of observations lying below it and 75% lying above it.

|  |  |  |  |  |  |  | MEDIAN POSITION |  |  |  |  |  |  |
|---|---|---|---|---|---|---|---|---|---|---|---|---|---|
| Position | 1 | 2 | 3 | 4 | 5 | 6 | 7 | 8 | 9 | 10 | 11 | 12 | 13 |
| Company No. | 10 | 1 | 5 | 9 | 11 | 3 | 6 | 12 | 7 | 2 | 8 | 13 | 4 |
| No. of employees | 12 | 15 | 15 | 15 | 19 | 21 | 23 | 25 | 26 | 35 | 35 | 50 | 60 |
|  |  |  |  |  |  |  | MEDIAN |  |  |  |  |  |  |

|  |  |  |  | LQU POSITION |  |  | MQU (MEDIAN) POSITION |  |  | UQU POSITION |  |  |  |
|---|---|---|---|---|---|---|---|---|---|---|---|---|---|
| Position | 1 | 2 | 3 | 4 | 5 | 6 | 7 | 8 | 9 | 10 | 11 | 12 | 13 |
| Company No. | 10 | 1 | 5 | 9 | 11 | 3 | 6 | 12 | 7 | 2 | 8 | 13 | 4 |
| No. of employees | 12 | 15 | 15 | 15 | 19 | 21 | 23 | 25 | 26 | 35 | 35 | 50 | 60 |
|  |  |  |  | LQU |  |  | MQU (MEDIAN) |  |  | UQU |  |  |  |

**Figure 9.1**

The middle quartile (MQU) is identical to the median since it has 50% of the observations above and 50% below.

Finally, the upper quartile (UQU) has 75% of the observations lying below it and 25% lying above it.

*These ideas are shown in the* **W9_2.xls** *file which should be loaded now.*

The sheet called Data contains the data from Table 8.1 (employee numbers), but it has been ranked in ascending order of number of employees.

The top section of all splits the data set in two around the median, while the second section then splits each half in two again to obtain the two quartiles. The effect is shown in Figure 9.1.

From inspection it is clear that:

LQU = 15 employees (position 4)

MQU = MEDIAN = 23 employees (position 7)

UQU = 35 employees (position 10)

For this small data set the calculations were simple. However, as the size of the data set increases it becomes more efficient to use the Excel =**QUARTILE** function. This has the following general syntax:

$$=QUARTILE(Data\ Range, Desired\ Quartile\ Number)$$

Notice that the function requires a number for the desired quartile, so we must remember that a value of 1 is the lower quartile, a value of 2 is the middle quartile and a value of 3 is the upper quartile.[2] Therefore:

$$LQU = QUARTILE(Data\ Range, 1)$$

$$MQU = QUARTILE(Data\ Range, 2)$$

$$UQU = QUARTILE(Data\ Range, 3)$$

These functions have been used in the sheet called Quartiles and confirm for this data set, the values previously obtained by inspection.

*Confirm this now.*

Notice that it only takes *three* quartile values (1, 2 and 3) to split the data set into *four* sections each with an equal number of observations.

We are now able to calculate the interquartile range (IQR) by subtracting LQU from UQU. That is:

$$IQR = (UQU - LQU).$$

For the illustrated data this evaluates to 20 employees, and gives the width of an interval that includes *the middle 50%* of observation values. That is, for our data set the middle 50% of observation span a range of 20 employees.

Compared to the range the IQR will always be smaller and will also be less affected by outlying observations. Like the range, however, a lot of information is ignored by the IQR and it makes no reference to the arithmetic worth of the other observations in the data set.

Nevertheless, the IQR is a useful measure of dispersion when the frequency distribution of the data set is not symmetrical (i.e. when the set contains a disproportionately high number of large observations or a disproportionately high number of small observations).

Finally, we should note that Excel has a related function called =PERCENTILE which allows more flexibility in dividing the data set into intervals of equal frequency. The general syntax is:

**=PERCENTILE(Data Range,Required Percentage)**

Clearly, the PERCENTILE function with an argument value of 25% will return the same value as the QUARTILE function with an argument value of 1.

More importantly, however, the PERCENTILE function allows a much greater degree of choice in controlling the equal portions into which the data are split. For example, suppose we want to split the current data set into five equal parts. This means that we need to compute the four *quintile* values that will do this.

Consequently, we use the PERCENTILE function with argument values of 20%, 40%, 60% and 80% respectively. This has been done in the sheet called Quintiles of the current file and computes the value of the four quintiles as 15, 20.6, 25.2 and 35 employees, respectively.

The implication of this is that the middle 60% of observations span a range of 20 employees (35–15) which happens, in this case, to be the same as the range encompassed by the middle 50% of observations (the IQR). Consequently, although this will not always be the case, considering 10% more observations has not increased the number of employees included in the defined span.

*Now attempt Exercise 9.3.*

## 9.6 **Exercises**

### Exercise 9.1

Load the W9_3.xls file. Here in the data sheet we have the data on the number of occupants and their ages variables.
 Calculate the range, variance and standard deviation for each variable.

### Exercise 9.2

For the data in Exercise 9.1 calculate the coefficient of variation for each of the data sets and state which has the greater degree of relative dispersion.

### Exercise 9.3

(a) For the data in Exercise 9.1 calculate the deciles (10% point values) for both the number of occupants and the age variables.

(b) Calculate the interquartile range for each variable.

## 9.7 **Solutions to the exercises**

### Solution to Exercise 9.1

Solutions are contained in the Solution(1) sheet of the file and show that when formatted to two decimal places the dispersion is absolutely greater for the age data than for the number of occupants.

### Solution to Exercise 9.2

The solution is contained in the Solution(2) sheet of the file, and shows that relative as well as absolute dispersion is still greater for the age data (coefficients of variation are 0.46 and 0.56 for the number of occupants and age respectively). However, this difference (0.1) is relatively small when compared with the larger difference in absolute dispersion 22.50 versus 1.16 for the comparative standard deviations).

### Solutions to Exercise 9.3

(a) The solution is contained in the Solution(3) sheet of the file, and shows that for the age data many of the deciles have the same value. This is only to be expected when there are only five different values of the variable and when we require the decile groups.

(b) The interquartile range is given as 1.00 for the number of occupants and 38.13 for the ages of these occupants. This means that the middle 50% of cars span only one occupant while the middle 50% of cars span an age range of 38.13 years. Again, this is only to be expected, given the difference in measurement units of the two variables.

However, relative to each of the median values, although the age data are still more widely dispersed than the number of occupants the relative difference is much less marked. This is because the IQR/Median would be evaluated for each data set as:

Number of occupants      $1/2 = 0.5$
Age      $38.13/40.25 = 0.94$

■ **NOTES**

1. Remember that the data are only samples of five individuals from each country. Whether this conclusion is valid for the nations as a whole is another matter.

2. Excel also allows values of 0 and 4 in the quartile function: 0 gives the minimum value in the data set, while 4 gives the maximum value.

# Data description— further methods

The following files from the online resource centre should be loaded as instructed:

| | | |
|---|---|---|
| W10_1.xls | W10_2.xls | W10_3.xls |
| W10_3A.xls | W10_4.xls | W10_5.xls |
| W10_6.xls | | |

## 10.1 Introduction

Previous chapters have indicated the techniques and statistical measures used in the description of simple data sets. However, sometimes the nature of the data requires the use of alternative methods of computing the standard statistical measures. This is particularly so if the original raw data are not available and only a collated frequency distribution can be obtained. Under these circumstances although the principles of calculating the various measures of central tendency and dispersion remain the same, the methods are slightly different.

## 10.2 Calculating the mean, variance and standard deviation from frequency distributions

*As an illustration of the problem load Workbook 10.1 (W10_1.xls) now.*

Here, the familiar data on number of occupants and their ages have been reproduced with a few amendments.

First, the mean, variance and standard deviation of both the number of occupants and their ages have been placed at the top of the sheet under appropriate labels. These are for comparison purposes later in the discussion.

Second, the histogram routine was used to prepare absolute frequency distributions of both variables (number of occupants and age) as indicated.

Now imagine that after these frequency distributions had been created, both raw data sets were destroyed and hence, along with them, the ability to compute the means, variances and standard deviations directly.

The question that arises is whether, in the absence of the raw data, the remaining frequency distributions provide sufficient information to allow us to calculate the means, variances and standard deviations.

The answer is a qualified 'yes', with the qualification being that sometimes when frequency distributions are used, the computed values for the mean, variance and standard deviation will only be estimates of their true values.

This is because the collation of the data into frequency distributions will usually (but not always) involve some loss of raw data.

For example, with the data on the number of occupants, the fact that every possible value for this data set was included in the bin means that by working backwards, the frequency distribution can be used to recreate the raw data set perfectly. In this case therefore, the estimates of the mean, variance and standard deviation will be identical to the statistics obtained from the raw data.

This is not the case, however, for the age data. Here, class intervals of 10 years were used and so the frequencies for each class interval do not tell us enough about the actual values that were observed, apart from the fact that they were located in those intervals. It would, for example, be impossible to replicate the raw data set perfectly, if only the frequency distribution data were available.

Clearly, in this case, any calculation to be performed must assume that the actual values were evenly distributed throughout each class interval, and if this were indeed the case then the estimated values for the mean, variance and standard deviation would be fairly accurate. However, to the extent that the actual values are not evenly distributed within each class interval, error will occur, and the calculated estimates will differ from the true values.

This means that when we are only presented with frequency distribution data, calculation of the mean, variance and standard deviation becomes slightly more difficult, since there are no dedicated Excel statistical functions that can be employed.

Nevertheless, Excel will still be of value in writing the formulae that have to be used.

Considering the data on the number of occupants first, we can start by calculating the arithmetic mean as follows.

The total number of occupants in the 100 cars is:

$$(1+1+\cdots+1) + (2+2+\cdots+2) + (3+3+\cdots+3) + (4+4+\cdots+4) + (5+5+\cdots+5)$$
$$\text{(22 terms)} \qquad \text{(32 terms)} \qquad \text{(27 terms)} \qquad \text{(12 terms)} \qquad \text{(7 terms)}$$

Thus the total **arithmetic worth** of these observations can be obtained by multiplying each different $x$ value (number of occupants) by its corresponding frequency (number of times which that occupancy value occurred) and then summing these products.

That is, with $f_i$ $(i = 1, \ldots n)$, representing the frequency of occurrence of each $x_i$ value:

$$\Sigma f_i x_i = f_1 x_1 + f_2 x_2 + f_3 x_3 + f_4 x_4 + f_5 x_5 = 22(1) + 32(2) + 27(3) + 12(4) + 7(5) = 250$$

This is the total **arithmetic worth** of all the observed $x$ values, i.e. the total number of occupants.

Furthermore, since the total number of cars $= \Sigma f_i = 100$, it follows that the arithmetic mean for this frequency distribution will be given by:

$$\bar{x} = \Sigma f_i x_i / \Sigma f_i = 250/100 = 2.5 \text{ occupants per car}$$

exactly the same as the value calculated in A2 from the raw data.

We can now use columns E and F of the current worksheet to perform these calculations.

*First, in E8 calculate the total number of frequencies (cars) from the formula:*

$$=SUM(E2:E6)$$

*Then, in F1 enter the label:*

fx

*and in F2 the formula:*

$$=D2*E2$$

*and copy this into F3:F6.*

This will compute the arithmetic worth of each of the five different observed $x$ values.

*Next, compute the total arithmetic worth in F8 from:*

$$=SUM(F2:F6)$$

*Finally, compute the arithmetic mean number of occupants in F9 from:*

$$=F8/E8$$

*and add the label:*

Mean =

*to the E9 cell.*

As we predicted, because this frequency distribution could recreate the raw data **exactly** the estimated mean and the true mean are identical (2.5 occupants in both cases).

To compute the variance and the standard deviation **directly** from the frequency distribution we need to employ the same principles.

Clearly, since there are 100 observations, there will be 100 deviations and 100 squared deviations from the mean that has just been computed in the F9 cell.

Thus, the deviations from the mean for each distinct value of $x$ are:

$$(x_i - \bar{x}) = (1\text{--}2.5) \qquad (2\text{--}2.5) \qquad (3 - 2.5) \qquad (4 - 2.5) \qquad (5 - 2.5)$$
$$(x_i - \bar{x}) = -1.5 \qquad\quad -0.5 \qquad\quad 0.5 \qquad\quad 1.5 \qquad\quad 2.5$$

The squared deviations are therefore

$$(x_i - \bar{x})^2 = (1 - 2.5)^2 \qquad (2 - 2.5)^2 \qquad (3 - 2.5)^2 \qquad (4 - 2.5)^2 \qquad (5 - 2.5)^2$$
$$(x_i - \bar{x})^2 = (-1.5)^2 \qquad\quad (-0.5)^2 \qquad\quad (0.5)^2 \qquad\quad (1.5)^2 \qquad\quad (2.5)^2$$
$$(x_i - \bar{x})^2 = 2.25 \qquad\qquad 0.25 \qquad\qquad 0.25 \qquad\quad 2.25 \qquad\quad 6.25$$

Once again, however, the **arithmetic worth** of each of these squared deviations must be computed on the basis of the **number of times** that the particular squared deviation occurred.

Thus, there are a total of 22 observations of $x = 1$ and therefore a total of 22 squared deviations of 2.25.

Their arithmetic worth is therefore:

$$22 \times (2.25)$$

A similar logic applies for the rest of the individual squared deviations and so the total sum of squared deviations (SSD) is:

$$\text{SSD} = 22(2.25) + 32(0.25) + 27(0.25) + 12(2.25) + 7(6.25) = 135$$

Given that the figures inside brackets are the individual squared deviations and the figures attached to them are the frequencies associated with those squared deviations, it therefore follows that:

$$\text{SSD} = f_1(x_1 - \bar{x})^2 + f_2(x_2 - \bar{x})^2 + \cdots + f_5(x_5 - \bar{x})^2 = \Sigma f_i(x_i - \bar{x})^2$$

Lastly, to standardize for the number of observations, we obtain the variance by dividing the SSD by the total number of observations. As with the calculations for the mean, the number of observations is given by the sum of the frequencies ($\Sigma f_i$), and so the variance is given by:

$$\text{Variance} = \Sigma f_i(x_i - \bar{x})^2 / \Sigma f_i$$

and the standard deviation by:

$$\text{Standard deviation} = \text{Variance}^{0.5}$$

To put these ideas into practice in the worksheet we need to use a new column (H).

*First, in H1 enter the label:*[1]

$$f(x - \text{mean})^2$$

*Next, in H2 enter the formula:*

$$\text{=E2*(D2-F\$9)\^2}$$

This is the first squared deviation times its frequency with the dollar sign attached to the F9 reference ensuring that it will **always** be the F9 cell (the mean) that is subtracted when copying is done.

*Now copy H2 into H3:H6.*

*Next, in H8 enter:*

=SUM(H2:H6)

This computes the SSD.

*Finally, to compute the variance number of occupants use H9 to contain:*

=H8/E8

i.e. the SSD divided by the sum of the frequencies.

*Then take the square root of the variance to obtain the standard deviation by using H10 to contain:*

=H9^0.5

The worksheet should now resemble the Solution(1) sheet of the W10_1.xls file.

*Confirm this now.*

As predicted earlier, these estimates of the variance and standard deviation are **identical** to the true values obtained from the raw data. This is entirely due to the fact that the data were whole numbers and that the values used in the frequency distribution were able to recreate the original raw data set perfectly.

When we address the age data then the fact that the frequency distribution used class intervals creates a problem that has already been encountered—namely, which of the interval values of $x$ to use. Once again, the remedy is to use the **midpoint** values of the intervals as representative of the $x$ values.

*Consequently, and still using Workbook 10.1, in F11 enter the label:*

$X_{mid}$

*and then fill F12:F20 with the values:*

5  15  25  35  45  55  65  75  85

These are the midpoint values of each of the class intervals.

Thereafter, the procedure is the same as with the data on the number of occupants explained above.

*Therefore, use G11 to contain the label:*

$fX_{mid}$

*and G12 to contain the formula*

=E12*F12

*Then copy G12 into G13:G20.*

*In E22 sum the frequencies from*

$$=\text{SUM(E12:E20)}$$

*and compute $\Sigma f X_{mid}$ in G22 from*

$$=\text{SUM(G12:G20)}$$

*Finally, calculate the mean in F23 from*

$$=\text{G22/E22}$$

*To compute the variance in age of the occupants in H11, add the label:*

$$f(X_{mid} - \text{mean})^2$$

*and in H12 the formula*

$$=\text{E12*(F12-F\$23)^2}$$

*Then copy this into H13:H20.*

*Next, in H22 calculate the SSD from*

$$=\text{SUM(H12:H20)}$$

*and the variance in H23 from*

$$=\text{H22/E22}$$

*The standard deviation can then be computed in H24 from*

$$=\text{H23^0.5}$$

When these calculations have been completed and appropriate labels added, the results should resemble the Solution(2) sheet of W10_1.xls.

*Consult this now to check your own solution.*

As you can see, the values for the mean, variance and standard deviation age of occupants calculated from the frequency distribution are not exactly the same as those obtained from the original raw data. The errors are not huge (496.84 versus 506.13, and 22.29 versus 22.50 for the variance and the standard deviation respectively) but they nonetheless exist, and represent the difference between the actual values of the mean variance and standard deviation and the estimated values.

The extent of such errors will depend upon two things.

First of all, the class intervals used to create the frequency distribution, and therefore the values of the midpoints. The fewer the number of intervals (i.e. the wider the class interval) then the greater is the likelihood of the errors' being large.

Secondly, the extent to which the raw data are evenly distributed within each of the class intervals. If this distribution is **completely even** then the midpoint values will be fairly representative and the estimation error will tend to be small. On the other hand, if many of the actual observation are concentrated at the top or at the bottom of the intervals, then the mid point values will underestimate or overestimate the actual worth of the values in the interval, and the scope for estimation error increases.

*Now attempt Exercise 10.1.*

## 10.3 Descriptive statistics from the Excel Data Analysis routine

In both this and the previous chapter the procedure has been to explain and develop **individual** Excel functions to calculate the various summary statistics (=AVERAGE, =MEDIAN, etc.). However, Excel contains a pre-programmed routine called Data Analysis that will produce all of the descriptive statistics automatically from raw data sets.

Now that we know what most of these statistics mean we can take advantage of that routine.

*First, load Workbook 10.2 (W10_2.xls).*

This reproduces the by-now-familiar data on car occupants and their ages.

*Now select Tools and then Data Analysis and then Descriptive Statistics.*

A dialogue box resembling the one in Figure 10.1 will appear.

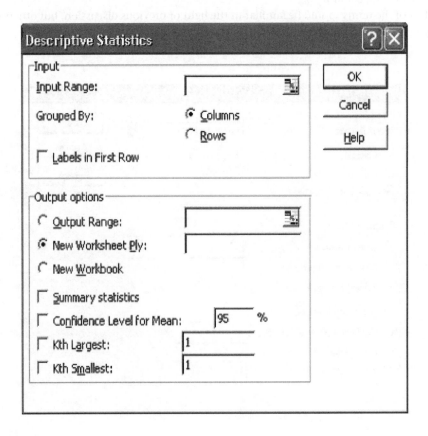

**Figure 10.1**

*First, enter the input range for the occupants data (A1:A251) in the top box and make sure that the data are grouped by columns. Since we have included the label contained in A1 in the input range, now make sure that the Labels in First Row box is checked.*

*Ignore the three boxes below for the moment, and click on the Output Range tab to make it checked.*

*Then choose a vacant range of the worksheet and enter its coordinates to the output range box.*

In the illustration we have chosen C1, so the Descriptive Statistics will appear in the range commencing at C1.

*Finally, click on the Summary Statistics tab*

The dialogue box should now resemble Figure 10.2.

*If it does, click OK.*

The results produced should resemble the Solution(1) sheet of the current file W10_2.xls (after widening column C).

Most of the terms should be familiar in the light of previous discussion, but others can only be understood later. Ignore them at the moment.

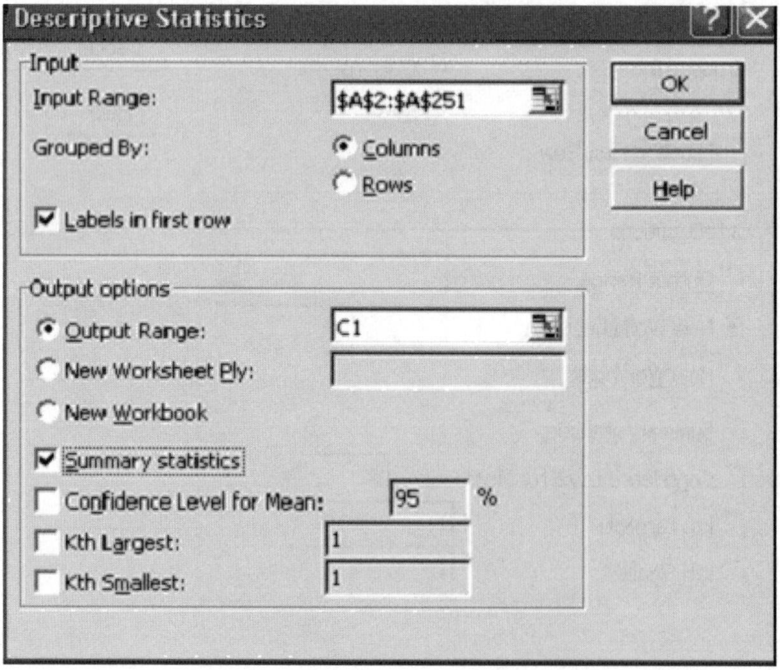

Figure 10.2

*To obtain the Descriptive Statistics for the age data set repeat the procedure outlined above, but define the Input Range as B1:B251 and the Output Range as E1.*

The results should resemble the Solution(2) sheet of the current file W10_2.xls

*Now attempt Exercise 10.2.*

# 10.4 **Statistical analysis of selected data subsets**

The previous discussion has shown how to compute the mean, variance and standard deviation for all of the observations in a given data set.

However, it will often be the case that we require measures of central tendency and dispersion that apply *only to certain selected observations* from the data set. This means that we are only concerned with what is known as a **data subset**.

For example, in a data set of the marks obtained by all of the students who sat a particular examination we may want to know the mean and standard deviation mark of *only* the female examinees, or of *only* those examinees who were over 25 years of age.

Computations such as these require that we re-deploy the data filtering process that was explained in Section 2 of Chapter 3, and then use some of the SUBTOTAL functions that were also explained in that section.

*To see how this selective data analysis can be achieved load Worksheet 10_3.xls now. Now select the A14:H14 area with the mouse and then select Data, Filter and then Autofilter.*

The data set can now be filtered as required to produce selected subsets.

Next, recall that to compute summary statistics in a filtered list requires that we use an appropriate SUBTOTAL function. These functions produce different summary statistics depending upon the numerical value adopted by their first argument. (The second argument is simply the range of each of the numerical fields for which calculations are to be performed: C15:C100, D15:D100, and so on to H15:H100 in this case).[2]

The full list of first argument numbers used in SUBTOTAL functions is:

1 = AVERAGE (i.e. the arithmetic mean)

2 = COUNT (i.e. the number of items in the list that are numbers)

3 = COUNTA (i.e. the number of items in the list that are numbers or text or messages)[3]

4 = MAX (i.e. the maximum value in the list)

5 = MIN (i.e. the minimum value in the list)

6 = PRODUCT (i.e. the product of all the values in the list)

7 = STDEV (i.e. the standard deviation of a sample data set)

8 = STDEVP (i.e. the standard deviation of a population data set)

9 = SUM (i.e. the sum of the values in the list)

10 = VAR (i.e. the variance of a sample data set)

11 = VARP (i.e. the variance of a population data set).

In the context of our *current knowledge* of statistics the relevant function arguments are 1, 2, 4, 5, 8 and 11.

*Consequently, to obtain these summary statistics for each of the fields, first of all enter the labels and numbers to the column A and B ranges as shown below:*

| | |
|---|---|
| A1: AVERAGE | B1: 1 |
| A2: COUNT | B2: 2 |
| A3: MAX | B3: 4 |
| A4: MIN | B4: 5 |
| A5: STDEVP | B5: 8 |
| A6: VARP | B6: 11 |

*Next, in E1 enter the formula*

$$=SUBTOTAL(\$B1,E\$15:E\$100)$$

*and copy it down into E2:E6.*

This uses the column B entries as the first argument of the SUBTOTAL functions, while the dollar signs ensure consistent copying both down and across the sheet. Clearly this process will produce the specified summary statistics for the SALARY field.

*To obtain equivalent statistics for the remaining fields, copy the E1:E6 block into F1:H6 and then format E1:H6 to two decimal places.*

The results should resemble the section shown in Figure 10.3 and contained in the Solution sheet of the current file W10_3.xls.

Now notice that, at the moment, the summary statistics refer to the entire data list (i.e. all of the observations in each of the fields). This is because the list has not yet been filtered.

So, suppose now that we want to compute the mean salary and the mean tax for the female subset.

*To do this, click on the GENDER field filter tab and select F from the list.*

The summary statistics at the top of the sheet will adjust automatically and if the model has been prepared correctly it is an easy matter to observe that for this subset (females) the mean salary is £33695.57 and the mean tax paid is £9145.30.

Finally, to obtain the summary statistics for all married females, say, *with the GENDER field still selecting females*, click on the MARSTAT field filter tab and select 1 (for married). The mean salary and the mean tax paid should be returned as £34549.17 and £8637.29 respectively.

*Now attempt Exercise 10.3.*

| | E1 | | ▼ | $f_x$ | =SUBTOTAL($B$1,E$15:E$100) | | | | | | | |
|---|---|---|---|---|---|---|---|---|---|---|---|---|
| | A | B | C | D | E | F | G | H | I | J | K | L |
| 1 | AVERAGE | 1 | | | 34757.36 | 9931.89 | 3054.54 | 21770.93 | | | | |
| 2 | COUNT | 2 | | | 14.00 | 14.00 | 14.00 | 14.00 | | | | |
| 3 | MAX | 4 | | | 56824.75 | 18752.17 | 5682.48 | 33395.98 | | | | |
| 4 | MIN | 5 | | | 889.64 | 222.41 | 80.96 | 578.27 | | | | |
| 5 | STDEVP | 8 | | | 17931.87 | 5711.52 | 1747.31 | 10888.26 | | | | |
| 6 | VARP | 11 | | | 321561998.40 | 32621484.50 | 3053102.76 | 118554269.55 | | | | |
| 7 | | | | | | | | | | | | |
| 8 | | | | | | | | | | | | |
| 9 | | | | | | | | | | | | |
| 10 | | | | | | | | | | | | |
| 11 | | | | | | | | | | | | |
| 12 | | | MARSTAT = 1 = MARRIED, MARSTAT = 0 = SINGLE | | | | | | | | | |
| 13 | | | SEX = F = FEMALE, SEX = M = MALE | | | | | | | | | |
| 14 | NAME ▼ | INITIA ▼ | MARSTAT ▼ | SEX ▼ | SALARY ▼ | TAX ▼ | SUPERAN ▼ | TAKEHOMI ▼ | | | | |
| 15 | ALLAN | L | 1 | M | 7058.27 | 1764.57 | 705.83 | 4587.88 | | | | |
| 16 | ALLEN | D | 0 | M | 43966.55 | 14508.96 | 4396.66 | 25060.93 | | | | |
| 17 | BROWN | G | 0 | M | 53531.38 | 17665.36 | 5353.14 | 30512.89 | | | | |
| 18 | BROWN | I | 1 | M | 889.64 | 222.41 | 80.96 | 578.27 | | | | |
| 19 | BROWN | L | 1 | M | 37085.07 | 9271.27 | 3708.51 | 24105.29 | | | | |
| 20 | COOPER | F | 0 | F | 50799.24 | 16763.75 | 3809.94 | 30225.55 | | | | |
| 21 | DAVIES | R | 1 | F | 33501.75 | 8375.44 | 2512.63 | 22613.68 | | | | |
| 22 | REDMOND | K | 0 | F | 12323.86 | 4066.87 | 924.29 | 7332.69 | | | | |
| 23 | REILLY | G | 1 | F | 14764.91 | 3691.23 | 1107.37 | 9966.32 | | | | |
| 24 | ROBERTS | F | 1 | F | 35054.07 | 8763.52 | 2629.05 | 23661.49 | | | | |
| 25 | SMITH | G | 1 | M | 51378.43 | 12844.61 | 5137.84 | 33395.98 | | | | |
| 26 | SMITH | P | 1 | F | 47981.05 | 11995.26 | 3598.58 | 32387.21 | | | | |
| 27 | SMITH | R | 0 | M | 56824.75 | 18752.17 | 5682.48 | 32390.11 | | | | |
| 28 | STEWART | R | 1 | F | 41444.09 | 10361.02 | 3108.31 | 27974.76 | | | | |
| 29 | | | | | | | | | | | | |

H ◄ ► H \ Sheet 1 / Sheet2 / Sheet3 / Sheet4 / Sheet5 / Sheet6 / Sheet7 / Sheet8 / Sheet9 / ◄ | ◄ |

**Figure 10.3**

Although using filters and subtotal functions is a simple but effective way of interrogating a database, these can only return the result of *one* filter at a time—since the results clearly change as the nature of the filter changes.

However, suppose that for the current data, we want to create *two* cells—one of which returns the average salary for males and the other for females. These two cells should *permanently* be available for inspection and/or access by other cells in the worksheet.

To do this we can use Excel database functions as follows.

The current data are reproduced in the W10_3A.xls file which should be loaded now.

Given our declared objectives, our first concern is with females in the GENDER field.

So, in the A1 cell enter the exact version of the field name to be used as the filter—i.e. GENDER in this case, and below in A2 enter F for female as the condition for the filter to use.

These two cells (A1:A2) are known as the **criterion range** and simply identify the search field and required record type in that field.

Now consider the =**DAVERAGE** function. This is simply the normal =AVERAGE function with its syntax modified to allow more selective application to a database.

All database functions take three arguments.

Argument 1: the range containing the database including field names. In the current file this constitutes A14:H28 and we have named it as DATA.

Argument 2: the address of the field for which we want to calculate the database statistic. In this case we want the average of the SALARY field so enter E14, i.e. the cell address of the salary field label.[4]

Argument 3: the criterion range, A1:A2 in this case.

Taken together this means that the relevant database function becomes:

=DAVERAGE(DATA,E14,A1:A2)

This has been entered to the D1 cell and returns a value of £33695.57 and is clearly the same result that was obtained from the SUBTOTAL function earlier.

Now, to calculate the equivalent value for the male clients we replicate this procedure except with the field criterion being changed from F to M.

That is, in A3 enter the label GENDER and in A4 enter M for male. Then use D3 to contain:

=DAVERAGE(DATA,E14,A3:A4)

These entries have been made to the A3:A4 range and the DAVERAGE function to the D3 cell, where it returns a value of £35819.16 for the average male salary.

Clearly we have achieved our declared objective, and the results confirm those obtained by simple filtering.

As in filtering, database functions can be used to ask more complex questions, i.e. using more than one field criterion.

For example, suppose we want the average salary of married females. Since we only want records that satisfy *both* criteria to be included in the calculations, the extra field and its criterion must be located immediately to the right of the original criterion range.

This means that we should use B1 to contain MARSTAT and B2 to contain a value of 1 (for married).

Now use E1 say to contain:

=DAVERAGE(DATA,E14,A1:B2)

Notice that the criterion range has been expanded to A1:B2 in the DAVERAGE function to incorporate this added condition.

A result of £34549.17 will be returned and once again replicates the answer obtained earlier by filtering.

It is left as an exercise to use E3 to house a database function that will calculate the average salary of married males (the answer will be £24102.85).

Finally, it should be noted that Excel supports a number of other database functions that replicate the number arguments of SUBTOTAL function. The most important of these are:

=DVARP (population variance)

=DSUM (sum)

=DSTDEVP (population standard deviation)

## 10.5 **Exercises**

### Exercise 10.1

Load the W10_4.xls file. The data are a frequency distribution of the number of accidents on a motorway network over a period of 365 days.
  Estimate the mean, variance and standard deviation of number of accidents.

### Exercise 10.2

Load the W10_5.xls file. The data are the annual profits earned by two groups of companies A and B.

(a) Use the Excel Data Analysis routine to compute the Descriptive Statistics for both groups of companies.

(b) Then answer the following questions.
   (i) Which group of companies has the highest mean profit?

   (ii) In which group of companies are the profit values most dispersed?

   (iii) Which group of companies has got the highest **relative** dispersion of profits?

   (iv) Calculate the mean profit earned by the **combined** group of companies.

   (v) Calculate the range of profits earned by the **combined** group of companies.

### Exercise 10.3

Load the W10_6.xls file.

(a) Use the Excel Data Filtering device in conjunction with appropriate SUBTOTAL functions to complete Table 10.1.

(b) Use the worksheet prepared in part (a) to determine:
   (i) The subject in which females performed best.

**Table 10.1**

| Mark in Economics | Count | Mean | St Dev | Max | Min | |
|---|---|---|---|---|---|---|
| Females | | | | | | |
| Males | | | | | | |
| Aged < 18 | | | | | | |
| Aged > 30 | | | | | | |
| Males with >40% in MATHS | | | | | | |
| Females with <40% in LAW | | | | | | |
| Females aged < 20 | | | | | | |
| Males aged < 20 | | | | | | |
| Over 40% in both LAW and MATHS | | | | | | |

**Table 10.2**

|  | F age < 20 | M age < 20 | F age >= 18 | M age >= 18 |
|---|---|---|---|---|
| LAW Mean |  |  |  |  |
| LAW St Dev |  |  |  |  |
| MATHS Mean |  |  |  |  |
| MATHS St Dev |  |  |  |  |
| ACCOUNTS Mean |  |  |  |  |
| ACCOUNTS St Dev |  |  |  |  |
| INFOTECH Mean |  |  |  |  |
| INFOTECH St Dev |  |  |  |  |
| ECONOMICS Mean |  |  |  |  |
| ECONOMICS St Dev |  |  |  |  |
| STATS Mean |  |  |  |  |
| STATS St Dev |  |  |  |  |

(ii) The subject in which males performed best.

(iii) The subject in which females performed worst.

(iv) The subject in which males performed worst.

(v) The subject with the least dispersion of marks for students aged under 18.

(vi) The subject with the greatest dispersion of marks for students aged over 20.

(c) Use the worksheet prepared in part (a) to complete Table 10.2 and then make some comments about the relative performance of the different groups of students in the different subjects.

Note: F = Female, M = Male

## 10.6 Solutions to the exercises

### Solution to Exercise 10.1

The solution is shown in Figure 10.4 and in the Solution sheet of the file (W10_4.xls).

The midpoint values of 2, 7, 12, 17, 22, 27, 32 and 37 were entered to the C2:C9 range directly and then the following formulae written:

In D2: =B2*C2, i.e frequency times midpoint value, copied into D3:D9.

In B10: =SUM(B2:B9), i.e. the sum of the frequencies = the total number of observations.

In D10: =SUM(D2:D9), i.e. the total worth of all the observations.

In B11: =D10/B10, i.e. the mean

In E2: =C2-B$11, i.e. the deviation of the mean from the first midpoint value, copied into E3:E9 to give the rest of the deviations from the mean.

| | A | B | C | D | E | F | G | H | I | J | K |
|---|---|---|---|---|---|---|---|---|---|---|---|
| | A15 | | $f_x$ | | | | | | | | |
| | A | B | C | D | E | F | G | H | I | J | K |
| 1 | No.of Accidents | No. of Days | Mid Points Xm | f*Xm | Xm - Mean | f*(Xm - Mean) | f*(Xm - Mean)² | | | | |
| 2 | 0 to 4 | 4 | 2 | 8 | -17.27 | -69.10 | 1193.56 | | | | |
| 3 | 5 to 9 | 21 | 7 | 147 | -12.27 | -257.75 | 3163.66 | | | | |
| 4 | 10 to 14 | 49 | 12 | 588 | -7.27 | -356.42 | 2592.62 | | | | |
| 5 | 15 to 19 | 121 | 17 | 2057 | -2.27 | -275.15 | 625.69 | | | | |
| 6 | 20 to 24 | 105 | 22 | 2310 | 2.73 | 286.23 | 780.28 | | | | |
| 7 | 25 to 29 | 36 | 27 | 972 | 7.73 | 278.14 | 2148.89 | | | | |
| 8 | 30 to 34 | 24 | 32 | 768 | 12.73 | 305.42 | 3886.84 | | | | |
| 9 | 35 to 39 | 5 | 37 | 185 | 17.73 | 88.63 | 1571.06 | | | | |
| 10 | Total | 365 | | 7035 | | | 15962.60 | | | | |
| 11 | Mean = | 19.27 | | | | | | | | | |
| 12 | Variance = | 43.73 | | | | | | | | | |
| 13 | Standard deviation = | 6.61 | | | | | | | | | |

Sheet1 \ Solution / Sheet3 /

**Figure 10.4**

In F2: =B2*(C2-B$11), i.e. frequency times the deviation from the mean, copied into F3:F9 to give the value of the rest of the deviations from the mean.

In F10: =SUM(F2:F9), i.e. the sum of all the deviations from the mean, equal to zero as always.

In G2: =B2*(C2-B$11)^2, i.e. frequency times the squared deviation from the mean, copied into G3:G9 to give the value of each of the squared deviations from the mean.

In G10: =SUM(G2:G9), i.e. the sum of squared deviations from the mean.

In B12: =G10/B10, i.e. the variance = sum of squared deviations divided by the sum of the frequencies.

In B13: =B12^0.5, i.e. the standard deviation = the square root of the variance.

## Solutions to Exercise 10.2

Use Tools, Data Analysis and then Descriptive Statistics. The input range for group A is B3:B202 and the output range is defined as D1. For group B the input range is C3:C202 and the output range is F1. The Summary Statistics tab was checked in both cases.

The results are shown in Figure 10.5 and in the Solution sheet of the current file.

(i) Group A has a higher mean profit than group B.

(ii) Both the range and the variance are higher for group A.

| | A | B | C | D | E | F | G | H | I |
|---|---|---|---|---|---|---|---|---|---|
| 1 | | Annual Group | Annual Group | A profits (£000s) | | B profits (£000s) | | | |
| 2 | Company no. | A profits (£000s) | B profits (£000s) | | | | | | |
| 3 | 1 | 21.81 | 3.49 | Mean | 48.404 | Mean | 35.564 | | |
| 4 | 2 | 77.34 | 52.16 | Standard Error | 2.0275 | Standard Error | 1.4205 | | |
| 5 | 3 | 36.91 | 44.99 | Median | 47.875 | Median | 37.898 | | |
| 6 | 4 | 87.83 | 1.58 | Mode | #N/A | Mode | #N/A | | |
| 7 | 5 | 27.71 | 42.07 | Standard Deviation | 28.673 | Standard Deviati | 20.09 | | |
| 8 | 6 | 84.14 | 0.51 | Sample Variance | 822.17 | Sample Variance | 403.59 | | |
| 9 | 7 | 80.36 | 62.13 | Kurtosis | -1.122 | Kurtosis | -1.244 | | |
| 10 | 8 | 48.49 | 36.41 | Skewness | 0.1281 | Skewness | -0.154 | | |
| 11 | 9 | 22.23 | 36.51 | Range | 98.307 | Range | 67.332 | | |
| 12 | 10 | 91.25 | 55.87 | Minimum | 0.7421 | Minimum | 0.5149 | | |
| 13 | 11 | 55.18 | 40.24 | Maximum | 99.049 | Maximum | 67.847 | | |
| 14 | 12 | 81.95 | 59.55 | Sum | 9680.7 | Sum | 7112.9 | | |
| 15 | 13 | 29.26 | 6.28 | Count | 200 | Count | 200 | | |
| 16 | 14 | 16.93 | 48.70 | | | | | | |
| 17 | 15 | 46.88 | 6.94 | | | | | | |
| 18 | 16 | 2.94 | 52.94 | | | | | | |
| 19 | 17 | 80.12 | 64.69 | | | | | | |
| 20 | 18 | 97.70 | 37.15 | | | | | | |
| 21 | 19 | 79.54 | 20.59 | | | | | | |
| 22 | 20 | 47.61 | 39.12 | | | | | | |

**Figure 10.5**

(iii) Calculate the coefficient of variation ($CV_A$ and $CV_B$) (see Section 9.4) for each group. Thus:

$$CV_A = 100(28.67/48.4) = 59.23\% \text{ and } CV_B = 100(20.09/35.564) = 56.48\%.$$

Relative dispersion is therefore slightly higher in group A.

(iv) Since there are an **equal** number of companies in the two groups the combined mean is obtained simply by summing the two individual means and then dividing by 2. Thus:

$$\text{Combined mean} = (48.4 + 35.564)/2 = 41.98$$

If, however, there had been an **unequal** number of companies in each group the combined mean would have to be computed in a way that takes account of the unequal numbers. This is called a **weighted** mean and is calculated as:

$$\text{Weighted mean} = (n_1\bar{x} + n_2\bar{x}2)/(n_1 + n_2)$$

(v) The range for the combined group is the **largest** maximum minus the **smallest** minimum. Hence:

$$\text{Combined range} = 99.05 - 0.5149 = 98.5351$$

## Solutions to Exercise 10.3

Select the A8:J8 range and then switch the Autofilter on.

**Table 10.3**

| Mark in Economics | Count | Mean | St Dev | Max | Min |
|---|---|---|---|---|---|
| Females | 11 | 44.09 | 28.01 | 89 | 8 |
| Males | 8 | 48.88 | 24.24 | 87 | 13 |
| Aged < 18 | 4 | 45 | 31.16 | 88 | 8 |
| Aged > 30 | 4 | 39.75 | 23.05 | 76 | 12 |
| Males with >40% in MATHS | 6 | 45.33 | 25.34 | 87 | 13 |
| Females with <40% in LAW | 4 | 46.25 | 25.17 | 89 | 24 |
| Females aged < 20 | 6 | 42.67 | 29.72 | 88 | 8 |
| Males aged < 20 | 5 | 47.6 | 27.2 | 87 | 13 |
| Over 40% in both LAW and MATHS | 10 | 45 | 25.51 | 87 | 8 |

Enter the numbers 2, 1, 8, 4, and 5 to the A1:A5 range and then the labels COUNT, AVERAGE, STDEVP, MAX and MIN, and to the B1:B5 range.

Then, in E1 enter the formula:

$$=SUBTOTAL(\$A1,E\$8:E\$100)$$

and copy this down into E5 and then along to J5.

This has been done in the Solution sheet of the file which should be consulted now.

The worksheet now contains the summary statistics for the **unfiltered** list. A specimen answer is contained in the Solution sheet of the file.

(a) To fill in the table click on the appropriate field filter tab, select the required filter and note the results. These are shown in Table 10.3 and in the Summary sheet of the current file.

(b) Once again use appropriate filters to produce the summary statistics for the selected list of observations and then choose the subject that meets the requirements of the question.

   (i) Infotech (mean = 83)

   (ii) Infotech (mean = 82.38)

   (iii) Economics (mean = 44.09)

   (iv) Accounts (mean = 47.28)

   (v) Accounts (standard deviation = 3.67)

   (vi) Economics (standard deviation = 23.28)

(c) The completed table is shown in Table 10.4 and in the Summary sheet of the current file.

The calculated statistics would suggest the following general conclusions.

(i) Males under 20 seem to be considerably better at maths than their female counterparts. The opposite is true for the 18-or-more age group. (Notice that 18- and 19-year-olds will be included in both of these groups.)

Table 10.4

| | F age < 20 | M age < 20 | F age >= 18 | M age >= 18 |
|---|---|---|---|---|
| LAW Mean | 53.83 | 51.2 | 53.5 | 56.29 |
| LAW St Dev | 19.83 | 15.43 | 22.53 | 15.93 |
| MATHS Mean | 58 | 67.6 | 64.25 | 55.86 |
| MATHS St Dev | 19.23 | 17.81 | 10.46 | 26.88 |
| ACCOUNTS Mean | 49.83 | 47.8 | 44.75 | 47.29 |
| ACCOUNTS St Dev | 6.72 | 5.38 | 7.28 | 6.88 |
| INFOTECH Mean | 80.33 | 83.8 | 83.63 | 83.71 |
| INFOTECH St Dev | 9.3 | 9.02 | 7.4 | 7.32 |
| ECONOMICS Mean | 42.67 | 47.6 | 45.63 | 47.29 |
| ECONOMICS St Dev | 29.72 | 27.2 | 24.95 | 25.52 |
| STATS Mean | 57.83 | 68.6 | 65 | 57 |
| STATS St Dev | 17.1 | 18.21 | 10.39 | 26.38 |

(ii) The accounts marks, although not producing the highest mean score for any of the groups, are clearly the least dispersed, since the standard deviations are lower than for any other subject group. This means that very few students did exceptionally well or exceptionally badly. (Remember that a zero standard deviation in this context would mean that each student obtained the same mark.)

(iii) The economics marks have similar means to those for accounts, but unlike the latter, the dispersion was very large for all of the student groups. There were, therefore, a number of students with extremes of good and poor performance.

(iv) The patterns observed for the maths marks are repeated for the stats marks (perhaps not surprisingly, since both are quantitative subjects and skills in one can be transferred easily to the other).

(v) The infotech marks are clearly the highest with a very low degree of dispersion across all of the student groups. In fact, the marks are so high with so little dispersion in comparison to those for the other subjects that one would want more information on either the standard of the examination or the method of marking, or both.

## ■ NOTES

1. To obtain the power symbol enter the text as $f(x - \text{mean})2$, then, on the formula bar, click and drag on the 2, select Format, Cells and then Superscript.

2. Notice that we have extended these ranges beyond the actual range of the data to allow new records to be added without having to edit the SUBTOTAL functions.

3. Neither COUNT nor COUNTA includes cells that are **blank** in the counting process.

4. Alternatively, as the second argument you could enter the field name inside double quotes *exactly* as it appears in the worksheet, i.e. ''SALARY''.

# 11 Data description—association

The following files from the online resource centre should be loaded as instructed:

W11_1.xls    W11_2.xls    W11_3.xls
W11_4.xls    W11_5.xls    W11_6.xls
W11_7.xls    W11_8.xls

## 11.1 Introduction

There will frequently be occasions when it will be desirable to see whether two or more data sets are associated with each other in a regular way. For example, we may suspect that examination performance is associated with attendance at lectures, or that house prices are associated with interest rates.

With quantitative data the most commonly used indicator of association is Pearson's correlation coefficient ($r$).

For qualitative ordinal data, where only rankings are available, there is an equivalent indicator known as Spearman's rank correlation coefficient.

Finally, when faced with qualitative categorical data, or with quantitative data that have been categorized, an indication of any apparent association can be obtained from a device known as contingency tables.

## 11.2 **Pearson's correlation coefficient**

The correlation coefficient ($r$) measures the extent to which there is a perfect linear association between pairs of observations on two statistical variables ($X$ and $Y$). It has a maximum value of 1 and a minimum value of $-1$. A value of 1 means that there is a perfect direct linear association between the pairs of $X$, $Y$ observations, with 'direct' meaning that as $X$ increases so too does $Y$.

For example, consider the following data set:

$X$: 1 2 3   4   5   6   7   8   9   10
$Y$:  3  6  9  12  15  18  21  24  27  30

In this example it should be clear that each value of $Y$ is always exactly 3 times the corresponding value of $X$, and so the correlation coefficient would be computed as 1.

On the other hand, consider:

$X$ :   1   2   3    4    5    6    7    8    9    10
$Y$:  $-3$  $-6$  $-9$  $-12$  $-15$  $-18$  $-21$  $-24$  $-27$  $-30$

In this case, the value of $Y$ is always exactly minus 3 times the value of $X$, and although still perfectly linear is indirect now in the sense that as $X$ increases $Y$ decreases.

For this reason the correlation coefficient would be computed as $-1$.

That is, there is a perfect negative linear association between $Y$ and $X$.

In general, if the values of one variable are always any constant multiple of the values of the other variable, then the correlation coefficient will be plus or minus 1.

Now consider the following data set

$X$:  1  2   3   4    5  6    7  8    9  10
$Y$:  $-3$  6  $-9$  12  $-15$  18  $-21$  24  $-27$  30

In this case, there is no perfect linear association to be observed. There *is* an apparent pattern: when $X$ is odd, $Y$ is minus 3 times $X$, while when $X$ is even, $Y$ is plus 3 times $X$. But, considering both odd and even values of $X$ leads us to conclude that there is no real linear association between $Y$ and $X$. This suggests that the computed correlation coefficient would lie somewhere between its maximum and minimum values of 1 and $-1$, and probably quite close to zero.

***To see if this is the case load* W11_1.xls.**

This contains the last data set.

Excel can compute the correlation coefficient with its $=$ CORREL function, the general syntax of which is:

$$=CORREL(Y\ range, X\ range)$$

***Consequently, in C2 enter the formula***

$$=CORREL(B2:B11, A2:A11)$$

When formatted to four decimal places a value of 0.1548 should be returned to C2, indicating that the strength of the linear association is far from perfect (±1).

Several points need to be explained about this number.

First, the value is positive in this case, because the sum of the positive $Y$ values (90) is greater than the sum of the negative $Y$ values ($-75$). However, if the opposite were the case (as shown in columns D and E of the current sheet), then the correlation coefficient would be computed as

$$-0.1548.$$

*This should be confirmed by entering:*

=CORREL(E2:E21,D2:D21)

*to the F2 cell*

Second, if we extend the data set to include 10 more observations, while retaining the existing odd–even pattern, then the value of the correlation coefficient will decline. This is shown in Sheet2 of the current file.

*Access this now and then in C2 enter:*

=CORREL(B2:B21,A2:A21)

A value of 0.0761 will be returned, which is almost half the value obtained when only

10 pairs of observations shared the same pattern (0.1548).

*Now make an equivalent entry to the F2 cell of Sheet2 of the current file to confirm that when the signs of the Y terms are reversed the correlation coefficient becomes −0.0761.*

This shows that, given any particular pattern of observations on $Y$ and $X$, the correlation coefficient will naturally be higher, the fewer are the number of observations. For example, it is easy to show that if either data set were extended for a further 60 observations (still with the odd–even pattern), then the correlation coefficient would fall to plus or minus 0.0188.

*(To see this look at Sheet3 of the current file.)*

Given this previous point, it would seem fair to ask what is a high correlation coefficient when it has been calculated as a value that is neither plus or minus one.

In other words, is a value of 0.8 indicative of high positive association, or would it have to be at least 0.9 or even 0.95?

The answer is that it depends—upon the number of pairs of observations and upon how much risk of error we are willing to bear.

Usually, we will be willing to risk no more than a 1% chance of error and so this means that we can derive some threshold values of the correlation coefficient that must be achieved before we can claim that the association is genuinely significant.

Once again, however, these threshold values vary depending upon the number of pairs of observations.

For example, with 10 pairs of observations (and with a 1% risk of error) the threshold value for the correlation coefficient can be shown to be 0.7646.

Only calculated absolute values that are greater than this figure can be said to indicate significant association.

If, however, the number of pairs of observations increased to 20, then the equivalent threshold figure decreases to 0.5614. Furthermore, if there were 40 pairs of observations the threshold value would be approximately 0.4.

Having established a rule-of-thumb method for determining the extent to which a given value of the correlation coefficient indicates strong association between the data sets, we should now discuss exactly what is meant by 'association'.

The first thing to note is that it cannot always be interpreted as meaning a causal relationship.

'Statistical association' simply means that the paired values of the two variables are tied together in a linear fashion.

In some cases the variables may be such that a causal tie is to be expected on the basis of theoretical analysis—life expectancy and tobacco consumption patterns, for example.

In other cases, even a highly significant correlation coefficient could be entirely spurious—in other words the result of pure chance.

A famous example of this is the reportedly perfect direct correlation ($r = 1$) between the annual number of storks nesting in Sweden and the annual Swedish birth rate.

However, although we would clearly be reluctant to accept any causal effect in cases such as this, there will always be others where the spuriousness of the association, in causal terms, is much less obvious.

*Now attempt Exercises 11.1 and 11.2.*


# 11.3 **Spearman's rank correlation coefficient**

Pearson's correlation coefficient requires quantitative data sets for its value to have any real statistical meaning.

However, when the researcher only has access to two or more respondents' ranked preferences (ordinal data), then it will useful to devise some measurement of the extent of agreement or disagreement between the individuals' ranked preferences.

For example, suppose that two individuals were asked to rank each of five terrestrial television channels in a range from most liked (1) to least liked (5).

Also suppose that the ranks for each individual (R1 and R2) were as shown in Table 11.1.


**Table 11.1**

| Channel | BBC1 | BBC2 | ITV1 | C4 | C5 |
|---------|------|------|------|----|----|
| Rank R1 | 2 | 5 | 1 | 3 | 4 |
| Rank R2 | 3 | 4 | 2 | 1 | 5 |

*To follow the discussion in Excel load the file called* **W11_2.xls.**

The first step towards obtaining a suitable index is to form the difference (*d*) between each of the ranks.

*Consequently, add the label: d to the A4 cell and in B4 enter the formula:*

$$=B2-B3$$

*Then copy this into C4:F4 and the differences will be computed.*

It will be noticed that there are positive and negative rank differences, and this means that if we attempt to add them up in order to gain an overall impression, then the negatives will tend to cancel out the positives. In fact, it is easy to show that the sum of the rank differences will always equal zero.

This creates a serious problem since it means that a value of zero will always be obtained *regardless* of how the ranks are paired. As a measure of the extent of agreement or disagreement between the respondents such an index is useless since it returns the same (zero) value for all possible rank combinations.

Therefore, to deal with this problem we square each of the rank differences so that the negative ones become positive. (Recall that we employed this device earlier in the discussion on calculating the standard deviation and the variance.)

*To do this in Excel, add the label: 'squared d' to A5, and in B5 write:*

$$=B4\char94 2 \quad or \quad =B4*B4$$

*Now copy B4 into C4:F4 and the squared differences will be calculated.*

*We now want to sum these differences so use A6 to contain the label:*

Sum of squared d

*And then in B6 enter:*

$$=SUM(B5:F5)$$

A value of 8 will be obtained.

We now define the Spearman rank correlation coefficient ($\rho$) as:[1]

$$\rho = 1 - (6 \times \text{sum of squared } d)/(n \times (n^2 - 1))$$

where *n* is the number of pairs of ranks (5 in this case), and the number 6 is **always** 6 regardless of the number of observations.

*We can now complete the calculation of $\rho$ by making the following entries:*

$A7 : n(n\text{squared} - 1) = \qquad B7 := 5*(5^2 - 1)$

$A8 : Rankcorrel.\text{Coeff.} = \qquad B8 := 1 - 6*B6/B7$

It will be found that B8 evaluates to 0.6—but what does this mean?

Like Pearson's coefficient, the rank correlation coefficient always lies between values of +1 and −1, with a value of +1 indicating perfect agreement between the rankings, and a value of −1 indicating perfect disagreement.

Each of these extreme outcomes is shown in the $\rho = 1$ and $\rho = -1$ sheets of the W11_2.xls file, along with a model Solution sheet.

*Consult these sheets now.*

For the current example we have $\rho = 0.6$ and, as it is positive, we conclude that there is a general (but not perfect) agreement between the respondents' preferences. (On the other hand, if we had calculated: $\rho = -0.6$, then general disagreement would have been the conclusion.)

Once again, like Pearson's correlation coefficient, we require threshold values to allow us to say whether any calculated rank correlation is 'high' or 'low'.

The argument, for a 1% risk of error, is exactly the same as with Pearson's coefficient, but the threshold values are slightly different.

Consequently, it should now be noted that for 5 pairs of observations the threshold value is given as 0.95, and since our calculated value of 0.6 is less than this we are unable to conclude that this rank correlation is significant.

However, had this figure of 0.6 in fact been obtained on the basis of 12 pairs of ranked observations, then the threshold value would be given as 0.5899, so our value of 0.6, being greater than this threshold, would now be significant.

*Now attempt Exercise 11.3.*

## 11.4  Cross-tabulation and contingency tables

The Histogram routine explained previously, counts the frequency of occurrence of each value of a single field variable. However, when the records contain data for two or more field variables then a different frequency counting routine must be used.

For example, consider a group of 20 randomly selected individuals. It would be an easy matter to describe them in a variety of ways.

Suppose we choose to use two descriptors (categories)—gender and hair colour.

Then, each individual could be classified in terms of two field variables.

Now suppose we define hair colour to be any one of Blond (B), Dark (D), or Red (R) and gender to be either Female (F) or Male (M).

Next, consider the data shown in Table 11.2 representing the result of such a classification process.

The purpose of cross-tabulation is to prepare a table showing the number of individuals in each of the two-way categories. That is, the numbers who are:

F and B    F and D    F and R    M and B    M and D    M and R

Clearly, such a classification procedure is most easily done in terms of a table, and it is called a *contingency table*.

The structure of such a table is shown in Table 11.3 and the task is to fill in the blank cells with appropriate values.

*To get the idea, after inspecting the raw data, complete the table manually.*

Table 11.2

| Individual no. | 1 | 2 | 3 | 4 | 5 | 6 | 7 | 8 | 9 | 10 |
|---|---|---|---|---|---|---|---|---|---|---|
| Gender | F | F | M | F | F | M | F | F | M | M |
| Hair colour | D | D | R | R | D | B | D | D | B | B |

| Individual no. | 11 | 12 | 13 | 14 | 15 | 16 | 17 | 18 | 19 | 20 |
|---|---|---|---|---|---|---|---|---|---|---|
| Gender | F | M | M | M | F | F | M | M | F | F |
| Hair colour | R | D | D | D | B | B | R | D | R | D |

Table 11.3

| | | Hair Colour | | |
|---|---|---|---|---|
| Gender | B | D | R | TOTAL |
| F | | | | |
| M | | | | |
| TOTAL | | | | |
| | | | | |

When finished, notice that even with a small data set such as this the required classification procedure is extremely tedious (and prone to error).

 *This is where Excel can help, and to see how, load the* W11_3.xls *file.*

*The Data worksheet contains the raw data from Table 11.2 in columns A, B and C.*

*Now select Data from the Menu bar and then Pivot Table and Pivot Chart Report.*

A Wizard routine supplying various prompts will be initiated.

*At the first of these ensure that the Microsoft Excel List or Data Base box is checked and then select Next.*

*At stage 2 of the Wizard tell Excel that the data range to be cross-tabulated is contained in B1:C21 and then click Next.*

*From the following screen select Layout to obtain the dialogue box as shown in Figure 11.1.*

*Now click and drag the gender button on the top right of the dialogue box into the ROW area and then click and drag the hair colour button into the COLUMN area.*

*Next, click and drag the gender button into the DATA area.*

The screen should now resemble Figure 11.2.

However, if the button in the Data area does not indicate Count of Gender, double-click on it and then select Count from the list that appears. (Excel automatically chooses the

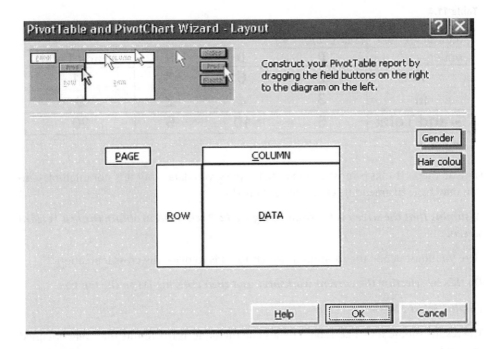

**Figure 11.1**

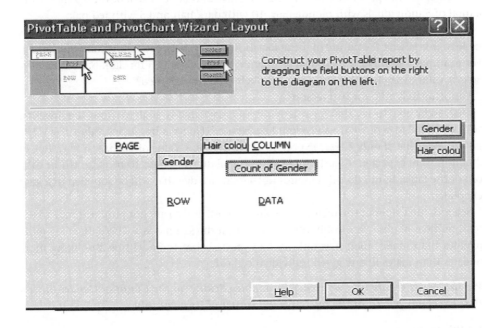

**Figure 11.2**

**Table 11.4**

| Count of Gender | Hair colour ▼ | | | |
|:---:|:---:|:---:|:---:|:---:|
| Gender ▼ | B | D | R | Grand Total |
| F | 2 | 6 | 3 | 11 |
| M | 3 | 4 | 2 | 9 |
| Grand Total | 5 | 10 | 5 | 20 |

statistic that it thinks is most appropriate for the given data—but it is not infallible—so you may have to amend its choice as explained.)

*Assuming that the screen is the same as Figure 11.2 select OK to obtain the last Wizard screen.*

Here you must define the location in which Excel is to place the cross-tabulation.

*Do this by selecting the current worksheet and then entering D1 to the top box.*

*Finally, select Finish.*

The results should look like Table 11.4 and be the same as the results that were obtained by hand.

Clearly the data have been cross-tabulated by gender and hair colour, and the totals for each of the categories computed. Thus we have a total of 11 females and 9 males and a total of 5 individuals with blonde hair, 10 with dark hair and 5 with red hair.

Although this is a purely descriptive statistic, it is only a short step to start using the table to investigate the nature of the association (if any) between hair colour and gender. For example, the highest *individual* frequency in the table is 6 for dark-haired females. So is it valid to say that females are more likely to be dark haired?

Unfortunately not, for two reasons.

First, to be able to say that a particular frequency value is 'high' or 'low' requires that we have some idea of what value would be *expected*. Hence a frequency value of say 100 is high if a value of only 1 were expected, while the same value of 100 is low if a value of 2 billion were expected. Clearly we need to calculate the values to be expected in each cell of the table, but to do this requires further knowledge that will be supplied in a later chapter.

Second, the values in the table are absolute values, and so are not proportionate to the total number of observations. In other words, if in the sample as a whole there are more females than males, then it is only to be expected that there will be absolutely more females than males in any given individual cell category.

*We can easily rectify this deficiency by double-clicking on the Count of Gender button that Excel has placed in the top left-hand corner of its pivot table.*

*Do this now.*

A dialogue box will appear.

Table 11.5

| Count as % of row total | | | | |
|---|---|---|---|---|
| | | Hair Colour | | |
| Gender | B | D | R | TOTAL |
| F | 0.18 | 0.55 | 0.27 | 1.00 |
| M | 0.33 | 0.44 | 0.22 | 1.00 |

Table 11.6

| Count as % of column total | | | | |
|---|---|---|---|---|
| | | Hair Colour | | |
| Gender | B | D | R | |
| F | 0.40 | 0.60 | 0.60 | |
| M | 0.60 | 0.40 | 0.40 | |
| TOTAL | 1.00 | 1.00 | 1.00 | |

*From this, select Options, and a number of choices are presented under the Show Data as: box.*

The most important are to express the absolute count as:

(i) a percentage of the row totals

(ii) a percentage of the column totals

(iii) a percentage of the grand total.

*Consequently, using the original pivot table as a template select each of these options and then select and then copy them in turn into vacant areas of the worksheet.*

Tables 11.5, 11.6 and 11.7 show the results of each of these calculations in turn, with the calculations also contained in the Count sheet of the current file.

This gives the percentage of individuals for each gender that are in each colour category, and could be used to compare gender characteristics. For example, we can say that there are proportionately more dark-haired females (55%) than there are females of any other hair colour (18% + 25% = 45%).

Table 11.7

| Count as % of grand total | | | | |
|---|---|---|---|---|
| | | Hair Colour | | |
| Gender | B | D | R | TOTAL |
| F | 0.1 | 0.3 | 0.15 | 0.55 |
| M | 0.15 | 0.2 | 0.1 | 0.45 |
| TOTAL | 0.25 | 0.5 | 0.25 | 1 |

Table 11.8

| Count of Gender | | Hair colour ▾ | | | |
|---|---|---|---|---|---|
| Gender ▾ | Smoke ▾ | B | D | R | Grand Total |
| F | NS | 2 | 4 | 3 | 9 |
| | S | | 2 | | 2 |
| F Total | | 2 | 6 | 3 | 11 |
| M | NS | 3 | 1 | 1 | 5 |
| | S | | 3 | 1 | 4 |
| M Total | | 3 | 4 | 2 | 9 |
| Grand Total | | 5 | 10 | 5 | 20 |

This gives the percentage of individuals for each colour category that are of each gender, and could be used to compare hair colour category characteristics. For example, we can say that there are proportionately more dark-haired females (60%) than there are dark-haired males (40%).[2]

This table gives the percentage of the total number of individuals sampled who are in a particular hair colour/gender category. For example, there are proportionately more dark-haired females (30%) than any other individual two-way category.

Up until now we have confined the analysis to data sets with only two field variables. However, suppose that each individual was further classified according to whether or not they smoked tobacco (S/NS).

Then imagine that the results are as contained in the Data(1) sheet of the current file (W11_3.xls).

*Access this now.*

Since we now have three field variables we must decide whether to add the new one (Smoke?) to the columns or the rows. Apart from this, however, the procedure is the same as before and will produce the results shown in Table 11.8 (when added as a row item) or Table 11.9 (when added as a column item). These results are also shown in the Solution sheet of the current file.

Notice that, since there no blond smokers of either gender, Excel has suppressed this category (B/S) from the output shown in Table 11.9.

Suppose now, that it was held, for example, that smoking was *exclusively* confined to red-haired males.

To justify this claim would require several statements to be true, viz.

Table 11.9

| Count of Gender | Hair colour ▾ | | Smoke ▾ | | | | | | | |
|---|---|---|---|---|---|---|---|---|---|---|
| | B | B Total | D | | D Total | R | | R Total | Grand Total |
| Gender ▾ | NS | | NS | S | | NS | S | | |
| F | 2 | 2 | 4 | 2 | | 6 | 3 | | 3 | 11 |
| M | 3 | 3 | 1 | 3 | | 4 | 1 | 1 | 2 | 9 |
| Grand Total | 5 | 5 | 5 | 5 | | 10 | 4 | 1 | 5 | 20 |

(i) All red-headed males must smoke (implying that there are no red-headed male non-smokers).

(ii) There must be no non-red-headed male smokers (implying that all non-red-headed males do not smoke).

(iii) There must be no female smokers (implying that all females are non-smokers).

If, and only if, each of these statements is true are we justified in claiming that smoking is exclusively a pursuit carried out by red-headed males. And even then, we should remember that this conclusion is based on a sample of only 20 individuals, and so it would be slightly rash to claim that such a conclusion was true for the entire population.

As a final aspect of cross-tabulation, notice that in the last illustration the raw data were already in categorical form (M/F, D/R/B and S/NS).

However, if one or more of the field variables is continuous or semi-continuous then we may have to use Excel to perform this categorization first, before we can use the cross-tabulation routine.[3]

We saw how to do this earlier in Section 7.6, where the raw data on company employment numbers were categorized into quartile categories using the = VLOOKUP function.

*Consequently, load the* **W11_4.xls** *file.*

Here the age data from the car occupants example have been supplemented with gender information for each individual.

The task is to perform a cross-tabulation of gender with age, after the latter data have been categorized according to quartile.

*The first thing to do is compute the quartiles of the age data in the E1:E4 range of the worksheet from:*

$$=QUARTILE(A2:A251,0) \qquad =QUARTILE(A2:A251,1)$$
$$=QUARTILE(A2:A251,2) \qquad =QUARTILE(A2:A251,3)$$

When formatted to two decimal places values of 0.13, 21.99, 40.25 and 60.12 should be returned.

*Now, in F1:F4 enter the labels:*

Q1, Q2, Q3 and Q4.

The E1:F4 range can clearly be regarded as a VLOOKUP table and then used to return the quartile associated with each age value. Thus, for example, any age value less than 21.99 will be classified as being in Q1, while any age value of 21.99 or more, but under 40.25 will be placed in Q2, and so on.

*Now add the label:*

Quartile

*to the C1 cell, and in C2 enter the formula:*

$$=VLOOKUP(B2,E\$1:F\$4,2)$$

**Table 11.10**

| Count of Gender | Age Quartile | | | | |
|---|---|---|---|---|---|
| Gender | Q1 | Q2 | Q3 | Q4 | Grand Total |
| F | 29 | 32 | 31 | 31 | 123 |
| M | 34 | 30 | 31 | 32 | 127 |
| Grand Total | 63 | 62 | 62 | 63 | 250 |

*and copy this into C3:C251.*

The data has now been categorized by both gender and age quartile in columns B and C.

*To obtain a cross-tabulation of these data use the Pivot Table routine as outlined above defining the E7 as the cell in which to start the pivot table (so that the data in E1:F4 are not overwritten).*

The results should resemble Table 11.10 and suggest that males and females appear almost equally often in each of the quartiles.

Furthermore, since there is a roughly equal split between females and males and between the quartiles, there is no real need to perform any of the percentage calculations explained earlier.

As a final topic in cross-tabulation notice that the values returned to the body of the pivot table need not *necessarily* refer to the variables used in the row and column tabulation. For example, with data on the number of occupants, their ages and their genders, suppose that we want to perform a cross-tabulation of gender with number of occupants but that we want the average age of the occupants (as opposed to the number of individuals) returned to the body of the table.

*To do this load the* W11_5.xls *file now.*

This is simply our previous data modified to provide the full information on the number of occupants in each car (i.e. without any gaps in the data in column A). Thus the data in column A become 1, 2, 2, 1, 3, 3, 3, 2, 2, 1, . . . ,etc. This is necessary so that the eventual cross-tabulation routine does not encounter blank cells.

*Now initiate the Pivot Table routine.*

*At the range prompt, however, define the area containing the data to be A1:C251.*

The subsequent prompt will now show three variables (number of occupants, age and gender) as being available for cross tabulation.

*Consequently, click and drag the Gender button to the Row area and the No. of occupants button to the Column area.*

*Then click and drag the Age button into the central area, double-click on it and select Average.*

*Finally, supply an output range commencing in E7.*

**Table 11.11**

| Average of Age | No. of occupai ▼ | | | | | |
|---|---|---|---|---|---|---|
| Gender ▼ | 1 | 2 | 3 | 4 | 5 | Grand Tota |
| F | 46.12 | 40.46 | 40.12 | 35.97 | 44.90 | 40.63 |
| M | 48.44 | 39.33 | 43.59 | 36.00 | 35.98 | 40.12 |
| Grand Total | 47.18 | 39.94 | 41.81 | 35.99 | 39.55 | 40.38 |

When you have finished the result should resemble Table 11.11 as well as the cross tabulation table contained in the Solution sheet of the file.

We can now note that:

The oldest average age is observed in cars with only 1 male occupant (48.44).

The youngest average age is observed in cars with 4 female occupants (35.97).

The average age of those individuals in cars with 2 occupants regardless of gender is 39.94.

The average age of females regardless of the number of occupants in the car is 40.63.

The average age of the entire sample is 40.38.

Cross tabulation is a very useful device for obtaining a 'feel' for data that have been categorized in two or more ways. Sometimes associations between categories will appear obvious, but until we have devised some method of deciding whether the obvious is simply what is to be expected, any claims of association must be heavily guarded until further tests have been carried out.

*Now attempt Exercise 11.4.*

## 11.5 Exercises

### Exercise 11.1

Load the W11_6.xls file.

   The data are the relationship between monthly sales of ice cream ($X$ litres) and monthly sales of peaches ($Y$ tonnes) in twenty selected supermarkets.

   By calculating the correlation coefficient between $Y$ and $X$ decide whether peaches and ice cream is a popular choice by the customers of this supermarket.

### Exercise 11.2

The data shown in Table 11.12 are the correlation coefficients between the examination marks obtained by a group of 100 students in four subjects.

Table 11.12

|  | MATHS | STATS | ECONOMICS | ENGLISH |
|---|---|---|---|---|
| **MATHS** | 1 | 0.9468 | 0.3812 | -0.8765 |
| **STATS** | 0.9468 | 1 | 0.1023 | -0.7945 |
| **ECONOMICS** | 0.3812 | 0.1023 | 1 | 0.9145 |
| **ENGLISH** | -0.8765 | -0.7945 | 0.9145 | 1 |

Suppose that in their next year of study the students have to specialize in any two of the four subjects.

Use the information provided by the correlation coefficient to suggest which two subjects should be taken by students whose marks are:

High in MATHS

Low in MATHS

High in STATS

Low in STATS

High in ECONOMICS

Low in ECONOMICS

High in ENGLISH

Low in ENGLISH

## Exercise 11.3

Load the W11_7.xls file.

The data are the rankings supplied by three individuals for a variety of leisure pursuits.

By calculating Spearman's rank correlation coefficients between each of the individuals decide which of the individuals are most and least 'compatible'.

## Exercise 11.4

Load the W11_8.xls file.

The data are the result of a market experiment in five regions of the UK: Southern England (SE), Northern England (NE), Scotland (S), Wales (W) and Northern Ireland (NI).

Consumers in each of these areas were asked to test a new product and then say whether they liked it (L), were undecided about it (U) or disliked it (D).

(a) Cross-tabulate these data by region and attitude.

(b) In which regions of the country might the product be expected to do best and worst?

(c) By considering the total number of respondents from each region, is there an indication of what type of sampling method was employed?

## 11.6 **Solutions to the exercises**

### Solution to Exercise 11.1

Make the following entry to any vacant cell:

=CORREL(B4:B23,C4:C23)

A value of 0.054573 should be returned. This value is very close to zero, indicating that there is neither a strong positive nor a strong negative linear association. If the correlation coefficient had been highly positive then it would suggest that peaches and ice cream are a common *joint* purchase, and that the products are complements. On the other hand, a large negative value for the correlation coefficient would indicate that the products are substitutes—when customers buy more of one they buy less of the other. The calculated value of the correlation coefficient being so close to zero, suggests that buying patterns of ice cream are not related (i.e. are independent of) buying patterns for peaches.

### Solution to Exercise 11.2

The general principle is that if a student is strong in a particular subject then they should specialize in **that** subject **and** the one with the highest positive correlation coefficient with that subject.

On the other hand, if a student is weak in a particular subject then they should specialize in those two subjects which are *least positively correlated* with the subject in which they are weak.

For example, if the correlation coefficient between Maths and English were −1, then a student who was very weak in Maths should specialize in English. The perfect negative correlation would suggest that they would be very strong in English.

Thus:

High marks in:

| | |
|---|---|
| MATHS | Specialize in MATHS and STATS ($r = 0.9468$) |
| STATS | Specialize in STATS and MATHS ($r = 0.9468$) |
| ECONOMICS | Specialize in ECONOMICS and ENGLISH ($r = 0.9145$) |
| ENGLISH | Specialize in ENGLISH and ECONOMICS ($r = 0.9145$) |

Low marks in:

| | |
|---|---|
| MATHS | Specialize in ENGLISH ($r = -0.8765$) and ECONOMICS ($r = 0.3812$) |
| STATS | Specialize in ENGLISH ($r = -0.7945$) and ECONOMICS ($r = 0.1023$) |
| ECONOMICS | Specialize in STATS ($r = 0.1023$) and MATHS ($r = 0.3812$) |
| ENGLISH | Specialize in MATHS ($r = -0.8765$) and STATS ($r = -0.7945$) |

### Solution to Exercise 11.3

The rank correlation coefficients between each of the individuals are calculated in the sheets called A with B, A with C and B with C, and produce values of:

Table 11.13

| Count of Attitude | Attitud ▾ | | | |
|---|---|---|---|---|
| Region ▾ | D | L | U | Grand Total |
| NE | 7 | 16 | 7 | 30 |
| NI | 1 | 3 | 2 | 6 |
| S | 3 | 5 | 2 | 10 |
| SE | 18 | 22 | 16 | 56 |
| W | 5 | 1 | 2 | 8 |
| Grand Total | 34 | 47 | 29 | 110 |

A with B      $p = -0.4706$
A with C      $p = 0.4471$
B with C      $p = -0.1206$

Clearly A and C have the greatest degree of 'compatibility', while A and B are the least 'compatible'. Furthermore, B and C seem to be neither compatible nor incompatible.

## Solution to Exercise 11.4

(a) Use the Pivot Table routine with a data range of A1:B111 and drag region into the Rows area and attitude into the Columns area. Then the attitude button was dragged into the centre of the Pivot table and Count of Attitude selected. The results should resemble Table 11.13.

(b) The absolute numbers who liked the product are highest in Southern England, which also possesses the highest number who disliked the product. However, in **relative** terms, i.e. as a percentage of the number of respondents in each region, then the highest proportion of respondents who liked the product was in Northern England. On the other hand the highest proportion of any region who disliked the product was in Wales (62.5%).

Table 11.14

| % of rows | | | | |
|---|---|---|---|---|
| Count of Attitude | Attitude ▾ | | | |
| Region ▾ | D | L | U | Grand Total |
| NE | 23.33% | 53.33% | 23.33% | 100.00% |
| NI | 16.67% | 50.00% | 33.33% | 100.00% |
| S | 30.00% | 50.00% | 20.00% | 100.00% |
| SE | 32.14% | 39.29% | 28.57% | 100.00% |
| W | 62.50% | 12.50% | 25.00% | 100.00% |
| Grand Total | 30.91% | 42.73% | 26.36% | 100.00% |

These percentage calculations are shown in Table 11.14, and were obtained by double clicking on the Count of Attitude tab, and then selecting options and % of rows from the option list that appeared.

(c) The number of respondents selected from each region is roughly in proportion to the populations of those regions. This is known as **quota sampling**.

■ **NOTES**

1. Excel does not have a dedicated statistical function that will calculate a rank correlation coefficient. Consequently, we must do it from first principles.

2. Notice that we can only really compare within categories whose totals sum to one in Tables 11.5 and 11.6.

3. If this is not done then the contingency table can become enormous when every single value of a continuous variable is used as a category.

# 12 Regression analysis

The following files from the online resource centre should be loaded as instructed:

W12_1.xls W12_3.xls W12_4.xls

W12_5.xls W12_6.xls W12_7.xls

W12_8.xls W12_9.xls

## 12.1 Introduction

As a general idea, statistical regression is the process of discovering any mathematical rule that governs the relationship between one set of data observations and another matching observation set.

For example, how are birth rates and income levels related? How is the level of unemployment related to the inflation rate?

With the first set of observations denoted as the dependent variable ($Y$) and the second set as the independent variable ($X$), then regression attempts to extract from these data a rule that allows $Y$ to be calculated from a given value of $X$.

In other words, given any value of $X$ and given the rule that has been discovered, it will be possible to determine the implied value of $Y$.

For example, if we know that the inflation rate was 2.1% then we might be able to predict that the level of unemployment would be 1.5 million.

Of course, a perfect rule may not exist; in this case the regression procedure will only be able to discover an approximate rule.

For example, a perfect rule would be that the value of $Y$ is always twice the value of $X$, while an approximate rule would be that the value of $Y$ is 'more or less' twice the value of $X$. This would mean $Y$ being slightly more for some $X$ values, slightly less for others, and exactly equal to twice the value of $X$ for others.

From this it should be clear that we not only need to discover a rule that links $Y$ to $X$, we also need to inspect the discovery with a view to how well it performs.

There is also the problem that there is a wide variety of possible mathematical rules available, which can make the task of finding the best one quite daunting.

Consequently, in order to simplify the introduction to the process, we will assume for the moment that the only rule available is a linear one.

That is, the relationship between $Y$ and $X$ can be portrayed as a straight line, and the implied rule is that the value of Y is given by some constant $a$, plus another constant $b$, times the value of $X$. In symbols we write:

$$Y = a + bX.$$

This is clearly a restrictive assumption, but we will wait until the ideas involved in linear regression have been absorbed before relaxing it.

## 12.2 **Simple linear regression**

Suppose you have been asked by a client to determine the effect of different levels of advertising expenditure on sales of a particular product.

Obviously, the first step must be to extract whatever relationship exists between sales and advertising expenditure, and to do this we must specify our model and its variables.

The model to be used will be a linear one (since at this stage we know of no other), and this is a perfectly valid first approach since linear regression can be performed easily and quickly within Excel.

However, it is as well to bear in mind from the outset that there is no necessary presumption in business or anywhere else, that relationships *must be linear*.

Indeed, as will be seen later, the linear model is often not justified in terms of the observed data, and may therefore have to be abandoned in favour of some alternative (non-linear) model.

At this stage, however, it is the logical first step, and provided we have some mechanism for *identifying its limitations*, it will get us started.

The presumed model is therefore **linear** and of the form

$$Y = a + bX.$$

where $a$ is the intercept[1] term and $b$ is the gradient term of the presumed line. But what are the dependent and independent variables (the $Y$ and $X$ terms) of this model?

In this case we would expect that it is advertising expenditure that influences product sales rather than vice versa, and as a consequence we can identify sales as the *dependent* variable ($Y$) and advertising expenditure as the independent variable ($X$). Our presumed model can therefore be stated verbally as:

Product sales is a linear function of advertising expenditure.

The task of linear regression is to determine the *precise nature* of this relationship by finding the implied values of the intercept and gradient terms, so that equations such as

$$Y = 5 + 0.9X \quad \text{or} \quad Y = 10 - 1.2x$$

can be obtained.

However, it is as well to note that it may not always be as easy to identify the dependent and independent variables as it was above. In many real-life applications the direction of *causation* (i.e. which variable influences which) will be far from clear, and this can cause untold difficulties. For the moment, however, we assume the relationship is properly defined in terms of causal direction.

Having defined the model generally, the next task is to make it more specific by collecting data on the relationship between sales and advertising expenditure. The standard approach is to perform a controlled investigation in which different chosen levels of advertising expenditure are applied to a set of identical market areas, and the sales recorded over a given time period.

Although this is easy enough to describe there are a number of potential difficulties that have to be considered. The most important of these are:

(i) The values of $X$ (advertising expenditure) chosen by the experimenter should include zero. This acts a 'control' in the sense that it provides us with information on the level of sales to be expected in the absence of any advertising expenditure.

(ii) The non-zero values of $X$ should span a 'reasonable' range, and should not increase in large jumps.

This, of course, begs the question of what is 'reasonable' and what is 'large'.

Consequently, the investigator will have to be guided by prior knowledge and a realization that it will usually be impossible to perform the investigation in such a way that completely continuous expenditure levels can be employed.

(iii) The expenditure levels must be completely under the investigator's control. Only if this is the case can the effects of other variables that influence the level of advertising expenditure be removed from the analysis.

This is a highly restrictive condition in reality, and is unlikely to be met fully. Yet it is of huge importance, since if advertising expenditure not only influences the level of sales, but is also influenced *by* these sales levels then neither of the two variables can properly be regarded as dependent or independent. They influence each other, perhaps in a highly complex way.

(iv) The conditions under which the experiment is carried out must be fully controlled in terms of all the other factors that influence sales. Only if this can be achieved is it possible to identify the *single* effect of advertising expenditure on sales, as opposed to the effect of advertising expenditure combined with these other factors.

Once again this is a demanding requirement, and it will often have to be accepted that in certain models the required degree of control will never be achieved. For example, we only have to think of the effect that a change in interest rates or the exchange rate can have upon a firm's sales to realise that these external factors are uncontrollable from the firm's viewpoint, yet nevertheless exercise a crucial influence.

(v) Finally, the presumed relationship should always reflect the logical reasons for expecting there to be a relationship to be discovered.

It is not acceptable to carry out a 'blanket' approach, whereby every independent variable that can be obtained is tried in a regression model until one that 'fits' is discovered, regardless of any apparent reason for expecting there to be a relationship. Provided these five points are fully accommodated in the design of the investigation then the designated independent variable ($X$) can truly be regarded as being independent.

Bearing these points in mind we might proceed to establish our application levels of advertising expenditure as:

$$X: \text{advertising expenditure } \pounds \text{ m}, 0, 1, 2, 3, 4, 5, 6, 7, 8, 9, 10$$

Once we have decided upon the advertising expenditure levels, the next problem is to decide what to apply them to.

Ideally, we should obtain a set of absolutely identical market areas then apply the chosen levels of advertising expenditure to each of them(i.e. the first market area receives £0m, the second area receives £1m, and so on).

However, the problem with this approach is that it is very difficult to be sure that the chosen market areas are truly identical. We have to accept that apparently identical market areas differ in their intrinsic characteristics and that this will exercise an effect upon their sales that is not related to the amount of advertising expenditure carried out.

There will also be other variables that influence sales that have not been included in the simple model.

To deal with this problem we should try to identify a number of market areas that have consistently shown equal sales volume in the recent past and apply each level of advertising expenditure to these comparable areas.

They should also be identical in terms of the other variables that influence sales such as price and household incomes.

Suppose now that this is what has been done and the results shown in Table 12.1 were obtained, where the sales values are measured in tens of thousands of units

*These data are contained in the* W12_1.xls *file and should be loaded now.*

Even a cursory examination of the data suggests that advertising expenditure has a marked effect upon sales at low application levels, but that this effect diminishes quite

**Table 12.1**

| £x million | 0 | 1 | 2 | 3 | 4 | 5 | 6 | 7 | 8 | 9 | 10 |
|---|---|---|---|---|---|---|---|---|---|---|---|
| y 0000s of units | 0.2 | 0.4 | 0.4 | 0.5 | 0.5 | 0.5 | 0.5 | 0.5 | 0.5 | 0.5 | 0.5 |

quickly (as saturation sets in) and eventually exercises an adverse effect as the market areas become overwhelmed by advertising.

This immediately casts doubt upon our linearity assumption, but we will overlook this for the moment until we have seen how to perform a linear regression on the data we have obtained.

We will, however, return to this problem at a later stage.

## 12.3 The scatter diagram

Our first step should always be to create a scatter diagram of the results obtained.

*To do this, use the Chart Wizard and define the data range as A3:B14. Then select an XY {Scatter} type of chart and use Sub-type 1. Next, supply titles as shown in Figure 12.1 and select Finish.*

The effect should resemble Figure 12.1.

Notice that this confirms our earlier observation that the relationship does not look particularly linear.

With the scatter of points established we must now try to fit a straight line through these points, and not just 'any old' straight line. Rather, we want to fit the straight line that *best fits* the given data observations.

To do this we use the trendline procedure.

*First, select the graph of the scatter points and then click once on any one of the data points. They will all become highlighted. Now click on the Chart menu and from this select the Add Trendline option.*

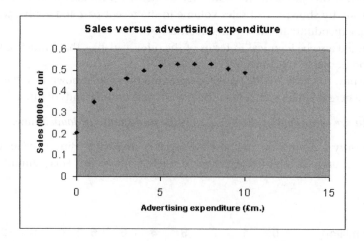

**Figure 12.1**

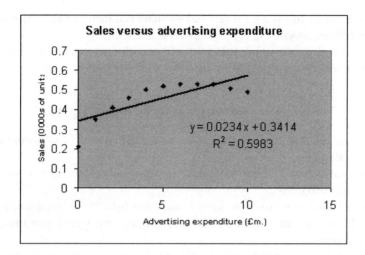

**Figure 12.2**

Excel will now offer six options—Linear, Logarithmic, Polynomial, Power, Exponential and Moving average—although not all of these options will necessarily be available at the same time.[2]

*In this case choose the Linear option, but before clicking OK, choose the Options tab and from this new screen check the bottom two options—Display equation on chart and Display R-squared value on chart.*

*Now click OK and the results will resemble Figure 12.2.*

As should be clear, the Trendline routine has fitted a straight line with the equation

$$Y = 0.3414 + 0.0234X$$

However, since this value of $Y$ is in fact a predicted value given the regression equation and the value of $X$, we should distinguish it from the value of $Y$ that was actually observed.

This is done by adding the caret symbol (^) on top. That is, $Y$ is the observed value of the dependent variable, $\hat{Y}$ is the predicted value.

Notice that this fitted equation is *generally* valid.

That is, it is defined for all positive values of $X$, including those that have not actually been observed.

For example, if advertising expenditure of £5.5 were to be applied, then from the equation we would predict that the level of sales would be:

$$\hat{Y} = 0.3414 + 0.0234(5.5) = 0.3414 + 0.1287 = 0.4701.$$

Remembering that the level of sales is measured in tens of thousands of units and that advertising expenditure is measured in millions of pounds, this means that when advertising expenditure equals £5.5m, the estimated level of sales is 4701 units.

However, whether this is a good or a bad estimate is difficult to say, since we did not actually observe an advertising expenditure level of £5.5m.

Consequently, suppose we use the calculated equation to estimate the value of sales for a level of advertising expenditure that was actually applied, £4m say. This would produce:

$$\hat{Y} = 0.3414 + 0.0234(4) = 0.3414 + 0.0936 = 0.435.$$

Now we should ask how this estimate relates to the actual level of sales observed when $X$ was set equal to £4m.

The latter was 0.5, and so our fitted equation has underestimated the true value by about 0.065 (i.e. 650 units).

This should come as no surprise, since it was clear from the original scatter diagram that it would be impossible to fit a single straight line that would pass through every observed data point.

What this means is that although the Trendline routine has fitted the 'best' straight line to the raw data, we need some measure of how *good* is the best that can be done.

This is where the $R^2$ figure that we asked to be included in the output becomes important.

To understand its significance, suppose that every observed data point lay on a single straight line. Under such circumstances we would have obtained a perfect fit since if we used the equation to predict the value of $Y$ for any given value of $X$ then the predicted and the actually observed values would all be identical. When this is the case we would be justified in claiming a 100% fit.

However, as the relationship between $Y$ and $X$ becomes less and less perfect, more and more data points will lie off the fitted straight line and positive and negative differences between the predicted and the observed values for $Y$ will start to emerge. The degree of fit will therefore be less than its perfect score of 100%.

This degree of fit is exactly what the $R^2$ statistic measures, either as a percentage or as a decimal lying between zero and one. This is also known as the **coefficient of determination** and is also equal to the square of the correlation coefficient (see Chapter p11).

Accordingly, we note from the graph that the calculated $R^2$ value for these data is 0.5983 (or 59.83%).

This means that of the total variation that takes place in the dependent ($Y$) variable 59.83% is explained by the variation that has taken place in the chosen values of $X$, and that there is therefore 41.17% of the total variation in $Y$ that is unexplained by our linear model.

Furthermore, it should be clear that using the calculated equation to predict sales levels becomes less and less accurate as the value of $X$ increases. This is simply because the scatter diagram showed that eventually sales levelled off and then started to decline, yet any straight line is unable to change direction. Consequently, if we were to use our equation to predict the level of sales when advertising expenditure was £15m we would obtain:

$$\hat{Y} = 0.3414 + 0.0234(15) = 0.3414 + 0.351 = 0.6924.$$

Yet it is clear from the scatter diagram that, if the trend continued, sales would be expected to be less than the maximum observed value of 0.53, and our estimated value would appear to be grossly inflated.

This raises the important question of how to re-specify the model when it is apparent that the linear form is inappropriate, but before we do this there are a few further points pertaining to the linear model that require attention.

The first of these relates to the fact that the Trendline routine does not supply us with readily usable values for the intercept and the gradient terms of the fitted line. That is, they would have to be entered manually to cells of the worksheet, if they were to be used in any further calculations (as is very likely).

For this reason we can now note that Excel has two dedicated functions that will calculate the values of the intercept and the gradient for any given set of $X$ and $Y$ values. These are:

$$=INTERCEPT(Y\ Data\ Range,\ X\ Data\ Range)$$

$$=SLOPE(Y\ Data\ Range,\ X\ Data\ Range)$$

*For example, to confirm the straight line parameters obtained from the Trendline routine above use E1 and G1 of the current sheet to contain:*

$$=INTERCEPT(B3:B13,A3:A13) \quad and \quad =SLOPE(B3:B13,A3:A13)$$

Notice that the $Y$ data range must precede the $X$ data range in these formulations. If they are ordered the other way round then the regression is of $X$ on $Y$ rather than $Y$ on $X$, and completely different results will be obtained.

These values for the intercept and the gradient can now be used to allow easy calculation of the predicted value of $Y$ for any value of $X$ that we care to choose.

*To do this, simply use the E2 cell to contain the value of X for which you want to predict the associated value of Y. Then, in G2 enter the formula:*

$$=E1+G1\char`^*E2$$

It is now an easy matter to confirm the predicted values that were calculated above, and these are shown in the Solution sheet of the file.

*Confirm that your calculations are correct now from the Solution sheet of* **W12_1.xls.**

These ideas can also be used to give a more detailed understanding of the process that took place in determining the equation of the best fitting line. However, since this is not a mainstream argument it is contained in the W12_2.xls file, and should only be consulted by interested readers who anticipate doing further regression analysis.

As well as functions to compute the intercept and the gradient of the best fitting straight line, Excel also has a dedicated function to calculate the $R^2$ value:

$$=RSQ(Y\ Data\ Range, X\ Data\ Range) = RSQ(B3:B13,A3:A13) = 0.5983$$

*Enter this now to a vacant cell of the sheet (H2 say) to confirm that it works.*

We can summarize the discussion to date in four points:

(i) The best fitting straight line that can be fitted to these data is defined by the equation:

$$\hat{Y} = 0.3414 + 0.0234.$$

(ii) Of the total variation in the values of $Y$, 59.83% is explained by the fitted regression line, and therefore by the observed values of $X$.

(iii) The fitted regression line leaves 41.17% of the variation in $Y$ unexplained.

(iv) Being linear, the fitted regression line cannot track the eventual slackening and decline that the sales data display.

It is to potential remedies for this last observation that we now turn our attention.

## 12.4 **Non-linear regression**

The real problem with the linear model that we fitted in the last section is that is cannot curve to follow the apparent pattern displayed by the scatter diagram. To do this requires that we fit a non-linear equation that is capable of changing direction.

 *This has been done in the Data sheet of* W12_3.xls *file which should be loaded now.*

Here, we have the same data, but this time the Polynomial Trendline option with an Order = 2 should be applied.

*Do this now by drawing the scatter diagram and then choosing Polynomial order 2 from the last dialogue box of the insert Trendline routine.*

This fits a polynomial equation of the form:

$$\hat{Y} = aX^2 + bX + c \quad (called\ a\ \textbf{quadratic equation}).$$

The results should look like Figure 12.3.

The effect of this new specification of the model is dramatic. The $R^2$ value has risen to 97.42%, and implies that the calculated polynomial equation

$$\hat{Y} = -0.0066X^2 + 0.0897X + 0.2419$$

provides a very good fit to the data and, importantly, tracks the change in direction that the data display.

We also note that compared to the linear equation the value of the intercept has fallen from 0.3414 to 0.2419.

Now, since these figures measure, for each of the models, the expected sales when no advertising expenditure is carried out, this reduction in the intercept value is important.

This is because in the linear model sales are much higher when advertising expenditure equals zero than with the quadratic model. If we trust in the linear model then we might be tempted not to advertise at all in the misguided belief that sales would be 3414 units anyway. However, with the better fitting quadratic model the consequences of zero advertising expenditure are that sales are estimated at only 2419.

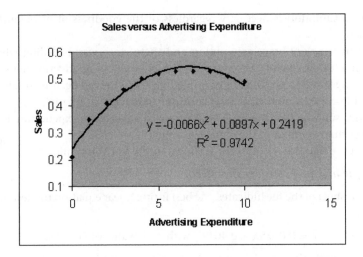

**Figure 12.3**

The reason for this change in the intercept value between the two models can be explained intuitively by recognizing that the intercept term has a tendency to pick up a large portion of the unexplained variation in the values of $Y$. Consequently, with a relatively low $R^2$ value the intercept also measures the extent of our ignorance. However, as the $R^2$ value increases, and with it the overall degree of explanation, the intercept becomes a much more reliable estimate of the value that $Y$ would adopt if the chosen $X$ value were zero.

Unfortunately, Excel does not support equivalent dedicated functions for the $a, b$ and $c$ terms of the fitted quadratic equation. Consequently, they must be transferred to an area of the worksheet manually. This has been done in the Solution sheet of the current file and then the predicted value of $Y$ calculated in the same way as before. This time, however the formula in G2 is:

$$=E1+G1*E2+I1*E2^2$$

Now suppose we want to predict, from this new model, the expected level of sales, if advertising expenditure were £15m. With the linear model our estimate was 6914 (0.6914 thousand) units and we noted that this seemed unlikely given the apparent behaviour of the data. However, with the quadratic model it is an easy matter to use the current worksheet to find that when advertising expenditure is £15m the predicted level of sales is 1024 units.

*Confirm this now.*

This prediction is clearly more in line with our intuitive expectation, but before we place too much faith in it we should recognize that we are making predictions on the basis of $X$ values that are *larger* than those that were actually applied.

Consequently, if these predictions are to be accurate then it requires that the discovered pattern continues as the values of $X$ increase.

Also, this assumption is necessary regardless of the goodness of fit obtained for the fitted model.

Clearly this is a very brave assumption and there is no way of telling whether it is valid or not without actually observing these higher values of advertising expenditure. Without doing this it is possible for example that the observed decline in sales is in fact a 'blip' that irons itself out before sales continue to behave 'normally'.

To see this, suppose that the investigator applied advertising expenditure levels up to £25m rather than £10m as in the current example.

Then suppose that the results were as shown in the W12_4.xls file.

*Load this file now and consider the effects.*

As the Linear sheet of the file indicates, the best fitting linear equation to these augmented data is:

$$\hat{Y} = 0.0075X + 0.4019 \quad \text{with an } R^2 \text{value of 50.73\%.}$$

Next, the Quadratic sheet finds that the best fitting quadratic equation is:

$$\hat{Y} = -0.0002X^2 + 0.0135X + 0.378 \quad \text{with an } R^2 \text{value of 53.03\%.}$$

Finally, we have used the Polynomial trendline option with an Order value of three to fit what is known as a cubic equation, and the best one that can be calculated is:

$$\hat{Y} = 0.0001X^3 - 0.0052X^2 + 0.0623X + 0.2864 \quad \text{with an } R^2 \text{value of 83.45\%}$$

Consequently, with these new data we conclude that the quadratic function that performed so well for $X$ values between 0 and 10 is now little better in terms of its $R^2$ value than the simple linear equation, and that both explain little more than 50% of the total variation in the $Y$ values.

On the other hand, the new cubic equation performs quite well by explaining roughly 84% of the total variation in the observed values of $Y$.

## 12.5 Regression using the Excel Data Analysis routine

The discussion to date has tried to give an intuitive understanding of the regression procedure and, importantly, by focusing on the $R^2$ values obtained has provided a simple diagnostic test of the reliability of the fitted model.

However, it should be appreciated that in what is in fact a highly complex process, other diagnostics should be obtained before any heavy reliance is placed upon the fitted model. Although discussion of these will be undertaken at a later stage, we can take the opportunity just now to illustrate a dedicated regression routine that not only confirms the results developed to date, but also provides further diagnostic statistics. These can be ignored for the moment in order to concentrate on the output from the routine with which we are currently familiar, but we will return to them at a later stage in the discussion.

*To follow the argument load the Data sheet of the W12_5.xls file.*

This is simply our original raw data set showing sales in terms of advertising expenditure.

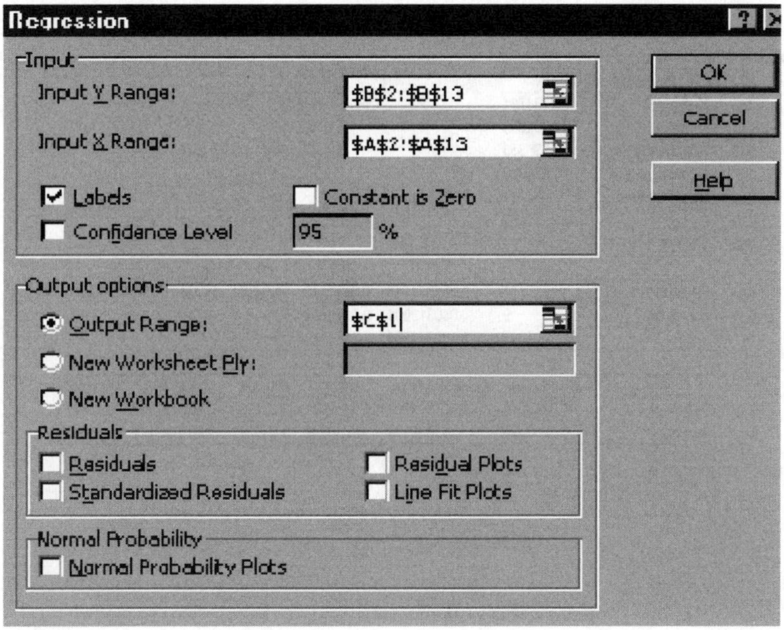

**Figure 12.4**

*To initiate the regression routine choose Tools and then Data analysis and then Regression.*

The dialogue box shown in Figure 12.4 will appear.

*Now fill in the boxes so that your own version looks like Figure 12.4, and click OK.*

(Notice the importance of ensuring that the Y and X values are placed in their correct boxes, and that the Labels box is checked if the first cell in the range is a label.)

The regression output commencing in C1 contains much more information than we have previously obtained. However, the $R^2$ value is contained in D5 and the intercept and gradient coefficients are housed in D18 and D19. Importantly, the same values as were previously obtained are returned, as the highlighted cells in Figure 12.5 and the Solution sheet indicate.

## 12.6 Time series analysis

An important application of the regression techniques developed above lies in an area known as **time series analysis**. What this means is that the independent variable (*X*) is taken to be the passage of time, and that the linear regression equation is used to extract any trend that the dependent variable adopts as time passes.

| | A | B | C | D | E | F | G | H | I | J |
|---|---|---|---|---|---|---|---|---|---|---|
| 1 | | | SUMMARY OUTPUT | | | | | | | |
| 2 | adv.exp | Sales | | | | | | | | |
| 3 | 0 | 0.21 | *Regression Statistics* | | | | | | | |
| 4 | 1 | 0.35 | Multiple R | 0.7734791 | | | | | | |
| 5 | 2 | 0.41 | R Square | 0.5982699 | | | | | | |
| 6 | 3 | 0.46 | Adjusted R Square | 0.5536333 | | | | | | |
| 7 | 4 | 0.5 | Standard Error | 0.066932 | | | | | | |
| 8 | 5 | 0.52 | Observations | 11 | | | | | | |
| 9 | 6 | 0.53 | | | | | | | | |
| 10 | 7 | 0.53 | ANOVA | | | | | | | |
| 11 | 8 | 0.53 | | *df* | *SS* | *MS* | *F* | *Significance F* | | |
| 12 | 9 | 0.51 | Regression | 1 | 0.060044545 | 0.0600445 | 13.4031 | 0.005227191 | | |
| 13 | 10 | 0.49 | Residual | 9 | 0.040319091 | 0.0044799 | | | | |
| 14 | | | Total | 10 | 0.100363636 | | | | | |
| 15 | | | | | | | | | | |
| 16 | | | | *Coefficients* | *Standard Error* | *t Stat* | *P-value* | *Lower 95%* | *Upper 95%* | |
| 17 | | | Intercept | 0.3413636 | 0.037754767 | 9.0416037 | 8.22E-06 | 0.255956355 | 0.426771 | |
| 18 | | | adv.exp | 0.0233636 | 0.00638172 | 3.6610248 | 0.005227 | 0.008927171 | 0.0378 | |

**Figure 12.5**

Unfortunately, however, when time is used as the independent variable there are a number of additional complications introduced to the regression technique. These stem from the fact that the dependent variable will often be subject to a number of influences that are highly sensitive to the units in which the passage of time is measured (months, quarters, years, etc.).

For example, if only annual data have been observed then it will be impossible to identify any seasonal influence (such as more fuel consumed in winter) that acts upon the data. To identify any such effects would require that quarterly or monthly data be collected. Similarly, in volatile financial markets such as the stock exchange there may be periods within each day at which the value of the dependent variable is uncharacteristically high or low. This would only become apparent, however, if hourly data were gathered.

Another difficulty stems from time lags between collection and compilation and publication of the data. With large complex data sets, it may be very difficult to obtain today an accurate value of the variable two or three days ago.

Finally, although published data may be nominally recorded on a monthly or quarterly basis, there is considerable discretion available in deciding exactly when the month or the quarter starts and ends. With a little ingenuity, it will usually be possible to choose the dates in such a way that the data behave in the most favourable way.

As long as we recognize these difficulties then we can accommodate them in our model and thereby develop a technique for splitting the raw time series data into their various component parts. This is the basic objective of time series analysis. As a simple starting point let us presume that any set of quarterly time series data is composed of three elements: a trend value (t), a seasonal element (s) and a residual component (r).

Having defined the components of our model we now have to decide upon the form that the model should take. In this simple illustration it will be assumed to be additive[3] and we adopt the following form:

$$Y = t + s + r$$

The first step in the analysis of time series is to establish the trend on the basis of a best fitting linear regression equation.

*To see how this is done load the* **W12_6.xls** *file.*

The data are average house price values in a particular area over a period of 20 quarters (5 years).

*Now compute the intercept and the gradient of the regression of Y on X trend line and use these to calculate the estimated trend in column C. The formulae are:*

In I1:     =INTERCEPT(B2:B21,A2:A21)

In I2:     =SLOPE(B2:B21,A2:A21)

In C2:     =I$1+I$*A2    copied into C3:C21

Column C therefore provides us with the linear trend values predicted by the regression equation of Y on X obtained from the INTERCEPT and SLOPE functions. That is:

$$\hat{Y} = 14.57895 + 0.79248X.$$

The next task is to calculate the de-trended series. In our additive case, the de-trended series will be given by:

$$\text{de-trended series} = Y - t.$$

*This means that the entries in column D should be obtained by subtracting the entries in column C from those in column B.*

*Do this now and then check your answers against the Solution sheet.*

The next task is to try and identify the seasonal component (if any) that is contained in the de-trended series.

To do this we must collect together all the de-trended values that relate to *the same quarter of the year* (i.e. quarters 1, 5, 9, 13, 17 and 2, 6, 10, 14, 18 etc.). Consequently, for the first quarter of year 1 the difference between the actual value of Y (20.00) and the trend value (15.37) is 4.63, and for the first quarter of year 2 the difference is 5.46.

These 'equivalent quarter' values have been placed in the block of cells commencing in B25, then summed and averaged to produce an average value for the season that they represent. They are shown in Table 12.2 and have been entered to the Solution sheet of the current file.

**Table 12.2**

|  | Quarter 1 | Quarter 2 | Quarter 3 | Quarter 4 |
|---|---|---|---|---|
| Year 1 | 4.63 | -1.16 | -6.96 | 0.25 |
| Year 2 | 5.46 | -1.33 | -7.13 | 0.08 |
| Year 3 | 6.29 | -0.50 | -4.30 | 0.91 |
| Year 4 | 7.12 | 0.33 | -5.47 | 1.74 |
| Year 5 | 6.95 | -0.84 | -7.64 | 1.57 |
| Average | 6.09 | -0.70 | -6.30 | 0.91 |

*Reproduce them now in the B24: E30 range of your own sheet (Data).*

It should be clear that the four entries in the row labelled 'Average' represent an estimate of the seasonal variation of the series across each of the quarters. That is, on average the Quarter 1 values are 6.09 above trend, while the Quarter 2 values are 0.70 below trend, and so on.

Consequently, the next step will be to place them in column E against their appropriate quarters and then subtract them from the actual series values to produce what is known as the **seasonally adjusted series**.

*Do this now in columns E and F of your worksheet by making the following entries.*

*First, in E2, E3, E4 and E5 enter:*

$$=B\$25 \ =C\$25 \ =D\$25 \ =E\$25$$

*and then copy E2:E5 into E6:E21.*

This will transfer the equivalent quarter seasonal variations to column E.

*Next, in F2 enter:*

$$=B2-E2$$

*and copy this into F3:F21*

These formulae subtract the seasonal variation ($s$) from the actual series values ($Y$) to give:

$$Y - s,$$

which is known as the *seasonally adjusted series*.

*Finally, the residual elements will be defined by:*

$$Y - s - t,$$

*and these should be placed in column G of your worksheet.*

*Do this now by entering the following formula to G2:*

$$=B2-E2-C2$$

*and copying it into G3:G21.*

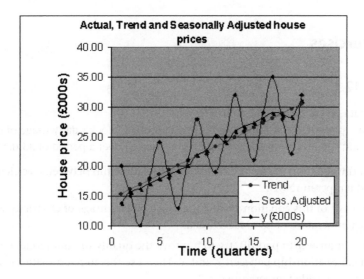

**Figure 12.6**

This completes the calculations and shows how the raw *Y* values can be apportioned between their trend, seasonal and residual components.

We should also recognize that the seasonally adjusted series is one of the most important results of this analysis, since it almost impossible to encounter any set of published statistics without finding that they have been seasonally adjusted in some way.

In its basic form, what the seasonally adjusted series does is to indicate what the behaviour of the dependent variable *would have been like* had it not been subject to seasonal variation.

If we now graph the actual series, the trend and the seasonally adjusted series on the same axes, then a more obvious indication of what has been done is obtained. The results should resemble Figure 12.6.

Clearly, the effect of seasonally adjusting the data has been to adjust the trend values upwards or downwards depending upon the effect of the seasonal influence, and this is the entire purpose of seasonal adjustment.

As a final consideration in this section, it should be realized that the analysis of time series is an extremely complex undertaking. This stems from the fact that the passage of time is the 'universal variable', i.e. just about everything changes with the advance of time. But whether it is the passage of time *per se* that is causing the dependent variable to change, or the influence of another variable or variables, is difficult to determine. This will often be of minor importance if all we are trying to do is describe and analyse the past behaviour of the dependent variable. But if, as is often the case, we are going to make *predictions* about the future on the basis of past experience then the influence of other variables cannot be ignored so easily.

## 12.7 **Exercises**

### Exercise 12.1

Load the data given in the W12_7.xls file.

The data represent the relationship between an office block's daily usage of electricity (in KWH) and the mean outside daily temperature (°C) over a period of 33 days.

(a) Obtain the equation of the best fitting linear relationship between electricity usage ($Y$) and temperature ($X$).

(b) On the basis of this equation predict the office block's usage of electricity when an outside temperature of 23°C is recorded.

(c) Given your answer to part (ii), try to improve the quality of your model by fitting a non-linear relationship between $Y$ and $X$. Then use this to re-estimate the kWh usage at an outside temperature of 23°C.

### Exercise 12.2

Load the file called W12_8.xls.

The data are the results of the following market research experiment by a large company.

The company's total market area was divided into 40 equally populated market areas, and the price to be charged for the product was set to be the same in each area.

Then, the weekly amount of advertising expenditure (£$x$) in each of these market areas was set as indicated in column A.

The weekly sales ($y$ units) in each market area was then recorded as shown in column B.

Use linear regression methods to estimate a linear equation describing how the value of sales ($Y$) varies with the level of advertising expenditure ($X$).

### Exercise 12.3

Load the file called W12_9.xls.

The data are a supermarket chain's monthly sales of turkeys over a period of 36 months.

(a) Prepare a workbook that will calculate the trend and the seasonally adjusted series for turkey sales.

(b) Prepare a suitably titled and labelled chart showing the actual series, the trend and the seasonally adjusted series on the same axes.

(c) What conclusions can be drawn from the above analysis?

## 12.8 Solutions to the exercises

### Solutions to Exercise 12.1

Full suggested solutions are contained in the Solution sheets (1), (2) and (3) of the current file (W12_7.xls).

(a) The best linear equation is given by:

$$\hat{Y} = 272.66 - 8.379X.$$

(b) When $X = 23$,

$$\hat{Y} = 272.66 - 8.379 \times 23 = 79.943.$$

The observed value when $X = 23$ was 164, so our estimate is less than half the observed value and would appear to be low. Clearly the linear trend is not tracking the rise in usage that occurs above 12°C.

(c) We fitted a cubic model to the data with the form:

$$\hat{Y} = 289.31 - 12.96X - 0.4797X^2 + 0.0366X^3.$$

So when $X = 23$,

$$\hat{Y} = 289.31 - 12.96 \times 23 - 0.4797 \times 23^2 + 0.0366 \times 23^3 = 182.75.$$

This is clearly a lot closer to the actual value when $X = 23$ of 164.

### Solution to Exercise 12.2

Full suggested solutions are contained in the Solution sheet of the file, where the estimated regression equation:

$$\hat{Y} = 3008.462 + 0.2179X$$

has been obtained in each of the three ways discussed—INTERCEPT and SLOPE functions, Trendline with linear trend and the Excel Data Analysis Regression routine.
  We note that the $R^2$ value of 0.9314 is satisfactorily high.

### Solutions to Exercise 12.3

A section of the solution is shown in Figure 12.7 and can also be found in the Solution sheet of the file.

(i) Cells H1:H2 were used to compute the intercept and slope of the $Y$ data (B5:B40) versus the $X$ data (A5:A40). Then the trend was computed in column C from the formula in C5:

$$=H\$1+H\$2*A5$$

copied into C6:C40.

| F5 | | | =B5-E5 | | | | | | |
|---|---|---|---|---|---|---|---|---|---|
| | **A** | **B** | **C** | **D** | **E** | **F** | **G** | **H** | **I** |
| 1 | Time | Monthly Sales | Trend | de-trended | seasonal | seasonally | a | 3.049714 | |
| 2 | (months) | of Turkeys | | series | variation | adjusted | b | 0.02934 | |
| 3 | | 000's | | | | | r | 0.208316 | |
| 4 | x | y | t | y - t | s | y - s | $R^a$ | 0.043395 | |
| 5 | 1 | 3.21 | 3.0790541 | 0.130945946 | 0.00553539 | 3.204464607 | | | |
| 6 | 2 | 2.7 | 3.1083938 | -0.40839382 | -0.60047104 | 3.300471042 | | | |
| 7 | 3 | 3 | 3.1377336 | -0.13773359 | -0.34647748 | 3.346477477 | | | |
| 8 | 4 | 4.25 | 3.1670734 | 1.082926641 | 1.13084942 | 3.119150579 | | | |
| 9 | 5 | 2.8 | 3.1964131 | -0.39641313 | -0.55515701 | 3.355157014 | | | |
| 10 | 6 | 2.5 | 3.2257529 | -0.7257529 | -0.77116345 | 3.271163449 | | | |
| 11 | 7 | 2.4 | 3.2550927 | -0.85509266 | -0.79716988 | 3.197169884 | | | |
| 12 | 8 | 2.5 | 3.2844324 | -0.78443243 | -0.83317632 | 3.333176319 | | | |
| 13 | 9 | 2.8 | 3.3137722 | -0.5137722 | -0.47918275 | 3.279182754 | | | |
| 14 | 10 | 2.4 | 3.343112 | -0.94311197 | -0.50518919 | 2.905189189 | | | |
| 15 | 11 | 3 | 3.3724517 | -0.37245174 | -0.54452896 | 3.544528958 | | | |
| 16 | 12 | 8.9 | 3.4017915 | 5.498208494 | 4.29613127 | 4.603868726 | | | |
| 17 | 13 | 3.4 | 3.4311313 | -0.03113127 | 0.00553539 | 3.394464607 | | | |
| 18 | 14 | 2.9 | 3.460471 | -0.56047104 | -0.60047104 | 3.500471042 | | | |
| 19 | 15 | 3.1 | 3.4898108 | -0.38981081 | -0.34647748 | 3.446477477 | | | |

Sheet2 / Sheet3 / Sheet4 / Sheet5 / Sheet

**Figure 12.7**

The de-trended series was calculated in column D by subtracting the trend values from the actual values.

Since turkey sales appear to be sensitive to the *month* rather than the *quarter* the seasonal variation was computed on a monthly basis.

The calculations for the seasonal variations are shown in Figure 12.8.

| E43 | | | =AVERAGE(B43:D43) | | | | | | |
|---|---|---|---|---|---|---|---|---|---|
| | **A** | **B** | **C** | **D** | **E** | **F** | **G** | **H** | **I** |
| 42 | | Year 1 | Year 2 | Year 3 | Average | | | | |
| 43 | Month 1 | 0.13095 | -0.031131 | -0.08320849 | 0.00553539 | | | | |
| 44 | Month 2 | -0.40839 | -0.560471 | -0.83254826 | -0.60047104 | | | | |
| 45 | Month 3 | -0.13773 | -0.389811 | -0.51188803 | -0.34647748 | | | | |
| 46 | Month 4 | 1.08293 | 1.2808494 | 1.028772201 | 1.13084942 | | | | |
| 47 | Month 5 | -0.39641 | -0.34849 | -0.92056757 | -0.55515701 | | | | |
| 48 | Month 6 | -0.72575 | -0.44783 | -1.13990734 | -0.77116345 | | | | |
| 49 | Month 7 | -0.85509 | -0.61717 | -0.9192471 | -0.79716988 | | | | |
| 50 | Month 8 | -0.78443 | -0.87651 | -0.83858687 | -0.83317632 | | | | |
| 51 | Month 9 | -0.51377 | -0.165849 | -0.75792664 | -0.47918275 | | | | |
| 52 | Month 10 | -0.94311 | 0.0048108 | -0.57726641 | -0.50518919 | | | | |
| 53 | Month 11 | -0.37245 | -0.204529 | -1.05660618 | -0.54452896 | | | | |
| 54 | Month 12 | 5.49821 | 3.9161313 | 3.474054054 | 4.29613127 | | | | |
| 55 | | | | | | | | | |

Sheet2 / Sheet3 / Sheet4 / Sheet5 / Sheet

**Figure 12.8**

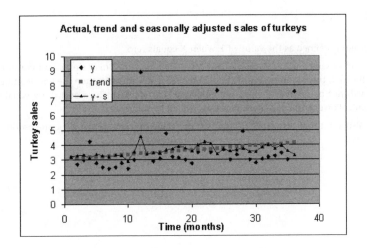

**Figure 12.9**

The average 'equivalent month' seasonal variations were then placed in column E, and in column F these were subtracted from the actual series values to give the seasonally adjusted data.

(ii) The data range for the chart was defined as A4:C40,F4:F40 and produces Figure 12.9.

(iii) Clearly, there are monthly peaks of turkey sales at Christmas and Easter. Nevertheless, the overall trend is of slowly increasing turkey sales (approximately $b = 0.03$thousand $= 30$ per month).

When the seasonally adjusted data are inspected, it would seem to suggest that although turkey sales are still a seasonal (monthly) event they are becoming *less so*. This could be due to the fact that people are increasingly consuming other types of meat on festive occasions, but also because they are consuming relatively more turkey at other times. This is indicated by the fact that the seasonally adjusted figure at Christmas for the first year (time period 12) is well above the trend value, whereas for the second and third years (time periods 24 and 36) the figures are below trend. Christmas sales of turkeys are therefore becoming less substantial in relation to turkey sales in the rest of the year.

As regards Easter sales (time periods 4, 16 and 28), the seasonally adjusted data shows that sales are roughly 'on trend' and so we conclude that the Easter turkey is retaining its traditional role more than the Christmas turkey.

## ■ NOTES

1. The intercept is defined as the value of $Y$ when $X$ equals zero.

2. If there is an observed value of zero for the $x$ variable then the Logarithmic and Power options will not be offered. If there is an observed value of zero for the $y$ variable, then the Power and Exponential options will not be offered. If there are values of zero for both the $x$ and the $y$ variable then the Logarithmic, Power and Exponential options will all be suppressed.

3. There is also a multiplicative model in which the value of $y$ is assumed to be the product of $t, s$ and $r$, i.e. $y = tsr$.

# 13 Financial arithmetic

## 13.1 Introduction

This chapter considers the effect that the passage of time, and the consequent payment of interest, exercises upon the value of any given sum of money after different lengths of time.

The simplest starting point is the notion that if any sum of money, called the *principal*, bears interest at a rate of $r\%$ per annum, then after one year has passed this principal has earned interest that is equal to the principal times $(r/100)$.

When this interest is added to the principal then the value of the account has become:

principal plus (principal times $r/100$).

For example, a principal of £200 that was deposited at an interest rate of 10% per annum would bear an annual interest payment of:

$$£200(10/100) = £20.$$

Furthermore, the value of the deposit when the annual interest has been included is easily seen to have increased from £200 to £200+ the annual interest payment, i.e.

$$£200 + £20 = £220.$$

In general then, we can state that

$$\text{the amount after 1 year} = \text{principal} + (\text{principal})(r/100)$$

Now, although we have referred to the interest rate as a percentage rate per annum, it will usually be more convenient to convert it to a **decimal** expression, denoted as i. This means that an interest rate of 15% per annum, for example, can be re-expressed as $15/100 = 0.15$.

In general, of course, we could say that an interest rate of $r$% per annum could be written in decimal form ($i$) as:

$$i = r\%/100.$$

This means that the expression above for the amount after 1 year can now be re-written as:

$$\text{amount after 1 year} = \text{principal} + (\text{principal})(i).$$

Furthermore, since the right-hand side of the last expression above can have the principal factored out of it, we can rewrite it as:

$$\text{amount after 1 year} = (\text{principal})(1 + i).$$

Obviously, it becomes extremely tedious to write out lengthy expressions like the ones above, and so we should use the following generally recognized symbols as abbreviations:

$t =$ the number of years for which the principal is deposited,

$i =$ the interest rate expressed as a decimal,

$P =$ the principal,

$A_t =$ a subscripted variable representing the amount after $t$ years have passed.

Taking these last two definitions together it should be clear that we can also write:

$$P = A_0.$$

That is, the principal is by definition the same as the amount after 0 years have passed. Furthermore, using these symbols more extensively, we can state that the amount after one year ($A_1$) is given by:

$$A_1 = P(1 + i) = A_0(1 + i)$$

For example, to find the amount after 1 year of a principal of £1500, if interest is paid at a rate of 6% per annum we would evaluate:

$$A_1 = 1500(1 + 0.06) = 1500(1.06) = £1590.$$

It should now be noted that the procedure illustrated above is perfectly adequate if **only one year's interest** is to be calculated, but it is easy to envisage circumstances in which we are required to find the value of a deposit after 2 or 3 or more years have passed.

In this case we must identify from the outset whether the annual interest rate is being applied on a **simple** or on a **compound** basis, since the calculation methods are significantly different in each of these two cases.

## 13.2 **Simple interest**

If interest is calculated on a **simple** basis then what this means is that at the end of each year for which the principal was deposited, a **constant** interest payment of $£iP$ is paid. This means that the annual interest received is the **same** regardless of the length of time for which the principal has been deposited.

Viewed in this way it is easy to see that simple interest can be represented in terms of an arithmetic progression in which the first term is the principal, and the common difference is $iP$. We therefore have:

$$A_0 = P,$$
$$A_1 = P + iP,$$
$$A_2 = P + iP + iP = P + 2iP,$$
$$A_3 = P + iP + iP + iP = P + 3iP.$$

Following this sequence through, it should be clear that the amount after $t$ years, denoted by $A_t$, will be given by:

$$A_t = P + iP + iP + \ldots + iP = P + tiP$$

and that this can then be rewritten as:

$$A_t = P(1 + ti).$$

For example, to find the amount after 5 years of a deposit of £2500, if the annual simple interest rate for the period is 13% per annum we should evaluate:

$$2500[1 + 5(0.13)] = 2500(1 + 0.65) = 2500(1.65) = £4125.$$

It should now be noticed that in the explanation to date we have made use of what is known as a **recursive** relationship. That is, that each term in the series is related to the previous term in a constant, known, fashion. Hence, for example, $A_t$ is always equal to $A_{t-1}$ plus the interest accruing during the year.

Identifying any recursive relationships that exist in a problem can often aid understanding and modelling, but on their own they are relatively **weak** computational aids. This is because before any chosen term can be evaluated, **all previous terms** must have been calculated.

Nevertheless, as we saw above, inspection of the recursive relationship often displays an expression that can be applied to any particular term to be evaluated. This was the

| | A | B | C | D | E | F | G | H | I |
|---|---|---|---|---|---|---|---|---|---|
| 1 | Principal (P) | 2500 | | | | | | | |
| 2 | Interest rate (i) | 13% | | | | | | | |
| 3 | Number of years (t) | 5 | | | | | | | |
| 4 | Amount after t years (A$_t$) | 4125 | | | | | | | |
| 5 | | | | | | | | | |

Sheet1 / Sheet2 / Sheet3 / Sheet4 / Sheet5 / She

**Workbook 13.1**

obviously the case in our simple example, since we were easily able to derive, from the recursive relationship, an expression for $A_t$. Namely,

$$A_t = P(1 + ti).$$

These ideas are easily translated into an Excel workbook as indicated in Workbook 13.1.

*Make this up now.*

The entries in B1:B3 will be the given data of any simple interest problem, and the terminal amount after the specified number of years is calculated in B4 from

$$=B1*(1+B3*B2)$$

*For example, with P = 2500, i = 13% and t = 5, use this worksheet to confirm the result obtained above for the terminal amount after 5 years (£4125).*

In the previous example it was required to find the amount after a specified number of years (i.e. $A_t$) but this need not always be the problem posed. Nevertheless, simple algebraic transposition of the expression for $A_t$ will always be sufficient to determine the value of any specified argument in the equation. To see this, suppose that it was required to find the annual simple interest rate which, if applied to the whole period, caused a principal of £2000 to amount to £3260 after 7 years.

To answer this we can start from

$$A_t = P(1 + ti)$$

and then write

$$A_t/P = 1 + ti$$

whereby

$$ti = A_t/P - 1$$

and

$$i = (A_t/P - 1)/t.$$

Therefore,

$$i = (3260/2000 - 1)/7 = (1.63 - 1)/7 = 0.09.$$

The required interest rate is 9% per annum.

As another illustration, suppose we were required to find the number of **years** that it will take for a principal of £4000 to amount to £6400 if the annual simple interest rate for the period is 12%.

To answer this we can again start from

$$A_t = P(1 + ti)$$

and then write

$$A_t/P = 1 + ti,$$

whereby

$$ti = A_t/P - 1$$

and

$$t = (A_t/P - 1)/i.$$

Therefore,

$$t = (6400/4000 - 1)/0.12 = (1.6 - 1)/0.12 = 5.$$

We therefore can conclude that it will take 5 years for a deposit of £4000 to amount to £6400 if the annual simple interest rate is 12% for the entire period.

Finally, it may be the case that we are required to find the principal that would need to be deposited **just now** in order to amount to a given sum after $t$ years when the interest rate is $i$ per annum.

Once again, we can start from

$$A_t = P(1 + ti),$$

whereby

$$P = A_t/(1 + ti).$$

For example, if a principal of £P amounts to £6000 after 5 years when the annual simple interest rate is 10%, then the principal that must have been deposited is calculated from

$$P = 6000/(1 + 5(0.1)) = 6000/1.5 = £4000.$$

Each of these transformations of the basic formula can be incorporated into Excel worksheets as shown in Workbooks 13.2, 13.3 and 13.4.

| | A | B | C | D | E | F | G | H | |
|---|---|---|---|---|---|---|---|---|---|
| 1 | Principal (P) | 2000 | | | | | | | |
| 2 | Number of years (t) | 7 | | | | | | | |
| 3 | Amount after t years (A_t) | 3260 | | | | | | | |
| 4 | Required interest rate (i) | 0.09 | | | | | | | |
| 5 | | | | | | | | | |

Sheet1 / Sheet2 / Sheet3 / Sheet4 / Sheet5 / She

**Workbook 13.2**

| | A | B | C | D | E | F | G | H | |
|---|---|---|---|---|---|---|---|---|---|
| 1 | Principal (P) | 4000 | | | | | | | |
| 2 | Interest rate (i) | 12% | | | | | | | |
| 3 | Amount after t years (A$_t$) | 6400 | | | | | | | |
| 4 | Required number of years (t) | 5 | | | | | | | |
| 5 | | | | | | | | | |

**Workbook 13.3**

| | A | B | C | D | E | F | G | H | |
|---|---|---|---|---|---|---|---|---|---|
| 1 | Interest rate (i) | 12% | | | | | | | |
| 2 | Amount after t years (A$_t$) | 7000.00 | | | | | | | |
| 3 | Number of years (t) | 6 | | | | | | | |
| 4 | Required Principal (P) | 4069.767 | | | | | | | |
| 5 | | | | | | | | | |

**Workbook 13.4**

*Make these up now.*

The given data of the problem should be entered to the B1:B3 range.
   Then the required interest rate is computed in B4 from:

$$=(B3/B1-1)/B2$$

The given data of the problem should be entered to the B1:B3 range.
   Then the required number of years is computed in B4 from:

$$=(B3/B1-1)/B2$$

The given data of the problem should be entered to the B1:B3 range.
   Then the required principal is computed in B4 from:

$$=B2/(1+B3*B1)$$

*Exercise 13.1 can be attempted now.*

# 13.3  Compound interest

The important point to have noted in the previous discussion was that because simple interest was being paid, the principal did **not increase** in magnitude as each subsequent year's interest was paid. However, this is contrary to our normal expectation that if a principal of £500 were deposited at a simple interest rate of 10% per annum, then after one year had passed the interest payment due would be £50, and that **this payment should then be added to the account**. The value of the account upon which the next year's interest is calculated would then become £550. This would once again attract interest at an annual rate of 10%, and would mean that the second year's interest payment would be £55 (as opposed to £50 under simple interest). When this payment is added to the account, then the value of the account at the start of the next period becomes £605, and the interest due at the end of the third year becomes £60.5.

This steady increase in the size of the interest payment that results from the previous period's interest payment being **added** to the account and being **left on deposit** to gain further interest, is the crucial feature of **compound** as opposed to simple interest. Furthermore, since compound interest is by far the most prevalent practice amongst financial institutions, it is crucial that its logic be fully understood.

This logic can be more generally appreciated as follows.

For the first year the situation is identical to simple interest. Hence:

$$A_1 = P + iP = P(1 + i).$$

After two years, however, it should be apparent that the amount accumulated is equal to the amount after 1 year plus $i$ times that amount. That is,

$$A_2 = A_1 + iA_1.$$

However, since we already know that $A_1 = P(1 + i)$, we can rewrite this last expression as:

$$A_2 = P(1 + i) + iP(1 + i).$$

Which, upon factoring the term in $P(1 + i)$ becomes:

$$A_2 = P(1 + i)(1 + i) = P(1 + i).$$

By a similar logic we could find the amount after 3 years to be:

$$A_3 = A_2 + iA_2.$$

Then, once again using our knowledge that $A_2 = P(1 + i)^2$, we can rewrite this as:

$$A_3 = P(1 + i)^2 + iP(1 + i)^2.$$

This, upon factoring the term in $P(1 + i)^2$, then produces:

$$A_3 = P(1 + i)^2(1 + i) = P(1 + i)^3.$$

Careful inspection of the relationships that have been built up here should provide an obvious expression for the amount after $t$ years. That is,

$$A_t = P(1 + i)^t.$$

To confirm this expression consider the process of finding the compounded amount after 3 years, of an initial deposit of £1000 if interest is compounded at a rate of 8% per annum for the period.

We therefore have:

$$P = A_0 = 1000,$$
$$i = 8/100 = 0.08,$$
$$t = 3.$$

| | A | B | C | D | E | F | G | H | I |
|---|---|---|---|---|---|---|---|---|---|
| 1 | Principal (P) | 1000 | | | | | | | |
| 2 | Interest rate (i) | 5% | | | | | | | |
| 3 | Number of years (t) | 6 | | | | | | | |
| 4 | | | | | | | | | |
| 5 | Amount (A,) | 1340.10 | | | | | | | |
| 6 | | | | | | | | | |

Sheet1 / Sheet2 / Sheet3 / Sheet4 / Sheet5 / She

**Workbook 13.5**

Therefore,

$$A_1 = £1000 + £1000(0.08) = £1080,$$

$$A_2 = £1080 + £1080(0.08) = £1166.4,$$

$$A_3 = £1166.4 + £1164.4(0.08) = £1259.71.$$

However, this result could have been obtained more easily from the expression that was derived above. That was:

$$A_t = P(1+i)^t,$$

which, upon substituting the given values produces:

$$A_3 = 1000(1+0.08)^3 = 1000(1.25971) = £1259.71.$$

These ideas can be translated into an Excel worksheet as indicated in Workbook 13.5.

*Make this up now.*

The given values for $P, i$ and $t$ are entered to the B1:B3 range, and then the compounded amount calculated in B5 from the formula

**=B1*(1+B2)^B3**

*Exercise 13.2 can be attempted now.*

As was the case in the discussion on simple interest, the basic compound interest formula derived above can be transformed to allow solution for any of the arguments that it contains.

For example, suppose it was required to find the annual compound rate that is being received on a principal of £2000 that amounted to £3500 after 5 years.

We can proceed as follows.

$$A_t = P(1+i)^t.$$

Therefore

$$A_t/P = (1+i)^t.$$

Now take the $t$th root of both sides to obtain:

$$\sqrt[t]{A_t/p} = (1+i),$$

whereby

$$i = \sqrt[t]{A_t/p} - 1.$$

| | A | B | C | D | E | F | G | H | I |
|---|---|---|---|---|---|---|---|---|---|
| 1 | Principal (P) | 2000 | | | | | | | |
| 2 | Amount (A$_t$) | 3500 | | | | | | | |
| 3 | Number of years (t) | 5 | | | | | | | |
| 4 | | | | | | | | | |
| 5 | Interest rate received | 0.118427 | | | | | | | |
| 6 | | | | | | | | | |

Sheet1 / Sheet2 / Sheet3 / Sheet4 / Sheet5 / She

**Workbook 13.6**

To aid eventual transfer to Excel this should now be written in index form as:

$$i = (A_t/P) - 1.$$

Thus, with $P$, $A_t$ and $t$ being given as £2000, £3500 and 5 respectively, we have:

$$i = (3500/2000)^{1/5} - 1 = 1.750^{0.2} - 1 = 1.118427 - 1 = 0.118427 = 11.8427\%.$$

The annual compound rate for the period must have been 11.8427% if a principal of £2000 amounted to £3500 after 5 years.

To assist computation, these relationships can be translated into an Excel worksheet as indicated in Workbook 13.6.

*Make this up now.*

The entries in B1:B3 are the given values of $P$, $A_t$ and $t$, and the interest rate being received is calculated in B5 from the formula

**=(B2/B1)^(1/B3)-1**

This is clearly the spreadsheet equivalent of the expression that was derived above and confirms the result that was calculated manually from that expression.

*Exercise 13.3 can be attempted now.*

Now suppose that it was required to find the number of **years** that it will take for a principal of £1000 to amount to £2000 if the annual compound rate of interest is 15%. As before, we start with the basic compound interest formula:

$$A_t = P(1 + i)^t.$$

Therefore,

$$A_t/P = (1 + i)^t.$$

Now take logarithms of both sides to obtain:

$$\log(A_t/P) = t\log(1 + i).$$

Therefore,

$$t = \log(A_t/P)/\log(1 + i).$$

With the values given, this means that

$$t = \log(2000/1000)/\log(1.15) = \log 2/\log 1.15 = 4.959 \text{ years.}$$

| | A | B | C | D | E | F | G | H | |
|---|---|---|---|---|---|---|---|---|---|
| 1 | Principal (P) | 1000 | | | | | | | |
| 2 | Amount (A$_t$) | 2000 | | | | | | | |
| 3 | Interest rate | 15% | | | | | | | |
| 4 | | | | | | | | | |
| 5 | Required number of years | 4.959484 | | | | | | | |
| 6 | | | | | | | | | |

Sheet1 / Sheet2 / Sheet3 / Sheet4 / Sheet5 / She

**Workbook 13.7**

It will therefore take almost 5 years for the principal of £1000 to double in value if the annual compound rate of interest is 15%.

Once again the calculations can be simplified by entering them to an Excel worksheet. This is done in Workbook 13.7.

*Make this up now.*

The given data of the problem, $P$, $A_t$ and $i$, are entered to the B1:B3 range and then the required number of years calculated in B5 from the formula

=LOG(B2/B1)/LOG(1+B3)

The result obtained earlier (4.959 years) will be obtained.

*Exercise 13.4 can be attempted now.*

Finally, it is an easy matter to perform the last logical transformation of the basic compounding equation to obtain the principal that must be deposited **just now** in order to receive a specified amount after $t$ years when the annual compound interest rate is $i$.

This is done simply by rewriting

$$A_t = P(1+i)^t$$

as

$$P=A_t/P(1+i)^t.$$

Hence, for example if an amount of £5000 is received after 6 years when the annual compound rate of interest is 8%, then the principal that must have been deposited in order to secure this terminal amount is calculated as:

$$P = 5000/(1.08)^6 = 5000/1.586874 = £3150.85.$$

A worksheet that can perform calculations of this type is shown in Workbook 13.8.

*Make this up now.*

The formula in B5 is:

=B1/(1+B2)^B3

When this is evaluated by Excel, the result obtained above (£3150.85) will be returned to the B5 cell.

| | A | B | C | D | E | F | G | H |
|---|---|---|---|---|---|---|---|---|
| 1 | Amount (A$_t$) | 5000 | | | | | | |
| 2 | Interest rate | 8% | | | | | | |
| 3 | Number of years | 6 | | | | | | |
| 4 | | | | | | | | |
| 5 | Required principal | 3150.848 | | | | | | |
| 6 | | | | | | | | |

◄◄ ◄ ► ►◄ \ Sheet1 / Sheet2 / Sheet3 / Sheet4 / Sheet5 / She ◄ ►◄

**Workbook 13.8**

*Exercise 13.5 can be attempted now.*

It should now be pointed out that in the previous discussion when the principal and the interest rate were **given**, the derived compounding formula calculated the amount accruing after a **selected** number of years ($t$). However, it will be instructive to investigate how the amount accruing **varies** with the passage of time. To do this we must evaluate $A_t$ for **each** of a specified number of years.

An Excel worksheet that can do this efficiently is shown in Workbook 13.9.

*Make this up now in line with the explanation.*

*First of all, enter the values and labels indicated in the A1:B3 range. Then name the B1 and B2 cells as P and i respectively (use Insert, Name, Define with the cursor located first in B1 and then in B2). Next, enter the year values 0 to 15 in the A4:A19 range. Finally, in B4 enter the formula*

$$=P*(1 + i)\char94 A4$$

This will return a value that is identical to the principal in year zero.

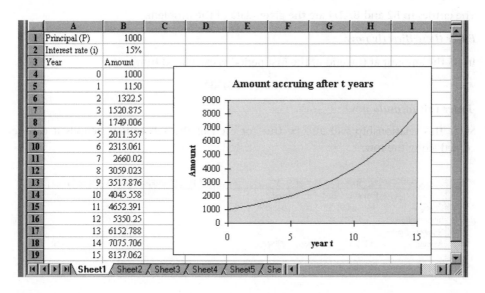

**Workbook 13.9**

*Now copy B4 into B5:B19.*

This will compute the amount accruing in each of the years 1 to 15.

The results shown in the illustrative worksheet should now be obtained.

*Now, chart the A4:B19 range as an XY scatter graph to obtain the diagram shown in Workbook 13.9.*

As is clear from this graph, the amount accruing rises steadily as the number of years increases, and does so at an **increasing** rate.

In all of the previous examples it will have been noticed that the interest rate was **constant** over the **entire** period under consideration. However, it is easy to envisage circumstances in which the rate changes from time to time.

To deal with this additional complication the problem can be approached as follows. Let $i_1, i_2, i_3$ etc. be the interest rates received respectively for periods of $t_1, t_2, t_3$ etc. years. It then follows that the amount after $t_1$ years ($A_{t_1}$) is given by:

$$A_{t_1} = P(1 + i_1)^{t_1}.$$

This amount can then be regarded as the **principal** to which the next period's interest rate ($i_2$) will apply for the whole of the next period ($t_2$). Consequently, the amount after $t_1 + t_2$ years will be given by:

$$A_{t_1+t_2} = P(1 + i_1)^{t_1}(1 + i_2)^{t_2}.$$

By a similar logic the amount after $t_1 + t_2 + t_3$ years will be given by:

$$A_{t_1+t_2t_3} = P(1 + i_1)^{t_1}(1 + i_2)^{t_2}(1 + i_3)^{t_3}.$$

These ideas can be transferred to an Excel worksheet as indicated in Workbook 13.10.

*Make this up now in line with the instructions.*

The entries in B2 and B3:D4 are the given data of the problem.

*Enter these directly now.*

In B5 the amount at the end of the first period is calculated from

$$=B2*(1+B3)^{\hat{}}B4$$

*Enter this formula now.*

Since this relationship will also be true for each of the subsequent periods it can be copied along the row.

| | A | B | C | D | E | F | G | H | I |
|---|---|---|---|---|---|---|---|---|---|
| 1 | | Period 1 | Period 2 | Period 3 | | | | | |
| 2 | Principal | 1000 | 1215.506 | 2088.466 | | | | | |
| 3 | Interest rate | 5% | 7% | 9% | | | | | |
| 4 | Number of years | 4 | 8 | 3 | | | | | |
| 5 | Amount | 1215.506 | 2088.466 | 2704.62 | | | | | |
| 6 | | | | | | | | | |

Sheet1 / Sheet2 / Sheet3 / Sheet4 / Sheet5 / She

**Workbook 13.10**

*So copy B5 into C5:D5.*

Then, the amount at the **end** of the first period must be transferred to the C2 cell to become the principal at the **start** of the second period.

*So make an entry in C2 of*

$$=B5$$

*and then copy it into D2.*

The model is now complete and can easily be extended to include further periods by copying the key formulae in D2 and D5 along the sheet.

*Exercise 13.6 can be attempted now.*

## 13.4 Fractional years

In all of the previous discussion the number of years for which the principal was deposited was always a **whole number**. But consideration should be given to situations in which a deposit is made for 2.5 or 3.6 years, or some other non-whole number of years.

In this respect it would be reasonable to expect that the basic compounding formula ($A_t = P(1 + i)^t$) would still apply, with the obvious difference being that $t$ no longer adopts an integer value.

In fact, this is **not the case**, since virtually all financial institutions evaluate interest payments on what is known as a 'daily basis'. What this means is that interest is compounded for the **integer** number of years for which the principal has been deposited, and any extra non-integer number of years is then treated on a 'pro rata' basis in relation to the annual interest rate.

For example, suppose £1000 were deposited at an annual compound interest rate of 7% for 2 years and 100 days. The amount after 2 years is easily calculated to be:

$$A_2 = 1000(1.07)^2 = £1144.9.$$

This amount then attracts that proportion of the interest rate that corresponds to the proportion of 365 days for which the funds have been deposited. Consequently, since the interest rate is 7%, and the funds have been on deposit for 100/365 of a year; the additional **interest payment** due is therefore given by:

$$1144.9(100/365)(0.07) = £21.96.$$

When this interest payment is added to the previous value of the account then we obtain:

$$£1144.9 + £21.96 = £1166.85.$$

| | A | B | C | D | E | F | G | H |
|---|---|---|---|---|---|---|---|---|
| 1 | Principal | 1000 | | | | | | |
| 2 | Interest rate | 7% | | | | | | |
| 3 | Number of years | 2.273973 | | | | | | |
| 4 | Integer number of years | 2 | | | | | | |
| 5 | Remaider number of years | 0.273973 | | | | | | |
| 6 | Compounded value | 1144.90 | | | | | | |
| 7 | Partial year value | 21.96 | | | | | | |
| 8 | Terminal value | 1166.86 | | | | | | |
| 9 | | | | | | | | |

Sheet1 / Sheet2 / Sheet3 / Sheet4 / Sheet5 / She

**Workbook 13.11**

The same result could, of course, have been obtained from the following expression:

$$A_{2,100} = [1000(1.07)^2][1 + (100/365)(0.07)] = £1166.85,$$

where $A_{2,100}$ represents the amount after 2 years and 100 days.

In general, then, if funds are deposited for $t$ years and $d$ days, at an annual compound rate of $i\%$ per annum, then the accumulated amount at the end of this period ($A_{t,d}$) is given by:

$$A_{t,d} = [P(1 + i)^t][1 + (d/365)(i)].$$

Notice that if the £1000 were deposited for 2 years and 365 days (i.e. 3 years) then the formula above remains correct, since

$$A_{t,d} = 1000[(1.07)^2][1 + (365/365)(0.07)]$$
$$= (1144.9)(1.07). = 1225.04,$$

which is identical to

$$A_3 = 1000(1.07)^3.$$

To perform this type of calculation on Excel consider Workbook 13.11.

*Make this up now in line with the instructions.*

*Enter the given data for the problem to B1:B3.*

Notice that 2 years and 100 days is the same as 2.273973 years.

*Now calculate the integer number of years in B4 from the formula*

=INT(B3)

This function returns the pre-decimal-point portion of any number.

*Next, calculate the remainder number of years in B5 from the formula*

=MOD(B3,1)

This function calculates the remainder of the first argument divided by the second argument.

Thus in our illustration B3 = 2.273973, so B3/1 also equals 2.273973. The remainder of this is clearly 0.273973 and this is the value that =MOD(B3,1) will return.

*Next, use B6 to calculate the value of the principal after the whole number of years contained in B4 from*

$$=B1*(1+B2)\hat{\ }B4$$

A value of £1144.9 will be returned.

*Then calculate the interest for the partial year in B7 from*

$$=B6*B2*B5$$

A value of £21.95 will be returned.

*Finally calculate the terminal value of the principal in B8 from*

$$=B6+B7$$

The answer obtained previously (£1166.85) will be returned.

*Exercise 13.7 can be attempted now.*

## 13.5 **Variations in the compounding period**

All of the discussion to date has assumed that interest is compounded on an **annual** basis (i.e. once a year). However, many financial organizations offer savings schemes on which interest is compounded on a half-yearly, quarterly, or even daily basis. Such variations in what is known as the **compounding period** exercise a considerable effect upon the eventual value of any given principal **even when the annual interest rate and the length of time of the investment are the same.**

To see this effect, consider a principal of £500 that is deposited for 2 years at an interest rate of 12% per annum.

Now, if interest is compounded annually, then it is an easy matter to calculate the amount after 2 years to be:

$$A_2 = 500(1.12)^2 = £627.2.$$

Suppose now, however, that interest were compounded **semi-annually** (i.e. twice per year). What this means is that after 6 months half a year's interest is actually credited to the account, and therefore increases the account's value accordingly. This larger value then forms the base upon which the next 6 months' interest is calculated, and so on.

Now, since the annual interest rate is 12%, this clearly implies that the appropriate rate for the half-year will be 12%/2 = 6%. Furthermore, since the funds are deposited for 2 years this means that the problem can be viewed in terms of four **half-year** periods in **each of which** the appropriate interest rate is 6%.

Bearing these points in mind means that the amount after 2 years can be calculated from

$$A_2 = 500(1.06)^4 = £631.24.$$

The fact that this new amount is £4.04 greater than under annual compounding is **entirely** due to the greater number of compounding periods (since all other factors are the same).

Continuing this line of reasoning, it should be clear that if interest were compounded quarterly, then the amount after 2 years could be derived from viewing the problem in terms of 8 periods of 3 months, in each of which the effective interest rate was $12\%/4 = 3\%$. Therefore,

$$A_2 = 500(1.03)^8 = £633.38.$$

Once again, the effect of increasing the number of compounding periods in the year (from 2 to 4) is seen to increase the amount after 2 years from £631.24 to £633.38.

Now, suppose that interest is compounded on a monthly basis. Clearly, the amount after 2 years can be calculated from evaluating the following expression:

$$A_2 = 500(1.01)^{24} = £634.86$$

(since there are 24 periods in which the interest rate for each period is $12\%/12 = 1\%$).

It should now be possible to generalize this result to deal with **any** number of compounding periods that are contained in a year. To do this it is simply necessary to recognize that if interest is compounded m times per annum, then any period of $t$ years contains m times $t = mt$ **compounding periods**. Furthermore, if the annual interest rate is represented, as usual, by $i$, then the relevant interest rate for each of these periods must be given by $i/m$.

This means that the amount after $t$ years will be given by:

$$A_t = P(1 + i/m)^{mt}.$$

For example, if interest were compounded weekly, then there would be 52 compounding periods in one year, and therefore $m = 52$. Consequently,

$$A_t = P(1 + i/52)^{52t}.$$

In order to keep our symbols consistent, however, we really should recognize the effect exercised by variations in the compounding period by including it in the symbol for the amount. Consequently, we should define $A_{t,m}$ to be the amount after $t$ years when interest is compounded m times per annum.

Of course, if interest is compounded on an annual basis, then $m = 1$ and the expression above becomes:

$$A_{t,1} = P(1 + i)^t,$$

which reproduces the basic compound interest formula.

In all other cases, however, the amount after $t$ years will be given by

$$A_{t,m} = P(1 + i/m)^{mt}.$$

| | A | B | C | D | E | F | G |
|---|---|---|---|---|---|---|---|
| 1 | Principal | 6000 | | | | | |
| 2 | Annual interest rate | 8% | | | | | |
| 3 | Number of years | 7 | | | | | |
| 4 | Number of compounding periods per annum | 1 | | | | | |
| 5 | Total number of compounding periods | 7 | | | | | |
| 6 | Interest rate per compounding period | 0.08 | | | | | |
| 7 | Terminal value | 10282.95 | | | | | |
| 8 | | | | | | | |

Sheet1 / Sheet2 / Sheet3 / Sheet4 / Sheet5 / She

**Workbook 13.12**

For example, to find the value after 1 year of £3000 deposited in an account that bears interest at a rate of 10% per annum, compounded quarterly, the following expression should be evaluated:

$$A_{1,4} = 3000(1 + 0.1/4)^4 = 3000(1.025)^4 = £3311.44.$$

Or, to find the value after 4 years of £5000 deposited in an account that bears interest at a rate of 9% per annum, compounded semi-annually, the following expression should be evaluated:

$$A_{4,2} = 5000(1 + 0.09/2)^8 = 5000(1.045)^8 = £7110.5.$$

A more efficient way of investigating the effects of variations in the compounding period can be seen in Workbook 13.12.

*Make this up now in line with the instructions.*

*Enter the given data of the problem directly to the B1:B4 cells.*

*Then, in B5 calculate the total number of compounding periods in the term of the investment from*

$$=B3*B4$$

*Next, in B6 calculate the interest rate for each compounding period from*

$$=B2/B4$$

*Finally, calculate the terminal amount in B7 from*

$$=B1*(1+B6)^B5$$

This is analogous to the algebraic expression derived earlier for $A_{t,m}$ when it is noticed that B6 has been forced to contain $i/m$ and B5 to contain $mt$.

From this worksheet it should be clear that the terminal value of a principal of £6000 that is deposited for 7 years at an annual interest rate of 8%, compounded quarterly, is £10446.15.

It is also an easy matter to use this worksheet to confirm that if interest were only compounded annually the terminal value would only be £10282.95.

*Now use Workbook 13.12 to confirm the two results obtained earlier (£3311.4 and £7110.5).*

It is now time to point out that an important result emerges if we choose certain values for $P, i, m$ and $t$ in the expression for $A_{t,m}$. To see this, consider the following example.

Find the value after 1 year of £1 deposited in an account that bears interest at a rate of 100% per annum, compounded annually.

*To find this value use Workbook 13.12 with values of 1 in each of the B1:B4 cells.*

A result of 2 will be returned to B7 since $A_{t,m} = P(1 + i/m)^{mt}$ will be evaluated as:

$$A_{1,1} = 1(1 + 1/1)^1 = 2.$$

Now suppose that interest is compounded semi-annually. This means that the entry in B4 should become 2.

*Make this entry now.*

The result in B7 will become 2.25.

Now suppose that we let the number of compounding periods in the year go through a steadily increasing sequence, and that we calculate the associated value of $A_{t,m}$ for each of these values of $m$.

Worksheet 13.13 performs the necessary calculations.

*Make this up now.*

*Enter the given values for P, i and t (all = 1) to the B1:B3 range.*

*Next, in B8:B16 enter the indicated values for the number of compounding periods in the year.*

| | A | B | C | D | E | F | G | H |
|---|---|---|---|---|---|---|---|---|
| 1 | Principal | 1 | | | | | | |
| 2 | Annual interest rate | 1 | | | | | | |
| 3 | Number of years | 1 | | | | | | |
| 4 | | | | | | | | |
| 5 | | Annual number | | | | | | |
| 6 | | of compounding | Terminal | | | | | |
| 7 | | periods (m) | amount | | | | | |
| 8 | | 1 | 2.0000 | | | | | |
| 9 | | 2 | 2.2500 | | | | | |
| 10 | | 4 | 2.4414 | | | | | |
| 11 | | 12 | 2.6130 | | | | | |
| 12 | | 52 | 2.6926 | | | | | |
| 13 | | 365 | 2.7146 | | | | | |
| 14 | | 8760 | 2.7181 | | | | | |
| 15 | | 525600 | 2.7183 | | | | | |
| 16 | | 31536000 | 2.7183 | | | | | |
| 17 | | | | | | | | |

Sheet1 / Sheet2 / Sheet3 / Sheet4 / Sheet5 / She

**Workbook 13.13**

These represent the process of annual, semi-annual, quarterly, monthly, etc. compounding, right down to B16 where interest is regarded as being compounded every second.

*Now use C8 to contain the formula*

$$=B\$1*(1+B\$2/B8)\hat{}(B\$3*B8)$$

*and copy this into C9:C16.*

This formula is equivalent to the expression for $A_{t,m}$ when it is noticed that B1, B2 and B3 contain the values for $P, i$ and $t$, while B8:B16 contain the varying values for $m$.

Clearly, what is happening is that the value of $A_{t,m}$ at first increases quite dramatically, but that as the number of compounding periods increases, then $A_{t,m}$ starts to increase less rapidly.

This suggests that the value of $A_{t,m}$ is approaching some **limit** as the value of $m$ increases and this limit can be shown to be e $= 2.7183$.

This limit is reached when the number of compounding periods in the year (i.e. the value of $m$) becomes infinitely large and, consequently, when the **time between** compounding periods becomes infinitesimally small.

In symbols it is said that the limit as $m$ tends to infinity of $1(1+1/m)^{m} = $ e $= 2.7183$.

## 13.6 **Continuous compounding**

As has previously been said, when $m$ becomes infinitely **large** the time between compounding periods becomes infinitesimally **small**, and can effectively be regarded as zero. When this happens we refer to such a situation as **continuous compounding**, since instead of there being a **countable** period of time between compounding periods there is so little time that the process can be regarded as continuous. It is almost as if the interest for a millisecond is added to the principal in the instant of its passing and hence forms an infinitesimally larger base upon which the interest for the next millisecond is calculated.

The sceptical reader will no doubt argue that few financial institutions would ever offer terms as beneficial to the lender as continuous compounding implies, and on this there is no dispute. However, many natural phenomena do not recognize the accounting habits of banks and building societies and insist upon growing in a fashion that is most appropriately modelled by continuous compounding and the use of e.

To see how this can be done, we should now relax some of the restrictive values that were imposed upon $P, i$ and $t$ in the illustration in the previous section (i.e. $P = i = t = 1$).

First of all, we should allow the value of the interest rate to be $i$ as usual, instead of 100%. When this is done the expression for $A_{t,m}$ can be written as:

$$A_{1,m} = 1(1 + i/m)^{m}.$$

Now we have already seen that if $i = 1$ then the limit of this expression as $m$ tends to infinity is $2.71828 = $ e.

So the question arises of what happens when $i$ adopts some value other than 1. In particular, does this expression also reach a definite limit, and if so, what is it? The answer is 'yes', although the algebra to prove it is beyond the scope of this text. Nevertheless, it can be taken on trust that the limit of

$$A_{1,m} = 1(1 + i/m)^m$$

as $m$ tends to infinity is given by:

$$A_{1,m} = 1(1 + i/m)^m = e^i.$$

This can be confirmed by an appropriate modification of the model in Workbook 13.13.

*To do this enter a value of 0.1 (for example) in B2, whereupon it will be found that a value of 1.1052 will be returned to the C16 cell.*

*This is indistinguishable from $e^{0.1}$, as is easily confirmed by entering the following formula to any vacant cell of the worksheet:*

$$=EXP(0.1)$$

Now suppose that the principal of £1 is deposited for **more than one year** and continuously compounded at an annual rate of $i$. The expression for $A_{t,m}$ becomes

$$A_{t,m} = 1(1 + i/m)^{mt}.$$

Now, if we rewrite this as

$$A_{t,m} = [1(1 + i/m)^m]^t,$$

it can be seen that since the limit of the expression inside the square brackets has already been stated to be $e^i$, we can write:

$$A_{t,m} = (e^i)^t = e^{it}.$$

In other words, the limit of $1(1 + i/m)^{mt}$ as $m$ tends to infinity is given by $e^{it}$.

Keeping the same figures as were used in the last example (that is, $i = 0.10, P = 1$), this result can be confirmed by making the following modifications to Workbook 13.13.

*In B3 enter a value of 5 (i.e. 5 years), and in any vacant cell enter:*

$$=EXP(B2*B3)$$

It will now be found that with hourly compounding the results returned to C14 onwards will be the same as that obtained from the exponential function (1.6487). This, of course, is because

$$1(1 + i/m)^{mt} = 1(1 + 0.1/8760)^{(5)(8760)} = 1.6487$$

and

$$e^{(5)(0.16)} = e^{0.8} = 1.6487.$$

Finally, if a principal of £P is deposited then we have:

$$A_{t,m} = P(1 + i/m)^{mt}.$$

It is left as an exercise to confirm that the limit of this expression as $m$ tends to infinity is given by:

$$A_{t,m} = Pe^{it}.$$

*Exercise 13.8 can be attempted now.*

## 13.7 The equivalent annual rate

The discussion in the previous section has produced the important implication that the **effective rate of interest** being paid on deposited funds not only depends upon the quoted nominal rate but also upon the frequency with which interest is compounded (i.e. the value of $m$). In other words, with any **nominal annual rate** of interest, a given principal will amount to more if that interest is compounded monthly than if it is compounded annually. Clearly, this implies that the **effective** rate on the monthly compounded funds exceeds that on the annually compounded funds.

This idea gives rise to the concept of the **equivalent annual rate** (EAR) which allows any nominal annual rate (NAR) to be expressed in terms that take account of the frequency with which interest is compounded. To do this, note that if interest is compounded $m$ times per annum at the quoted NAR then the amount after $t$ years is given by

$$A_{t,m} = P(1 + \text{NAR}/m)^{mt}.$$

However, in the simplest case of annual compounding, the fact that $m = 1$ means that this expression reduces to

$$A_{t,1} = P(1 + \text{NAR})^t.$$

This implies that only under annual compounding will the nominal and the equivalent rates be the same, and this knowledge allows us to rewrite the last expression as

$$A_{t,1} = P[1 + \text{EAR}]^t.$$

If we now equate the right-hand sides of the first and third of these last expressions we obtain

$$P(1 + \text{EAR})^t = P(1 + \text{NAR}/m)^{mt}.$$

Eliminating $P$ from both sides and then raising both sides to the power of $1/t$ produces:

$$(1 + \text{EAR}) = (1 + \text{NAR}/m)^m.$$

Therefore,

$$\text{EAR} = (1 + \text{NAR}/m)^m - 1.$$

For example, if a savings scheme offers quarterly compounding at a nominal annual rate of 12%, then the last expression above would become (with NAR = 0.12 and $m = 4$)

$$\text{EAR} = (1 + 0.12/4)^4 - 1 = 1.03^4 - 1 = 0.1255.$$

The effect of quarterly compounding has been to make the nominal annual rate of 12% become **equivalent** to an annually compounded rate of 12.55%.

Furthermore, if the compounding process were continuous then it should be clear that the expression for the EAR becomes:

$$EAR = (e^{NAR}) - 1$$

which, if NAR = 0.15 for example, implies that the annual equivalent rate of a nominal rate of 15% compounded continuously is given by

$$e^{0.15} - 1 = 0.1618, \text{i.e.} 16.18\%.$$

This is clearly the **highest** value, **for any given nominal rate**, that the equivalent annual rate can adopt.

In short, the result of this discussion is the conclusion that the EAR increases steadily with any increases in the number of compounding periods in the year, and approaches a limit of $e^{NAR}$ as $m$ approaches infinity.

These results are summarized in Table 13.1.

| Annual number of compounding periods ($m$) | EAR |
|---|---|
| 1 | NAR |
| 2 | $(1 + NAR/2)^2 - 1$ |
| 4 | $(1 + NAR/4)^4 - 1$ |
| 12 | $(1 + NAR/12)^{12} - 1$ |
| ... | ... |
| M | $(1 + NAR/m)^m - 1$ |
| ... | ... |
| $\infty$ | $e^{NAR}$ |

Furthermore, it is an easy matter to translate these expressions into Excel terms to create a worksheet that can perform the necessary calculations.

This is shown in Workbook 13.14.

*Make this up now in line with the explanation.*

*Enter the given labels and values as indicated A1:B2 as shown.*

*Next, in A3 enter the label*

Equivalent annual rate

*and in B3 the formula*

=(1+B1/B2)^B2-1

| | A | B | C | D | E | F |
|---|---|---|---|---|---|---|
| 1 | Nominal annual rate | 10% | | | | |
| 2 | Number of compounding periods per annum | 4 | | | | |
| 3 | Equivalent annual rate | 0.103812891 | | | | |
| 4 | | | | | | |

Sheet1 / Sheet2 / Sheet3 / Sheet4 / Sheet5 / She

**Workbook 13.14**

*Now use this workbook to confirm the result obtained above—that a nominal annual rate of 12% is equivalent to a rate of 12.55% if interest is compounded quarterly.*

*Exercises 13.9 and 13.10 can be attempted now.*

## 13.8 Growth rate calculations

It has already been suggested that although financial institutions do not offer continuously compounded interest rates, there are a number of naturally occurring processes in which the growth in the variable's value is of a continuous or almost continuous nature. Population growth, the rate of inflation, gross national product, and the appreciation or depreciation of company assets, are all examples of such continuous growth processes. In each of these cases the most important feature is that although analysts may measure the value of the variable at **one point in time** and then measure it again at some later date, the variable is in fact changing **continuously** throughout the duration of the measurement period. In other words, it does not remain constant for 99.99% of the measurement period and then **suddenly** change its value at the time of the second measurement.

What this means is that the arbitrary choice of the **length** of the measurement period will influence how the growth in the value of the variable is perceived and calculated. Of course, continuous monitoring of the variable's value is the only way to remove this problem completely, though this would be a time-consuming and expensive practice.

Nevertheless, knowledge of the process of continuous compounding and its relationship with the exponential function allows us to calculate the appropriate growth rate **as if** it had been subject to continuous monitoring.

To see this, consider the following example.

An accountant estimates the value of a company's assets to be £1.64 million on the 1st of January 1997, and to be £2.14 million 2 years later. The task is to calculate the implied rate of growth of the company's assets over the period.

To deal with this problem it must be decided whether the growth process is to be regarded as simple or compound, and, if it is compound, the assumed number of compounding periods per annum must be determined.

Each of these alternatives can be considered as follows.

### Simple growth
In this case the value of $i$ can be calculated from transposition of the formula for simple interest. That is,

$$A_t = P(1 + ti)$$

implies that

$$i = [A_t/P - 1]/t.$$

Therefore,

$$i = [(2.14/1.64) - 1]/2 = 0.1524.$$

The simple growth rate is 15.24% per annum.

## Annual compound growth

In this case, the most recent version of the compound interest formula should be used and then transposed to produce an expression for $i$ as follows:

$$A_t = P(1 + i/m)^{mt}$$
$$A_t/P = (1 + i/m)^{mt}$$
$$(A_t/P)^{1/mt} = (1 + i/m)$$
$$(A_t/P)^{1/mt} - 1 = i/m$$
$$m[(A_t/P)^{1/mt} - 1] = i.$$

Now, since for annual compounding we have $m = 1$, and can write

$$1[(2.14/1.64)^{1/2} - 1] = i,$$

implying that $i = 0.1423$. The annually compounded growth rate is 14.23% per annum.

## Quarterly compound growth

In this case, we have $m = 4$, and so

$$4[(2.14/1.64)^{1/8} - 1] = i = 0.13453.$$

The quarterly compounded growth rate is 13.53% per annum.

## Monthly compound growth

For this case, we have $m = 12$, and so

$$12[(2.14/1.64)^{1/24} - 1] = i = 0.1337.$$

The monthly compounded growth rate is 13.37% per annum.

## Continuous compound growth

In this case, we must make use of the expression for continuous compound growth as follows:

$$A_t = Pe^{it}.$$

Therefore,

$$A_t/P = e^{it}$$
$$\ln(A_t/P) = it \ln e$$

But $\ln e = 1$ by definition, so

$$[\ln(A_t/P)]/t = i.$$

For the figures of the example this produces:

$$i = [\ln(2.14/1.64)]/2$$
$$0.1330.$$

The continuous compound growth rate is 13.3% per annum.

As is clearly illustrated from these calculations the calculated growth rate is highly sensitive to the number of compounding periods used. Nevertheless, as might be expected by now, the growth rate approaches a lower limit that is provided by the continuous compound rate as the number of compounding periods in the year approaches infinity.

*Exercise 13.11 can be attempted now.*

## 13.9 Annuities

So far we have only considered the process of calculating the future or terminal value of a **single** principal that has been placed on deposit for some specified number of years. However, many popular savings schemes allow for a **number of equal principals** to be deposited at periodic (usually annual) intervals.

Such schemes are known as **annuities**, and to calculate their terminal value **immediately after the last principal has been deposited**, requires that account is taken of **all** of the deposits, and **all** of the interest payments that each of these deposits attracts. The method of doing this can be illustrated as follows.

Suppose that starting today, four annual deposits of £2000 are made to an account that bears interest at an annual rate of 11% per annum, compounded annually over the entire period during which the deposits are made.

The task is to calculate the terminal or **future value** of the account immediately after the fourth deposit has been made.

To do this we can argue as follows.

The first deposit will attract interest at the prevailing rate for 3 years, and consequently will have a terminal value given by

$$A_3 = 2000(1.11)^3 = £2735.26.$$

Similarly, the second deposit will attract interest for a period of 2 years, and will therefore have a terminal value of

$$A_2 = 2000(1.11)^2 = £2464.20.$$

The third deposit will only bear interest for 1 year and therefore has a terminal value of

$$A_1 = 2000(1.11)^1 = £2200.00.$$

Finally, since it is required to calculate the value of the account **immediately** after the fourth deposit has been made, this fourth deposit must be included in the calculations **without any interest added to it.** Hence:

$$A_0 = 2000(1.11)^0 = £2000.00.$$

Clearly the total future value (FV) of the account can be obtained by adding each of these individual terminal values together, to produce:

$$FV = £2735.26 + £2464.20 + £2200 + £2000 = £9419.46.$$

Viewed in this methodical way the calculation of the terminal value of an annuity is easily understood. However, such an approach is needlessly laborious, since Excel has a dedicated function that can perform such calculations.

The function is called **future value** (=FV) and has the following general syntax:

FV(Interest rate,Number of periods,Periodic equal payment,*Present value,type*)

where those arguments in *italics* are **optional**, and need not necessarily be included. Their exact meaning is explained below.

**Interest rate** is the interest rate per period. It will be the annual rate if interest is compounded annually, but the equivalent annual rate $(1 + i/m)^m - 1$, if interest is compounded $m$ times per annum, and payments to the annuity are on an annual basis.

If interest is compounded with the **same** annual frequency as deposits are made to the annuity then the appropriate value for this argument is the periodic rate $i/m$.

**Number of periods** is the total number of periods in which payments are made to the annuity. If payments are made on an annual basis then the number of periods is the number of years of the annuity (its term) plus one. (Remember that an annuity with a term of 3 years consists of four equal payments if the first payment is made just now.) If payments are made more frequently than annually, and if interest is compounded with the same frequency ($m$ times per annum say), then the number of periods is the term of the annuity plus 1 times the frequency of payments in the year. For example, an annuity with a term of 3 years has 4 annual payments, 8 semi-annual payments, 16 quarterly payments, 48 monthly payments, etc.

Consequently, an annuity with a term of $t$ years and with $m$ payments per annum will consist of a total of $(t + 1)m$ periods, in each of which the interest rate is $i/m$ if the annual interest rate is $i$.

**Periodic equal payment** is the payment made to the annuity in each period. It cannot change over the life of the annuity.

*Present value* is an optional argument that is not relevant to the discussion at the moment. It is assumed to be 0 if it is omitted.

*Type* is another optional argument that indicates when the future value of the annuity is to be calculated. If omitted its value is assumed to be 0 and means that the future value is to be calculated **immediately** after the last payment has been made. On the other hand, if *Type* is set to 1 then the last payment is assumed to remain on deposit for **one more period** and so will attract an extra period's interest.

For example, to replicate the result that was obtained for the future value of the annuity illustrated earlier (£9419.46), take a blank worksheet and make the following entry to any vacant cell:

=FV(11%,4,-2000,0,0)

A result of £9419.46 will be returned, and since the Type argument has been set to 0, indicates that this future value is based on the value of the annuity **immediately after the last payment has been made**.

However, suppose that this future value (£9419.46) had been left on deposit for a further year at the going interest rate of 11%. Clearly it will then amount to 9419.46(1.11) = £10455.60.

This would be the value returned by the FV function if its last argument had been set to 1.

*Confirm this now.*

*Exercise 13.12 can be attempted now.*

Now consider the following situation.

An annuity with a term of 15 years has annual payments of £1500. The interest rate for the period is 10% per annum compounded quarterly. Calculate the future value of the annuity immediately after the last payment has been made.

To answer this we note that there are 16 annual payments of £1500, and the value of the account is to be calculated immediately after the last deposit is made. Also, since interest is compounded on a quarterly basis, but payments are made annually, we need to calculate the equivalent annual rate implied by the quarterly compounding. This is easily done from

$$EAR = (1 + i/m)^m - 1 = (1 + 0.1/4)^4 - 1 = 0.10381 = 10.381\%.$$

Consequently, the interest rate to be used as the first argument of the FV function should be 10.381%. Taken together these observations mean that the completed FV function should be

$$=FV(10.381\%,16,-1500,0,0)$$

*Enter this now to a vacant cell of a worksheet to obtain an answer of £55722.11.*

Notice that if the annual interest rate of 10% had in fact only been compounded annually, then the future value of the annuity would decline to £53924.59.

*Confirm this now by changing the first argument value from 10.381% to 10%.*

*Exercise 13.13 can be attempted now.*

Now consider an annuity with a term of 13 years to which **quarterly** payments of £500 are made. The interest rate attracted is 8% per annum compounded quarterly. To calculate the future value of this annuity immediately after the last deposit has been made we can note that the frequency of the payments to the annuity (quarterly) **also matches** the frequency with which interest is compounded.

Consequently, the annuity can be thought of as 14(4) = 56 quarterly payments of £500 that attract a quarterly interest rate of 8%/4 = 2% in each quarter.

The future value of this annuity is therefore calculated from

$$=FV(2\%,56,-500,0,0)$$

*Enter this formula to a vacant cell of a worksheet to obtain a result of £50779.13 as the future value of this scheme.*

*Exercise 13.14 can be attempted now.*

As a final point in this section the role of the optional present value argument should be explained.

Reconsider the simple annuity that was illustrated at the start of the section. That was four equal annual payments of £2000 to an account that provided interest of 11% per annum compounded annually.

Now recall that the future value of this annuity, immediately after the last payment was made, was £9419.46.

However, suppose that the account to which these annuity payments were made contained an initial amount of £1000. The future value of the **account** (as opposed to the annuity itself) will clearly be greater as a result of this initial amount.

To be exact, after the last deposit of £2000 has been made, the account will be worth £9419.46 plus the initial deposit of £1000, plus the interest received on the initial deposit over a period of 3 years.

That is, the future value will be:

$$£9419.46 + £1000(1.11)^3 = £9419.46 + 1367.63 = £10787.09.$$

This is the value that the Excel future value function *should* return when a value of -1000 is used as the optional present value argument.

In fact, however, on many versions of Excel there is a 'bug' in the function that has the effect of returning a result that is only consistent with the initial value of the account having attracted interest for one more year than it actually did.

To see this, use any vacant cell of a worksheet to contain

$$=FV(11\%,4,-2000,-1000,0)$$

A result of £10937.53 will be returned.

Clearly this exceeds the previously calculated future value of £10787.09 by an amount of £150.44.

This is **exactly** the amount of interest that would be paid on a sum of £1000 invested for 3 years at 11% per annum (£1367.63) plus the annual interest for another year on that amount, namely $0.11 \times £1367.63 = £150.44$.

This means that, as constituted, the Excel FV function must be modified downwards if the future value of the account is to be computed satisfactorily when the account to which the annuity payments are made contains an initial sum, and when the value of the account is to be calculated immediately after the last deposit has been made. In other words we must write:

$$=FV(11\%,4,-2000,-1000,0)-1000*0.11*(1.11)^3$$

*Now confirm that this amended version of the function returns the correct result (£10787.09).*

It should be noticed, however, that this 'bug' **does not exist** in the FV formula when the last argument (Type) is set to a value of 1.

To see this, suppose that the account with an initial deposit of £1000, and with four annual payments of £2000, all receiving interest at an annually compounded rate of 11% per annum, was allowed to gather one more year's interest.

The future value would then become

$$£9419.46 + £1000(1.11)^3 = £9419.46 + 1367.63 = £10787.09$$

after 3 years, plus one year's interest on £10787.09.

This clearly gives

$$£10787.09(1.11) = £11973.67.$$

*Now, remembering that the last argument of the FV function should be 1 rather than 0 (since we require the future value one year after the last deposit was made), take a vacant cell of the worksheet and enter:*

$$=FV(11\%,4,-2000,-1000,1)$$

A result of £11973.67 will be obtained, thereby indicating that the Excel future value function performs correctly when its last argument value is 1, but not when it is 0.

*Exercise 13.15 can be attempted now.*

Now recall that it was shown earlier that an annuity with a term of 3 years and with four annual payments of £2000 had a future value of £9419.46 when the interest rate was 11% per annum compounded annually.

However, suppose that we now asked the following question.

How many annual payments of £2000 must be made to an account in order to ensure a terminal value of £9419.46, if the interest rate for the period is 11% per annum compounded annually?

Clearly the answer is 4.

But the issue to be addressed now is whether an equivalent answer could be obtained to variations on this type of problem.

In other words, we are required to calculate the total number of equal periodic payments that must be made to an annuity if a future value of FV is to be obtained, immediately after the last payment is made, and if the interest rate for the period is *i* per annum.

The solution to this type of problem is provided by the Excel function called NPER (short for number of periods). It has the following general syntax.

$$=NPER(\text{Interest rate}, \text{Equal periodic payment}, \text{Present value}, \textit{Futurevalue}, \textit{Type})$$

where those arguments in italics are optional, and need not necessarily be included. Their exact meaning is explained below.

**Interest rate** is the interest rate per period. It will be the annual rate if interest is compounded annually, but the equivalent annual rate $(1+ i/m)^m - 1$ if interest is compounded *m* times per annum, and payments to the annuity are on an annual basis.

**Equal periodic payment** is the amount that is paid in to the annuity in each period of the term of the annuity.

**Present value** is the value **just now** of the account into which the periodic payments are made. If the account is established with a balance of zero, then the value of this argument is 0.

*Future value* is an optional argument representing the future amount that is to be secured by the annuity.

*Type* is another optional argument that indicates when the future value of the annuity is to be calculated. If omitted it is assumed to be 0 and means that the future value is to be calculated immediately after the last payment has been made. On the other hand, if *Type* is set to 1 then the last payment is assumed to remain on deposit for one more period and so will attract an extra period's interest.

Consequently, to obtain the result that was obtained above by simple inspection (four periods) we should enter:

$$=NPER(11\%,-2000,0,9419.46,0)$$

*Do this now and confirm that a result of 4 is obtained.*

Now reconsider the solution to Exercise 13.15.

This showed that nine equal annual payments of £1000 to an account containing £5000 to start with, would produce a future value of £25382.94, one year after the last deposit was made, if interest were paid at an annual equivalent rate of 9.2025%.

Consequently, we should expect that the NPER function would evaluate to 9 if the arguments were set to values of 9.2025%, −1000, −5000, 25382.94 and 1 respectively.

*Confirm this now by using any vacant cell of a worksheet to contain*

$$=NPER(9.2025\%,-1000,-5000,25382.94,1)$$

A value of 9 should be returned.

*Exercise 13.16 can be attempted now.*

## 13.10 Sinking funds

A sinking fund is simply the process of setting up a series of equal periodic payments that are designed to secure some specified future value when the number of payments and the interest rate that they attract are given.

For example, suppose that the basic annuity example from the previous section was rephrased in the following way.

An annuity with a term of 3 years is to supply a future value of £9419.46 when the interest rate that it attracts is 11% per annum compounded annually. What is the required size of the four equal annual payments to the annuity if the specified future value is to be achieved?

Once again, the answer is easily obtained by inspection and prior knowledge to be £2000.

However, to replicate this result in Excel, use must be made of the PMT function. This has the following general syntax:

=PMT(Interest rate,Number of periods,Present value,*Future value*, *Type*)

The exact meaning of each of these arguments is the same as with the FV and NPER functions.

Consequently, use any vacant cell of a worksheet to contain

**=PMT(11%,4,0,9419.46,0)**

A value of $-£2000$ will be returned, thereby confirming what is already known—that four equal annual payments of £2000 are required to secure a future value of £9419.36 in three years' time if the interest rate furnished by the annuity is 11% per annum compounded annually.

Now consider the solution to Exercise 13.15 again. There it was shown that nine equal annual payments of £1000 to an account containing £5000 to start with, would produce a future value of £25382.94, one year after the last deposit was made, if interest were paid at an annual equivalent rate of 9.2025%.

So, suppose that the necessary annual payments required to achieve this target future amount were unknown. They can easily be calculated from the PMT function if the following argument values are used:

**=PMT(9.2025%,9,-5000,25382.94,1)**

*Now confirm that this function will return the required value of £1000.*

*Exercise 13.17 can be attempted now.*

## 13.11 Debt repayments

The Excel PMT function can also be used to calculate the periodic repayments that will have to be made in order to repay any debt that is incurred just now.

For example, suppose that a loan of $£D$ is secured at an annually compounded interest rate of $i$%. This debt is to be repaid in three equal annual instalments of $£X$, with the first repayment being made **immediately**.

If the debt is administered on a **reducing balance** basis the task is to calculate the size of the three equal annual repayments required to pay off the debt.

Since the first repayment is to be made immediately, this means that the size of the debt on which interest is charged is given by

$$(D - X).$$

This outstanding debt then attracts interest charges so that at the end of the first year the outstanding debt becomes

$$(D - X)(1 + i).$$

When the second payment of £X is made, this outstanding debt reduces to

$$[(D - X)(1 + i) - X],$$

which then attracts interest charges in such a way that at the end of the second year the outstanding debt is

$$[(D - X)(1 + i) - X](1 + i).$$

When the third and final repayment of £X is made, then the debt must be cleared (i.e. outstanding debt = 0). We can therefore derive the following equation for this example:

$$[(D - X)(1 + i) - X](1 + i) - X = 0.$$

Collecting terms and simplifying, gives

$$(D - X)(1 + i)^2 - X(1 + i) - X = 0.$$

Therefore,

$$D(1 + i)^2 - X(1 + i)^2 - X(1 + i) - X = 0$$

and

$$D(1 + i)^2 - X[(1 + i)^2 + (1 + i) + 1] = 0.$$

Consequently,

$$X = D(1 + i)^2 / [(1 + i)^2 + (1 + i) + 1].$$

For example, if a debt of £10000 is incurred just now at an annual interest rate of 10%, and is to be repaid in three equal annual instalments, with the first instalment being paid just now, then the size of each instalment is given by

$$X = 10000(1.1)^2 / [1.21 + 1.1 + 1] = 12100/3.31 = £3655.59.$$

The debt will then be cleared after 2 years.

However, many reducing balance debts allow the debtor to have a one-period delay before the first payment has to be made. This being the case, then for the last example (with one year's delay) we have:

$$\text{Initial debt} = D$$
$$\text{Debt after 1 year} = D(1 + i)$$
$$\text{Debt after 1st repayment} = D(1 + i) - X$$
$$\text{Debt after 2 years} = [D(1 + i) - X](1 + i) = [D(1 + i)^2 - X(1 + 2i)]$$
$$\text{Debt after 2nd repayment} = [D(1 + i)^2 - X(1 + i) - X]$$
$$\text{Debt after 3 years} = [D(1 + i)^2 - X(1 + i) - X](1 + i) = [D(1 + i)^3 - X(1 + i)^2$$
$$-X(1 + i)]$$
$$\text{Debt after 3rd repayment} = [D(1 + i)^3 - X(1 + i)^2 - X(1 + i) - X].$$

Setting this last term equal to 0, collecting terms and solving for X as before produces:

$$X = [D(1 + i)^3 / [(1 + i)^2 + (1 + i) + 1].$$

For example, with the same figures as before, the three equal annual instalments are given by:

$$10000(1.1)^3/(1.21 + 1.1 + 1) = 13310/3.31 = £4021.15.$$

Three equal annual instalments of £4021.15 will be required to pay off this debt after 3 years when the first repayment is made in one year's time. Notice how this contrasts with the lower figure obtained earlier of £3655.59 if the first repayment is to be made immediately.

To replicate these results with the PMT function we can write

$$=PMT(10\%,3,10000,0,1)$$

*Enter this now to a vacant cell of a worksheet and confirm that by setting the last argument value to 1, this forces the function to regard the repayments as being immediate.*

Also notice that the optional future value argument has been set to zero. This is because the repayments must **exactly** clear the debt, with neither surplus nor deficit.

*Now confirm that if the first repayment is delayed by one year, then the result obtained earlier (£4021.15 as opposed to £3655.59) can be obtained from*

$$=PMT(10\%,3,10000,0,0)$$

In other words, by setting the *Type* argument value to 0 the function has been forced to regard the repayments as commencing in one period's time.

Also notice that both functions will return **negative** values, since these are the **repayments** necessary to pay off the initial positive loan.

*Exercise 13.18 can be attempted now.*

## 13.12 Exercises

### Exercise 13.1

(a) Calculate the amount after 20 years, of a principal of £2000 if simple interest is paid at an annual rate of 8.25%.

(b) Calculate the length of time required for a principal of £3000 to amount to £5400 if simple interest is paid at a rate of 8% per annum.

(c) Calculate the principal that must have been deposited, if an amount of £6000 is received after 15 years and simple interest paid at a rate of 10% per annum.

(d) Calculate the simple interest rate being received if a principal of £4000 amounts to £8000 after 10 years.

## Exercise 13.2

A principal of £3000 is deposited for 20 years at a compound interest rate of 7.75% per annum. Calculate the compounded amount after 20 years.

## Exercise 13.3

Find the annual compound rate of interest being received on a principal of £10000 that amounts to £20000 after 7 years.

## Exercise 13.4

Calculate the length of time for which £3500 must be deposited if it is to amount to £10000 when the annual compound rate of interest is 5.5%.

## Exercise 13.5

Calculate the size of the principal that must be deposited just now if a terminal sum of £20000 is to be obtained after 10 years when the annual compound rate of interest for the period is 9.9%.

## Exercise 13.6

A principal of £6000 is deposited just now. The annual interest rate for the coming year is 8%. This interest rate increases at a compound rate of 5% per annum for all subsequent years.

Modify the model created in Workbook 13.10 (W13_10.xls) to allow calculation of the value of the account after 10 years have passed.

## Exercise 13.7

Find the amount accruing to a principal of £5000 that is deposited at an annual interest rate of 8% per annum, for a period of 5.7824 years.

## Exercise 13.8

Use Workbook 13.13 to compare the terminal value of a principal of £2500 that is compounded by the second at an annual rate of 11.5% for a period of 7 years, with the amount that would accrue if interest were only compounded once per annum.

Also demonstrate that continuous compounding is indistinguishable from compounding by the second, when calculated to two decimal places.

## Exercise 13.9

Find the equivalent annual rate being supplied by an account that bears interest at a nominal annual rate of 25% compounded daily.

## Exercise 13.10

Calculate the required number of compounding periods in a year if a nominal annual rate of 10% is to have an equivalent annual rate of 10.5%.

## Exercise 13.11

Calculate the continuous compound annual rate of inflation if the index of retail prices was 134.67 on the 1st of January 1995, and had risen to 204.78 by the 1st of January 2000.

## Exercise 13.12

Calculate the future value, immediately after the last deposit has been made, of an annuity with a term of 12 years, consisting of annual payments of £5000, if the interest rate is 9% per annum compounded annually.

## Exercise 13.13

Calculate the future value, immediately after the last deposit is made, of an annuity with a term of 19 years, in which annual payments of £10000 attract interest at an annual rate of 18% compounded monthly.

## Exercise 13.14

Calculate the future value of an annuity with a term of 25 years, immediately after the last deposit has been made, if the monthly payments are £50, and if the rate of interest is 18% per annum compounded monthly.

## Exercise 13.15

An account containing £5000 is to be the recipient of an annuity with a term of 8 years, and a periodic payment of £1000. The interest rate for the period is 9% per annum compounded semi-annually.

Calculate the future value of the account one year after the last deposit has been made.

## Exercise 13.16

Calculate the number of equal annual payments of £6000 that are required to supply a future value of £306528.05 immediately after the last payment is made, if the account is empty to start with, and gathers interest at a quarterly compounded rate of 15% per annum.

## Exercise 13.17

An annuity scheme attracts interest at a monthly compounded rate of 10% per annum. It is intended to make 20 equal annual payments to this fund, with the objective of securing a future amount of £300000. The fund contains an amount of £10000 when the first payment is made.

(a) Calculate the required size of the 20 equal annual payments if:

    (i) the future sum is to be available immediately after the last payment is made;

    (ii) the future sum is to be available one year after the last deposit is made.

(b) Repeat both of these calculations if the account were empty when the first annuity payment is made.

(c) Suppose that the value of the account when the first payment is made is £50000.

Calculate the size of the 20 equal annual payments that are required to supply the future value of £300000 immediately after the last deposit is made.

## Exercise 13.18

Calculate the size of the 15 equal annual payments required to pay off a debt of £7,000 incurred at an interest rate of 17% per annum if the first repayment is to be made:

(a) 1 year from now;

(b) immediately.

# 13.13 Solutions to the exercises

## Solutions to Exercise 13.1

(a) Enter values of 2000, 8.25% and 20 to the B1, B2 and B3 cells of Workbook 13.1. (W13_1.xls). The amount after 20 years will be returned to B4 as £5300 when formatted to two decimal places.

(b) Enter values of 3000, 8% and 5400 to the B1, B2 and B3 cells of Workbook 13.3 (W13_3.xls). The required number of years will be returned to B4 as 10.00 years when formatted to two decimal places.

(c) Enter values of 10%, 6000 and 15 to the B1, B2 and B3 cells of Workbook 13.4 (W13_4.xls). The principal that must have been deposited will be returned to B4 as £2400 when formatted to two decimal places.

(d) Enter values of 4000, 10 and 8000 to the B1, B2 and B3 cells of Workbook 13.2 (W13_2.xls). The required simple interest rate will be returned to B4 as 0.1 (10%) when formatted to two decimal places.

## Solution to Exercise 13.2

Enter values of 3000, 7.75% and 20 to the B1, B2 and B3 cells of Workbook 13.5 (W13_5.xls). The compounded amount will be returned to B5 as £13349.56 when formatted to two decimal places.

## Solution to Exercise 13.3

Use the B1:B3 cells of Workbook 13.6 (W13_6.xls) to contain 10000, 20000 and 7 respectively. The compound rate of return being received is calculated in B5 as 0.10409, i.e. 10.409%.

## Solution to Exercise 13.4

Enter values of 3500, 10000 and 5.5% to the B1:B3 cells of Workbook 13.7 (W13_7.xls).

The required number of years will be computed in B5 as 19.6 when formatted to two decimal places.

## Solution to Exercise 13.5

Enter values of 20000, 9.9% and 10 to the B1:B3 cells of Workbook 13.8 (W13_8.xls).

The required principal will be calculated in B5 as £7781.31.

## Solution to Exercise 13.6

Enter the principal of £6000 to the B2 cell, and then copy D1 into E1:K1 to give 10 periods.

Make the number of years for each period equal to 1 by entering 1 to D4 and copying this into E4:K4.

Copy D2 and D5 into E2:K2 and E5:K5.

Next, enter 8% to the B3 cell and 1.05*B3 to the C3 cell. This calculated the increase in the interest rate in the second period.

Finally, copy C3 into D3:K3 to obtain the interest rate in each of the subsequent years.

This completes the model, and the terminal value of the account should be returned to K5 as £15638.07.

## Solution to Exercise 13.7

Use Workbook 13.11 (W13_11.xls) to contain the following values.

In B1: 5000   In B2: 8%   In B3:5.7824

The worksheet will evaluate the terminal amount to be £7806.48.

## Solution to Exercise 13.8

Enter values of 2500, 11.5% and 7 to B1:B3.

The terminal amount when interest is compounded by the second case is returned to C16 as £5591.74, as opposed to the value in C8 of £5356.29 representing annual compounding.

For continuous compounding the terminal amount can be obtained by using any vacant cell of the worksheet to contain

$$=B1*EXP(B2*B3)$$

A value of £5591.74 will be returned when formatted to two decimal places.

## Solution to Exercise 13.9

Enter values of 25% and 365 to the B1 and B2 cells of Workbook 13.14.

The EAR will be calculated in B3 as $0.2839 = 28.39\%$.

## Solution to Exercise 13.10

There is no easy way to solve this problem manually since we require to find $m$ such that

$$0.105 = (1 + 0.1/m)^m$$

and this is not amenable to simple manipulative solution methods.

However, if you use Workbook 13.14 (W13_14.xls) then the Excel Solver can be used.

First, enter the given NAR of 0.1 to the B1 cell.

The target cell is B3 and the target cell value is to be 0.105.

The changing cell is B2 and this must be constrained to be greater than zero.

When these entries and Solver settings are made to the worksheet a result for m = 32 is obtained.

Interest must therefore be compounded 32 times per annum if the nominal annual rate of 10% is to have an equivalent annual rate of 10.5%.

## Solution to Exercise 13.11

We have

$$P = 134.67, \quad t = 5, \quad A_5 = 204.78.$$

Therefore,

$$i = [\ln(204.78/134.67)]/5 = \ln(1.5206)/5 = 0.4191/5$$

0.0838.

The continuously compounded inflation rate for the period was therefore 8.38% per annum.

## Solution to Exercise 13.12

The periodic interest rate is the annual rate in this case, i.e. 9%.

The number of periods is the term plus $1 = 12 + 1 = 13$.

The equal periodic payment is $-5000$.

The present value argument is entered as 0 or omitted.

The future value is to be found immediately after the last deposit has been made, so the Type argument value is 0.

Consequently, we should enter:

$$=FV(9\%,13,-5000,0,0)$$

and obtain a value of £114766.92.

## Solution to Exercise 13.13

The equivalent annual rate must be calculated before the Excel FV function can be used, since payments are annual but interest is compounded monthly.

Therefore, we require

$$EAR = (1 + i/m)^m - 1 = (1 + 0.18/12)^{12} - 1 = 0.1956 = 19.56\%.$$

This can then be used in the FV function as follows.

$$=FV(19.56\%,20,-10000,0,0)$$

A value of £1770040.18 will be obtained.

## Solution to Exercise 13.14

The periodic rate is $18\%/12 = 1.5\%$ per month, and this matches the periodic payments of £50 per month. There are $26(12) = 312$ periods in the term of the annuity, in each of which the payment is £50. Consequently, the structure of the required future value function is:

$$=FV(1.5\%,312,-50,0,0)$$

A result of £343,630.28 for the future value will be returned.

## Solution to Exercise 13.15

First calculate the equivalent annual rate from

$$\text{EAR} = (1 + 0.09/2)^2 - 1 = 0.092025 = 9.2025\%.$$

Then remember that the Type argument should be set to 1 since the future value is to be calculated one year after the last deposit is made. This also means that the FV function performs properly unlike the case when the Type argument value is 0.

The future value can therefore be obtained from

=FV(9.2025%,9,-1000,-5000,1)

This should return a value of £25382.94.

## Solution to Exercise 13.16

First, the equivalent annual rate must be calculated from

$$(1 + 0.15/4)^4 - 1 = 0.15865 = 15.865\%.$$

The answer is then given by the NPER function with the following argument values:

=NPER(15.865%,-6000,0, 306528.05,0)

This should return a value of 15 for the required number of annual payments to be made over a timespan of 14 years.

## Solution to Exercise 13.17

First calculate the equivalent annual rate from

$$(1 + 0.1/12)^{12} - 1 = 0.1047 = 10.47\%.$$

(a)(i)  The answer is obtained from:

=PMT(10.47%,20,-10000,300000,0)

The 20 required annual payments are £3752.46 and this will secure the required annual amount after 19 years (20 payments).

(a)(ii)  All that is needed is to change the last argument value from 0 to 1. Hence,

=PMT(10.47%,20,-10000,300000,1)

The 20 required annual payments are £3396.81 and this will secure the required annual amount after 20 years.

(b)(i)  Change the present value argument from $-10000$ to 0, and then enter:

=PMT(10.47%,20,0,300000,0)

The 20 required annual payments are £4964.96 and this will secure the required annual amount after 19 years.

(b)(ii) Use a present value argument of 0 and a Type argument of 1. Then enter:

$$=PMT(10.47\%,20,0,300000,1)$$

The 20 required annual payments are £4494.39 and this will secure the required annual amount after 20 years.

(c) Change the present value argument to −50000 and set the Type argument to 0. That is,

$$=PMT(10.47\%,20,-50000,300000,0)$$

Now notice that Excel returns a **positive** amount (£1097.54) for this function. This is because the initial account value of £50000 **on its own** will amount to **more than** £300000 after 19 years' compound interest. (The £50000 will be worth £331673.2 to be exact.) Consequently, there is no need to make any annual **payments** to the account in order to secure the target sum. In fact, the value returned by the PMT (£1097.54) function in this case indicates the annual amount that the account can **pay out** and still have a future value of £300000.

## Solution to Exercise 13.18

The answers are obtained from:

(a) =PMT(17%,15,7000,0,0)
A value of £1314.75 should be returned.

(b) =PMT(17%,15,7000,0,1)
A value of £1123.72 should be returned.

# 14 Investment Appraisal

The following files from the online resource centre should be loaded as instructed:

W14_3.xls    W14_4.xls       W14_5A.xls

W14_6.xls    W14_11A.xls

## 14.1 Present value

The ideas of compounding explained in the previous chapter have an important extension in an area known as **discounting**. To understand the issues involved ask the following question:

When is a pound not a pound?

One answer would be:

When it is received at some future date rather than at the present.

What this means is that £1 (or any other amount) that is to be received 10 years from now, is worth less than £1 that is to be received 5 years from now, which is worth less than £1 that is to be received 1 year from now. Only if the funds are received **just now** is their **present** worth the same as their **nominal** worth.

This idea can be stated more formally as follows.

Any two or more **nominally** equal monetary sums must be regarded as **unequal** in current magnitude unless they are received at **exactly** the same time. Furthermore, the current magnitude of these monetary sums is only equal to their nominal magnitude if the funds are received just now.

This explicit introduction of the time dimension to the calculation of the present worth of funds that are to be received at some future date, means that any future sum must have its nominal value modified downwards in order to take account of the reduction in present value caused by the time lapse that exists before the funds are received.

This reduction stems **entirely** from the fact that the recipient of the funds must **wait** for a finite period of time before the money is available to be spent or re-invested, and the reduction in current value compared to nominal value therefore represents the lost interest cost to the individual of having to wait for the funds to be received.

The procedure of modifying nominal values into current values is known as **discounting**, and there are two things that must be understood about it.

First, the word 'discount' is **not used** in the popular sense of the word to mean a reduction in the price paid for an article expressed as a percentage of the higher price. Discounting as used here, *does* mean a systematic reduction in the nominal value of monetary sums, but, as will be seen, it is not done in a simple percentage manner.

Secondly, the cost of having to wait mentioned above has got **nothing** to do with the existence of a positive inflation rate. It is true that if inflation exists, then the penalty of having to wait becomes higher, but this penalty exists whether there is inflation or not, and is to be understood in terms of the interest payments that have to be **given up** as a result of having to wait for the funds to be received.

As in the case of some of our previous analyses, a simple transposition of a basic equation is sufficient to illustrate the basic idea. This is because it will be remembered that the basic compounding formula developed in Chapter 13 stated that

$$A_t = P(1 + i)^t.$$

Now, if a principal of £$P$ amounts to £$A_t$ after $t$ years when the interest rate is given by $i$, it follows that if a sum of £$A_t$ is to be received after $t$ years, then this is equivalent to a principal just now of

$$P = A_t/(1 + i)^t.$$

When this transposition is made, the term $P$ is usually referred to as the **present value** (PV) of the future amount $A_t$ and the $i$ term is known as the **discount rate** (i.e. the interest rate used for discounting purposes). We therefore have:

$$PV = A_t/(1 + i)^t.$$

For example, to find the present value of an amount of £1000 that is to be received in 10 years' time when the interest rate for the period is 10% per annum, we must evaluate

$$PV = 1000/(1 + 0.1)^{10} = 1000/1.1^{10} = £385.54.$$

The implication of this calculation is that an individual would be **indifferent** between the choice of £1000 to be received in 10 years' time, and £385.54 to be received just now. This is because the present sum of £385.54 could be placed on deposit for 10 years

| | A | B | C | D | E | F | G | H | I |
|---|---|---|---|---|---|---|---|---|---|
| 1 | Start value for t | 0 | | | | | | | |
| 2 | Step value for t | 2 | | | | | | | |
| 3 | Future amount | 1000 | | | | | | | |
| 4 | Discount rate % | 0% | 5% | 10% | 15% | 20% | 25% | | |
| 5 | t (periods) | PV | PV | PV | PV | PV | PV | | |
| 6 | 0 | 1000 | 1000.00 | 1000.00 | 1000.00 | 1000.00 | 1000.00 | | |
| 7 | 2 | 1000 | 907.03 | 826.45 | 756.14 | 694.44 | 640.00 | | |
| 8 | 4 | 1000 | 822.70 | 683.01 | 571.75 | 482.25 | 409.60 | | |
| 9 | 6 | 1000 | 746.22 | 564.47 | 432.33 | 334.90 | 262.14 | | |
| 10 | 8 | 1000 | 676.84 | 466.51 | 326.90 | 232.57 | 167.77 | | |
| 11 | 10 | 1000 | 613.91 | 385.54 | 247.18 | 161.51 | 107.37 | | |
| 12 | 12 | 1000 | 556.84 | 318.63 | 186.91 | 112.16 | 68.72 | | |
| 13 | 14 | 1000 | 505.07 | 263.33 | 141.33 | 77.89 | 43.98 | | |
| 14 | 16 | 1000 | 458.11 | 217.63 | 106.86 | 54.09 | 28.15 | | |
| 15 | 18 | 1000 | 415.52 | 179.86 | 80.81 | 37.56 | 18.01 | | |
| 16 | 20 | 1000 | 376.89 | 148.64 | 61.10 | 26.08 | 11.53 | | |
| 17 | 22 | 1000 | 341.85 | 122.85 | 46.20 | 18.11 | 7.38 | | |
| 18 | 24 | 1000 | 310.07 | 101.53 | 34.93 | 12.58 | 4.72 | | |

| ◄ ◄ ► ►| \ **Sheet1** / Sheet2 / Sheet3 / Sheet4 / Sheet5 / She | ◄ |

**Workbook 14.1**

at the 10% compound interest rate and would eventually amount to

$$385.54(1.1)^{10} = £1000.$$

As has already been said, the **further** into the future a given sum is to be received, then the **less** is its present value for any given discount rate.

*This can be confirmed by preparing a worksheet similar to Workbook 14.1.*

*Do this now.*

The crucial formula is contained in B6:

=$B$3/((1+B$4)^$A6))

*Now copy this formula down the sheet to show how the present values change as the number of periods increases and then copy the whole block in B6:B8 along the sheet to show how the present values change as the discount rate increases*

The results shown in Workbook 14.1 should be obtained.

Furthermore, when the A4:G18 range is graphed as an XY scatter graph using the first two rows for the legend text, Figure 14.1 is produced.

*Prepare this graph now and when you have finished save the file as* **W14_1.xls.**

Clearly, as the time before the funds are received increases, the present value of any given amount decreases, and this decrease in present value is greater, the greater is the discount rate.

Figure 14.1 also shows that there is one special case when present and future values are the same—namely, when the discount rate is **zero.** This should be intuitively obvious since if no interest is paid on deposited funds then there is no penalty involved in having to wait for the funds to be received.

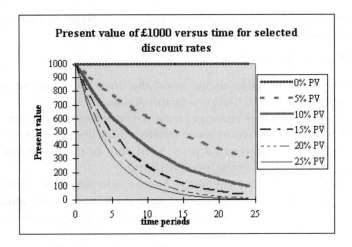

**Figure 14.1**

*Exercise 14.1 can be attempted now.*

## 14.2 **Discounting multiple amounts**

The ideas involved in the basic notion of discounting can of course be extended to situations in which there is **more than one** future payment. In this respect, consider the following example.

Imagine a situation in which a sum of £1000 was to be received just now, and after 1 year, and after 2 years and after 3 years. Also assume that the interest rate is 14% per annum compounded annually. What is the present value of this **stream** of income receipts?

To answer this question notice that the £1000 that is received just now simply has a present value of £1000 (i.e. its nominal worth), while the receipt of £1000 that is to be received in one year's time has a present value of £1000/(1.14) = £877.19.

By a similar logic the final two receipts will have present values of £1000/(1.14)$^2$ = £769.47 (for the receipt after 2 years) and £1000/(1.14)$^3$ = £674.97 (for the receipt after 3 years).

Consequently, the combined present value of all four income receipts (i.e. the present value of the entire income stream) must be given by:

$$£1000 + £877.19 + £769.47 + £674.97 = £3321.63.$$

What this means is, that with an annual interest rate of 14%, a lump sum payment just now of £3321.63 is equivalent to an income stream of four annual receipts of £1000 with the first receipt being received immediately and the remaining equal receipts of £1000 being received after 1, 2 and 3 years respectively.

In other words, £3321.63 is the present value of the stream of four equal annual receipts of £1000 when the first receipt is received just now.

*Exercise 14.2 can be attempted now.*

Now, a moment's consideration should reveal that there are numerous savings and pension schemes available which use exactly this notion.

For example, suppose that in exchange for a specified (but as yet unknown) lump sum payment just now, a savings scheme guaranteed to provide five payments of £5000 after 1 year, 2 years, 3 years, 4 years and 5 years. What must be the size of this lump sum payment if the interest rate over the period is 12.5%?

Clearly the answer to this question can be obtained by finding the present value of the guaranteed income stream, since no rational saver would agree to pay **more** than this present value as the initial lump sum payment required to secure the specified income stream.

Similarly, no rational borrower would be willing to accept **less** than the present value of the income stream as the initial payment.

In either case, the size of the initial payment would differ from the present value of the income stream that the initial payment was designed to secure.

This initial lump sum payment must therefore be equal to the present value of the secured income stream, which is given by

$$5000/1.125 + 5000/1.125^2 + 5000/1.125^3 + 5000/1.125^4 + 5000/1.125^5 = £17802.84.$$

From what we have done it should be clear that we can derive a general expression for the present value of any given income stream of £$R$ per annum, receivable at the end of each of $t$ years, when the interest rate is $i(= r/100)\%$ per annum.

Assuming that the first income receipt is received a year from now this would be

$$PV = R/(1+i) + R/(1+i)^2 + \cdots + R/(1+i)^t.$$

Of course, it is possible that the first receipt in an income stream is actually received **just now**, in which case the last expression becomes

$$PV = R/(1+i)^0 + R/(1+i)^1 + R/(1+i)^2 + \cdots + R/(1+i)^t,$$

where, of course, $R/(1+i)^0 = R$.

Clearly, if several years are involved, then these calculations although arithmetically simple can become extremely tedious. This is where Excel can help with its dedicated present value function, the general syntax of which is

= PV(Interest rate,Number of periods,Equal periodic amount,*Futurevalue,*

*Year start or end*)

where, as usual, optional arguments have been italicized.

Consequently, to reproduce the answer obtained in the last illustration (£17802.84) we can identify the following arguments of the Excel PV function:

Interest rate = 12.5%,

Number of periods = 5,

Equal periodic amount = 5000,

Future value = 0, since it is an optional argument that is not relevant to the current discussion.

Year-start or year-end = 0. This is a simple **switch** argument—enter 0 or omit the argument if the payments or receipts occur at the **end** of the period, or enter 1 if they occur at the **start** of the period. In the worked illustration the first receipt of £5000 was to be received after one year, i.e. at the end of the period, and so a value of 0 should be used in this case.

Taken together, these figures mean that the PV function should be specified as:

$$=PV(12.5\%,5,5000,0,0)$$

*Enter this now to any vacant cell of a workbook and confirm that the present value of this stream of income is £17802.84.*

Also notice that Excel in fact returns the present value as a negative amount. This is because the constant amounts were positive, representing receipts as opposed to outgoings (in which case they should be entered as negative amounts). This means that the calculated present value represents the **negative** amount that would have to be laid out just now in order to secure the specified future stream of positive receipts.

Now suppose that the scheme illustrated promised an **immediate** return of £5000, followed by a further four returns of £5000 after 1, 2, 3 and 4 years.

The effect of this alteration to the problem is to bring the **whole** stream of payments **forward** by one year.

Consequently the present value would be given by

$$PV = 5000/1.125^0 + 5000/1.125^1 + 5000/1.125^2 + 5000/1.125^3 + 5000/1.125^4$$
$$= £20028.20.$$

To reproduce this result in Excel all that needs to be done is to alter the last argument of the previous PV function from 0 to 1.

*Do this now and confirm that the correct answer (£20028.20) is obtained.*

*Exercise 14.3 can be attempted now.*

Before leaving the Excel PV function, the role of the optional fourth argument (future value) should be explained.

Consider a savings scheme that, in exchange for a lump sum payment just now of £3000 promises to pay four equal annual amounts of £600 after 1, 2, 3 and 4 years. Additionally, however, a terminal bonus of £1000 is paid along with the last payment of £600.

If the interest rate for the period is 9% per annum compounded annually, calculate the present value of the scheme.

This problem differs from the previous illustrations in the sense that the payments (including the terminal bonus) are not all **equal**, and so the PV function is not immediately applicable.

However, if we regard the problem in terms of the present value of the following income stream, then a solution can be obtained:

$$\text{PV} = 600/1.09 + 600/1.09^2 + 600/1.09^3 + 600/1.09^4 + 1000/1.09^4 = £2652.26.$$

Clearly this is simply the present value of the four equal receipts of £600 plus the present value of the 'one-off' payment of £1000 received after 4 years.

In terms of the PV function this one-off payment is regarded as the **future value** argument.

*Consequently, make the following entry to a blank cell of a worksheet.*

=PV(9%,4,600,1000,0)

The answer obtained above (£2652.26) should be returned, and represents the amount of the lump sum payment that has to be laid out just now in order to secure the given stream of equal annual amounts, **plus** the one-off terminal bonus.

The result of this discussion is that the optional future value argument in the PV function is to be used if the stream of constant amounts also contains **one (and only one)** additional and perhaps different amount that accrues with the last constant amount.

Furthermore, since, in the illustration, a lump sum of £3000 was required to be laid out just now in order to secure a future stream of income with a present value of £2652.26, it can be deduced that the savings scheme offered is less attractive than simply placing the £3000 on deposit at the prevailing interest rate of 9%. This is because the savings scheme is equivalent to giving away £3000 just now in exchange for a return of £2652.26 received just now, in other words, a **net present** giveaway of £347.74.

Finally, the future value argument can also be used to allow calculation of the present value of a **single** future amount simply by setting the equal periodic amount to zero and using the single future amount as the future value argument.

For example, earlier in this chapter the present value of a **single** payment of £1000 to be received in 10 years' time when the discount rate was 10% per annum was calculated as £385.54 (i.e. $1000/1.1^{10}$).

*Confirm that this result could also be obtained from*

=PV(10%,10,0,1000,0)

*Exercise 14.4 can be attempted now.*

## 14.3 Variations in the discounting period

It will have been noticed that the foregoing discussion has only considered situations in which interest is discounted on an **annual** basis. Yet, as was the case with compounding, account should be taken of situations in which interest is discounted **more frequently** than once per year.

For example, consider an amount of £2000 that is to be received 5 years from now. If the current interest rate is 7% compounded annually, then the present value of this amount is easily obtained from

$$PV = 2000/(1.07^5) = £1425.97$$

or, in Excel from,

**=PV(7%,5,0,2000,0)**

Now suppose that the interest rate of 7% per annum was compounded half-yearly. Then, in the same way that any sum deposited just now would be worth **more** after a given number of years than under annual compounding, any sum received in the same given number of years will be worth **less** than if annual discounting prevailed. To be exact:

$$PV = 2000/(1 + 0.07/2)^{5(2)} = 2000/(1.035^{10}) = £1417.83.$$

The figure above results from the fact that there are now 10 discounting periods in each of which the interest rate is 3.5%.

By a similar logic, if interest were compounded quarterly, monthly, weekly or daily, then the present values would be given by:

Quarterly:

$$PV = 2000/(1 + 0.07/4)^{5(4)} = 2000(1.00875^{20}) = £1413.65.$$

Monthly:

$$PV = 2000/(1 + 0.07/12)^{5(12)} = 2000(1.00583^{60}) = £1410.81.$$

Weekly:

$$PV = 2000/(1 + 0.07/52)^{5(52)} = 2000(1.00135^{260}) = £1409.70.$$

Daily:

$$PV = 2000/(1 + 0.07/365)^{5(365)} = 2000(1.00019^{1825}) = £1409.42.$$

Inspection of the pattern in these results should now suggest that if some future amount (A) is to be received in $t$ years' time when the interest rate is $i = r/100\%$ per annum, compounded $m$ times per annum, the present value will be given by

$$PV = A/(1 + i/m)^{mt} = A(1 + i/m)^{-mt}.$$

That is, the present value is to be viewed in terms of $m$ times $t$ periods in each of which the interest rate is $i/m$.

Phrased in these terms, it should now be clear how the PV function can be adapted to take account of variations in the compounding period.

Hence, the semi-annual, quarterly, monthly, weekly and daily discounted amounts produced above would be obtained from the following versions of the Excel present value function.

*Confirm these results now in your own worksheet.*

Semi-annual      =PV(7%/2,5*2,0,2000,0)
Quarterly          =PV(7%/4,5*4,0,2000,0)

| | A | B | C | D | E | F | G |
|---|---|---|---|---|---|---|---|
| 1 | Single future amount | 2000 | | | | | |
| 2 | Annual discount rate | 7% | | | | | |
| 3 | Number of years | 5 | | | | | |
| 4 | Number of compounding periods per annum | 12 | | | | | |
| 5 | Total number of compounding periods | 60 | | | | | |
| 6 | Interest rate per compounding period | 0.00583333 | | | | | |
| 7 | | | | | | | |
| 8 | Present value | -£1,410.810 | | | | | |
| 9 | | | | | | | |
| 10 | | | | | | | |

Sheet1 / Sheet2 / Sheet3 / Sheet4 / Sheet5 / She

**Workbook 14.2**

| Monthly | =PV(7%/12,5*12,0,2000,0) |
|---|---|
| Weekly | =PV(7%/52,5*52,0,2000,0) |
| Daily | =PV(7%/365,5*3652,0,2000,0) |

Furthermore, it is an easy matter to write a more general version of the present value function that will never need editing for any variations in the compounding period.

This is shown in Workbook 14.2.

*Make this up now.*

The entries in B1:B4 are the given data of the problem and are therefore entered directly. The value in B5 is obtained from

$$=B3*B4$$

which is the number of years of the investment times the number of compounding periods in the year.

The value in B6 is the discount rate per compounding period and is obtained from

$$=B2/B4$$

Finally, the present value is calculated in B8 from

$$=PV(B6,B5,0,B1,0)$$

*Now use this model to confirm the results that were obtained above by making successive alterations to the value in B4.*

As was the case with compounding, the effect of increasing the frequency with which interest is discounted, is at first quite dramatic, but eventually exercises an almost negligible additional effect. Clearly the expression for the present value is approaching some **limit** as the frequency of discounting increases.

Now it should be remembered that as compounding became effectively continuous (i.e. as the number of compounding periods ($m$) tended to infinity), the expression

$$A_t = P(1 + i/m)^t \quad \text{tended towards } Pe^{it}.$$

By a similar logic we would therefore expect that the equivalent discounting expression,

$$PV_t = A/(1 + i/m)^{mt} \quad \text{would tend towards } A/e^{it}.$$

This is indeed correct, and is the discounting equivalent of continuous compounding. That is, if an interest rate of $i$ is discounted $m$ times per annum, then the present value of an amount of £$A$ to be received $t$ years from now is given by

$$PV_t = A/(1 + i/m)^{mt} \quad \text{which tends towards} A/e^{it} \text{as} m \text{tends to infinity.}$$

Using the figures from our last illustration, this means that with continuous discounting we would obtain

$$PV = 2000/e^{0.07(5)} = 2000/e^{0.35} = £1409.376.$$

This figure is, of course, almost identical to the one obtained on the basis of daily discounting (£1409.42).

*Confirm this now in Workbook 14.2 by imagining that the annual interest rate was discounted by the second. There are therefore 365(24)(60)(60) = 31536000 periods of 1 second in a year. So enter this value to the B4 cell and the present value will be computed as 1409.376 (when formatted to three decimal places).*

Clearly the difference between continuous discounting and discounting every second can only be observed if more than three decimal places are used.

*Exercise 14.5 can be attempted now.*

Now, in just the same way as continuous compounding was used to model growth processes that did not fall into discrete accounting patterns (population growth etc.) continuous discounting should be used to calculate the present value of such processes.

For example, suppose that a forestry enterprise has planted an area of young trees that is expected to have a value of £10 million in 15 years' time. If the value of usable wood is believed to grow at a **continuous** exponential rate of 4% per annum, calculate the present value of the tree plantation.

To answer this, note that since growth is taken to be at an exponential rate of 4% per annum we have:

$$PV = 10/e^{0.04(15)} = 10/e^{0.6} = £5.48 \text{ million.}$$

As a final point in this section it should now be shown how the Excel present value function can be used in situations where there are a series of equal periodic payments or receipts, but where these periods are **not necessarily** of one year.

For example, suppose that in order to buy a car, an individual agrees to a loan with the following scheme of repayments.

Twenty-four monthly repayments of £200, with the first repayment being made in one month's time.

If the annual interest rate is 12% compounded monthly, calculate the size of the sum borrowed.

To answer this question we note that the monthly interest rate is 12%/12 = 1%, and that over the term of the debt there are a total of 24 monthly periods. Consequently we

require

$$=PV(1\%,24,-200,0,0)$$

*Now confirm that this evaluates to £4248.68 as the sum that was borrowed.*

 A generic worksheet model that can solve problems of this type is on the online resource centre in the file called W14_3.xls.

*Load this now and study its structure.*

*Exercise 14.6 can be attempted now.*

## 14.4 Net present value

The techniques illustrated above have important applications in any attempt to evaluate the relative merits of financial projects that yield **differing** returns at different points in time.

For example, consider a firm that is trying to decide whether to purchase a new machine with an initial cost of £10000. Suppose also, that this machine is expected to provide revenue of £6000 at the end of both its first and second years of use. Thereafter, the machine is scrapped **without** any scrap value.

If the market interest rate is 12% per annum, compounded annually, does this machine represent a viable investment?

It should be clear that the stream of income furnished by the machine must be brought back to the present so that it can be compared with the current cost of £10000. Consequently, we must evaluate

$$PV = 6000/(1.12) + 6000/(1.12^2) = £10140.30.$$

This figure, representing the value **just now** of the **future** stream of income from the machine, must be compared with the cost of £10000 that must be laid out just now in order to produce the income stream. Consequently, we can form the difference between the present value of the income stream and the initial cost, to obtain a figure that is known as the **net present value** (NPV). That is,

$$NPV = PV - C,$$

where $C$ represents the initial cost of the machine.

Now, in our example, the NPV is £140.30(£10140.30 − £10000) and since this figure is **positive** we would recommend that that the machine be purchased in preference to the alternative available—with that alternative being to place the funds on deposit at the going market rate of interest of 12%.

This means that the implication of a positive (negative) NPV is that the project being appraised provides an implied rate of return that is greater (less) than the currently available market rate of return.

To see this, imagine that the funds had been placed on deposit for two years at the prevailing rate of 12% per annum (compounded annually). The amount accruing after 2 years is easily calculated as

$$£10000(1.12)^2 = £12544.00.$$

Now this raises an apparent difficulty in the light of our declared preference for the project, since simple arithmetic suggests that the machine will provide a terminal sum of £6000 + £6000 = £12000, which is **less** than the £12544 that could have been obtained from the bank.

Yet this is to forget that the first return of £6000 from the machine occurs after 1 year and is therefore available to be **placed on deposit** at the going market rate (which is assumed to be 12%).

When this is done the terminal value of the returns from the machine is calculated to be

$$£6000(1.12) + £6000 = £12720.00.$$

This figure exceeds the terminal value that would have been obtained from the bank by £176.00, thereby confirming our conclusion that purchasing the machine is a superior financial project to the alternative use of the funds.

A problem arises, however, when we attempt to **measure** this superiority. This is because we have two apparently conflicting measures. On the one hand, on the basis of the net present value calculation, the machine appears to be £140.30 superior to a 12% rate of return, whereas on the other hand, when viewed at the **end** of the period, this superiority has also been calculated to be £176.00.

In fact, there is no conflict here, since it should be clear that a **terminal** superiority of £176.00 is identical to a **current** superiority of £140.30 if the current market rate of interest is 12%. This is because the present value of £176.00, discounted at 12% for 2 years is £140.32.

The net result of this discussion is twofold.

First, the net present value technique assumes that the incoming funds are placed on deposit at the going market rate **immediately** they become available.

Second, the net present value figure gives the **current** net superiority of the project being appraised, in comparison with the rate of return available from the alternative uses of the funds. This last rate of return is the figure to be used as the discount rate in the net present value calculations, and will usually be taken as the current market rate of interest.

Excel can carry out net present value calculations with its NPV function, the general syntax of which is:

= NPV(discount rate,Range of amounts from year 1 onwards) + Initial cost

*For example, to reproduce the result from the last example, make the following entries to a blank worksheet.*

*In A1:A5 enter the labels:*

Initial Cost   First return   Second return   Discount rate   Net present value

*Then in B1:B4 enter the values:*

−10000   6000   6000   12%

*Finally in B5 calculate the NPV from the formula*

$$=NPV(B4,B2:B3)+B1$$

The previously obtained result of £140.30 should be returned.

Notice how Excel has been forced to obtain the present value of the year-1 and year-2 receipts and then add on the (negative) initial cost at its nominal value.

This means that correct usage of the NPV function requires that the stream of returns from year 1 onwards are entered in the range specified in the second argument. The first element in this range should always be the receipt to be received one year from now, and the last element in the range should always be the last receipt. All cost items should be entered as negative terms, but initial (i.e. immediately incurred) costs (as opposed to recurring costs) should not be entered in the second argument of the function. Rather, they are added on at their nominal worth outside the NPV function.

Also notice that the crucial distinction between the PV function and the NPV function is that the former can **only** calculate the present value of a stream of **equal** amounts and a single terminal amount (future value). The NPV function, on the other hand, does not require that the amounts **are all equal**.

As might be imagined, the net present value figure obtained for any problem is highly dependent upon the discount rate that is used. This can be seen more clearly in Workbook 14.4 where the NPV for the last example has been calculated for a variety of discount rates.

*Load workbook (W14_4.xls) now and study the formulae in D2:D14.*

When the results are graphed Figure 14.2 is obtained.

As should be clear, the NPV declines steadily as the discount rate increases, and becomes negative for rates in excess of about 13%. This is an important point, since it

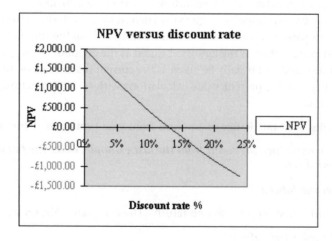

**Figure 14.2**

indicates the **threshold** value of the discount rate that will make viable projects non-viable. In this sense, as will be seen in the next section, the value of the discount rate that makes the value of NPV = 0 can be interpreted as a measure of the **rate of return** being supplied by the project.

The full power of the NPV function in saving calculation time can be appreciated in the following example.

A power station is to be constructed just now at an initial capital cost of £100 million. Its expected useful lifetime is 16 years, and during this time it is expected to produce an average of one million megawatt-hours (MWh) per annum. The operational costs of the power station are estimated to be £10 million per annum in its first year of operation, and these are expected to increase at an average rate of 6% over the power station's operational life.

The electricity produced is sold at a price of £25 per MWh in its first year of operation, but this price will be raised at an annual rate of 4% per annum.

Assuming that all costs and revenues (apart from the initial capital cost) accrue at the end of each operational year and that the company employs a discount rate of 15%, calculate the net present value of the project and comment on its financial viability.

The cash flows are indicated in Workbook 14.5.

*Make up this model now in line with explanation below.*

Three formulae have been used to generate the cost, revenue and net income entries. These are:

In B4: =B3*(1.06) which is then copied into the cells B5:B18.

In C4:=C3*(1.04) which is then copied into the range C4:C18.

In D2:=C2+B2 which is then copied to the range D4:D18.

| | A | B | C | D | E | F | G | H | I | J |
|---|---|---|---|---|---|---|---|---|---|---|
| 1 | Year | Costs | Revenue | Net income | NPV | | | | | |
| 2 | 0 | -100 | | -100 | £0.84 | | | | | |
| 3 | 1 | -10 | 25 | 15 | | | | | | |
| 4 | 2 | -10.6 | 26 | 15.4 | | | | | | |
| 5 | 3 | -11.236 | 27.04 | 15.804 | | | | | | |
| 6 | 4 | -11.9102 | 28.1216 | 16.21144 | | | | | | |
| 7 | 5 | -12.6248 | 29.24646 | 16.6216944 | | | | | | |
| 8 | 6 | -13.3823 | 30.41632 | 17.03406678 | | | | | | |
| 9 | 7 | -14.1852 | 31.63298 | 17.44778434 | | | | | | |
| 10 | 8 | -15.0363 | 32.89829 | 17.86199189 | | | | | | |
| 11 | 9 | -15.9385 | 34.21423 | 18.27574551 | | | | | | |
| 12 | 10 | -16.8948 | 35.5828 | 18.68800572 | | | | | | |
| 13 | 11 | -17.9085 | 37.00611 | 19.09763016 | | | | | | |
| 14 | 12 | -18.983 | 38.48635 | 19.50336582 | | | | | | |
| 15 | 13 | -20.122 | 40.02581 | 19.90384075 | | | | | | |
| 16 | 14 | -21.3293 | 41.62684 | 20.29755508 | | | | | | |
| 17 | 15 | -22.609 | 43.29191 | 20.68287163 | | | | | | |
| 18 | 16 | -23.9656 | 45.02359 | 21.05800571 | | | | | | |
| 19 | | | | | | | | | | |

Sheet1 / Sheet2 / Sheet3 / Sheet4 / Sheet5 / She

**Workbook 14.5**

Finally, the NPV is calculated from the formula in E2 as

$$=NPV(15\%,D3:D18)+D2$$

Since the NPV is positive (£0.84 million) this means that the power station is supplying a rate of return in excess of the 15% discount rate that was applied to the project. Assuming that 15% is the best alternative rate of return that can be achieved, then building and operating the power station is the superior use of the funds.

*Exercises 14.7 and 14.8 can be attempted now.*

Up until now the NPV technique has only been used to compare the benefits of carrying out a **single** project with the alternative of placing the funds on deposit at the going market rate of interest (the discount rate). However, it will often be the case that the NPV approach will be of value in allowing rational choices to be made between two or more **alternative projects**. For example, suppose that in the last illustration there had been an alternative type of power station available with its own different initial and recurring costs (the output and revenue stream can be assumed to be the same).

These new cost data have been added to Workbook 14.5A along with some labels to identify the power stations as A and B.

*Now load the workbook (W14_5A.xls).*

The NPV for power station B has been calculated in H3 from the formula

$$=NPV(15\%,F4:F19)+F3$$

As can be seen, the NPV for power station B is greater than that for station A and so, **if only one of the power stations is to be built** it should be station B—because of its greater NPV. However, although B is superior to A at the 15% discount rate that was employed, it does not **necessarily** follow that B will **always** be superior to A at **all** discount rates.

To see whether this is the case we should evaluate the NPV values of both projects over a range of different discount rates.

This has been done in the J1:L22 range of Workbook 14.5A for discount rates between 0% and 20% in steps of 1%. Furthermore, when these data are graphed, Figure 14.3 is produced.

As is clear from this diagram the NPV values of the two stations **cross over** at a discount rate of about 14%. For discount rates less than this, station A is superior to station B, while for discount rates in excess of 14% station B is superior to station A.

This said, however, it is also clear that the superiority of station B at discount rates in excess of 14% is only a **viable superiority** for discount rates that are less than roughly 16%. In other words, both projects have negative NPVs for discount rates in excess of about 16% and so neither is really viable in comparison with placing the funds on deposit at a going rate of about 16%.

*Exercise 14.9 can be attempted now.*

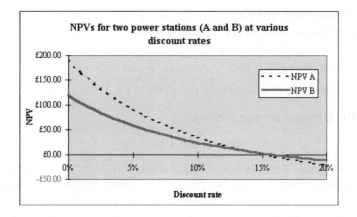

**Figure 14.3**

## 14.5 The internal rate of return

If we now reconsider the machine example of the previous section, then it will be remembered that it was shown that with a discount rate of 12% the NPV of the project was £140.32. Now this must surely mean that the implied rate of return on this project was somewhat in excess of 12%, otherwise the net present value would be zero.

Nevertheless, 'somewhat in excess of 12%' is not a sufficiently exact statement, so the question arises of how to obtain an **exact** figure for the implied rate of return provided by the project.

The answer to this question is supplied by a concept known as the **internal rate of return** (IRR), which defined as that rate of return ($i$), which, if used as the discount rate, would make the NPV of the project exactly equal to 0. In other words:

$$\text{IRR} = i \quad \text{such that PV} - C = 0.$$

If we apply this idea to the machine illustration then we are required to find
$i$ such that:

$$6000/(1 + i) + 6000/(1 + i)^2 - 10000 = 0.$$

This should be recognized as a quadratic equation which has two solutions: $i = 0.1306$ or $-1.5306$, and when we ignore the meaningless negative solution we have:

$$\text{IRR} = i = 0.1306 \quad (\text{i.e.}13.06\%).$$

This confirms our earlier statement that the IRR would be 'somewhat in excess of 12%'. You can also confirm that this is indeed the IRR by substituting a value of $i = 0.1306$ into the NPV expression, whereupon you will find that the NPV does in fact become zero. This will only be the case for the data in our example if $i = 0.1306$. That is,

$$6000/(1.1306) + 6000/(1.1306^2) - 10000 = 0.$$

As a further illustration of this concept consider the following example.

Find the internal rate of return of the following cost and income stream: an initial expenditure of £12000, followed by revenue of £8000 after 1 year and revenue of £6000 after 2 years.

To do this we require $i$ such that

$$PV - C = NPV = 8000/(1+i) + 6000/(1+i)^2 - 12,000 = 0,$$

which has the following positive solution:

$$i = 0.11506 = 11.506\%.$$

There are, however, a number of potential difficulties with the IRR technique when more difficult problems are considered. In particular, where the costs and/or revenues are spread over more than two years, then solving for $i$ involves finding the solution of difficult equations. Fortunately, Excel has a dedicated internal rate of return function called IRR which, provided we recognize its limitations, can eliminate these computational difficulties.

The structure of the IRR function is

$$= IRR(\text{Range of outgoings and receipts,Guess})$$

This means that on the basis of a (preferably realistic) guess of the IRR, the Excel IRR function will calculate the internal rate of return of the range of costs and revenues entered as the first argument. This range should be constructed so that initial costs precede first-year costs and revenues, which in turn should precede second-year costs and revenues etc. Once again, costs should be entered as negative items and revenues as positive items.

The results of the last illustration can now be confirmed.

*To do this take a blank worksheet and make the following entries.*

*In A1:A4 enter the labels:*

    Initial Cost   First year Revenue   Second year Revenue   Internal Rate of Return

*Then in B1:B3 enter the values:*

$$-12000 \quad 8000 \quad 6000$$

*Finally in B4 enter the formula.*

$$=IRR(0.1,B1..B3)$$

It will be found that the previously obtained result (11.506%) for the IRR is returned to B4.

*Now use the IRR function to find the internal rate of return of the stream of costs and revenues associated with the two power stations example from the last section. To do this load Workbook 14.5A and use G4 and H4 to contain the labels:*

       IRR station A   and   IRR station B

*Then use G5 and H5 to contain the formulae:*

=IRR(E3:E19,0.1)   and   =IRR(F3:F19,0.1)

Results of 15.16% and 15.91% will be obtained.

As was hinted at earlier, however, there are limitations upon the validity of the IRR under certain **patterns** of cash flows. In particular, an unambiguous result will only be obtained from any Excel IRR calculation if the signs of the net cash flows correspond to one of the following patterns:

(a) $-+++$, i.e. costs just now, revenues later.

(b) $--++++$, i.e. costs just now and after 1 period, revenues thereafter.

(c) $-++++++-$, i.e. costs just now and at the end of the project, revenues in between.

If the actual pattern of net cash flows does not correspond to one of these forms then the IRR as calculated can often be ambiguous and even misleading.

Furthermore, in complex problems spanning several years the IRR as calculated by Excel is sensitive to the initial guess. For this reason it is always advisable to try several guesses to see if the calculated IRR changes.

*Exercises 14.10, 14.11 and 14.12 can be attempted now.*

## 14.6 **The annual percentage rate**

The notion of the annual percentage rate (APR) as frequently quoted in credit terms stems from the idea that if each of the stream of repayments needed to repay a given debt are **not on the same time basis** as quoted in the nominal rate of interest, then the **effective** rate of interest will differ from this nominal rate.

As will be seen, the APR is very closely related to the IRR concept, but before we make this association explicit consider the following illustration.

A lender quotes a **flat rate** of 10% per annum, and requires that a debt of £5000 is to be repaid in two equal annual instalments with the first repayment being made one year from now. The fact that it is a **flat rate** that has been quoted has two important implications. First, it means that the repayments are not treated on a reducing balance basis. Secondly, it means that interest is calculated on a **simple** rather than a **compound** basis. This means that the total interest on the debt is calculated to be $0.1(5000) = £500$ for each of the two years for which the debt is outstanding. This gives a total interest requirement of £1000 and a total debt to be repaid of $£5000 + £1000 = £6000$.

From this it is easy to see that two annual instalments of £3000 are needed to repay the debt plus interest.

Now, if the first repayment is to be made in one years' time, and if the second is to be made in 2 years' time, then we can calculate the annual **compound** percentage rate of interest that will make the present value of this stream of repayments **exactly** equal to the sum that was borrowed. In other words, we can solve for $i$ in the following expression:

$$3000/(1 + i) + 3000/(1 + i)^2 = 5000.$$

Now the similarity with the IRR concept should be clear, since this last expression can be solved for $i$ by using the Excel IRR function.

*Do this now in any cell of a blank worksheet and confirm that a value of 13.06% is obtained.*

This figure is called the **annual percentage rate** (APR), and in the context of the illustration indicates that the quoted flat rate of 10% is **in fact** equivalent to an effective compound rate that is slightly in excess of 13%.

Several points are worth noting about the APR:

(a) Like the IRR it is frequently difficult to calculate, and subject to the same reservations when complex loan arrangements are considered.

(b) If the repayments on the debt are made on an annual reducing balance basis, then the APR and the nominal rate are the same. To see this, suppose that a debt of £5000 is to be repaid in two equal annual instalments on a reducing balance basis. If the nominal interest rate is 10% compounded annually, then the Excel PMT function will calculate the required repayments to be:

$$=PMT(0.1,2,5000) = -£2880.95.$$

*Confirm this now.*

In other words, two equal annual payments of £2880.95 are needed to pay off the £5000 debt after 2 years—with the first repayment being made one year from now.

Now, since these repayments have been said to be on a reducing balance basis, and since it is assumed that the first payment will be made after 1 year, the APR on this debt can be found from calculating the value of $i$ such that

$$2880.95/(1 + i) + 2880.95/(1 + i)^2 = 5000.$$

*Now confirm in the current worksheet that the IRR for this expression is 10%.*

This shows that equal annual repayments on an annual reducing balance basis at a nominal annual interest rate of $i$ represent the only situation in which the calculated APR is the same as the quoted nominal rate.

Of course, very few debts are actually repaid on an annual basis, as anyone who has a mortgage or a bank loan will appreciate. In these cases **monthly** repayments tend to be the norm, and this means that any quoted annual rate (even if repayments are on a reducing balance basis) will **not** represent the APR unless the repayments are **also annual**. This can be seen in the following two examples.

Suppose that the following credit terms are offered by a kitchen unit manufacturer for one of its range of kitchen units.

| | |
|---|---|
| SPECIAL CREDIT OFFER    3% INTEREST | (APR = 5.65%) |
| UNIT LIST PRICE | £3637.82 |
| LIST PRICE LESS 25% DEPOSIT | £2728.37 |
| FIRST YEAR'S INTEREST (3% FLAT) | £81.85 |
| SECOND YEAR'S INTEREST (3% FLAT) | £81.85 |
| TOTAL DEBT PLUS INTEREST | £2892.07 |
| NUMBER OF MONTHLY INSTALMENTS | 24 |
| MONTHLY REPAYMENTS (2892.07/24) | £120.50 |

The question that needs to be addressed is how a flat rate of 3% becomes equivalent to an APR of 5.65%, and the answer derives from finding the value of $i$ such that

$$2728.37 = 120.5/(1+i) + 120.5/(1+i)^2 + \ldots + 120.5(1+i)^{24}.$$

*To solve this on Excel use A1 to contain the total debt (2728.37) and then A2:A25 to contain the 24 monthly repayments (−120.5).*

*Now use A26 to contain:*

**=IRR(A1:A25,0.1)**

A result of 0.4713% will be obtained when formatted to four decimal places.

However, since the repayments are monthly, this last figure is the **monthly** rate and so to obtain the APR it must be multiplied by 12 to obtain 5.65% per annum.

As another example, suppose that a £30000 mortgage is taken out over 25 years at a guaranteed nominal rate of 13% per annum. The repayments on this debt are made monthly, but the debt is serviced on an annual reducing balance basis. The task is to calculate the size of the monthly repayments and the APR on this debt.

*To do this open a new workbook and in B1 enter*

**=PMT(0.13,25,30000)**

This will evaluate to −£4092.77, and implies that 25 equal annual repayments of this amount are required to repay the mortgage.

Consequently, the **monthly** repayments are:

$$4092.77/12 = -£341.06.$$

The APR on this debt is $i$ such that

$$30000 = 341.06/(1+i) + 341.06(1+i)^2 + \cdots + 341.06(1+i)^{300}.$$

*Accordingly, enter the sum borrowed in A1 and the 300 repayments of **£341.06** as negative items in A2..A301. Then in B2 enter.*

**=IRR(A1:A301,0.01)**

A value of 1.0933% will be returned and so the APR on this debt is 12(1.0933%) = 13.1198% per annum, and exceeds the nominal rate (13%) for no other reason than the fact that the repayments are made on a **monthly** basis while the outstanding balance of the debt is only **reduced annually**.

*Exercise 14.13 can be attempted now*

## 14.7 Exercises

### Exercise 14.1

Use Workbook 14.1 to indicate how the present value of £500 varies over a period of 12 years at discount rates of 1%, 2%, 4%, 8%, 16% and 32% respectively.

### Exercise 14.2

Use Workbook 14.1 to calculate the present value of £2000 to be received at the end of each of the next 5 years if the discount rate is 11% per annum.

### Exercise 14.3

Reconsider Exercise 14.2.

Write an Excel function that will provide the same answer as was obtained in that exercise.

### Exercise 14.4

Find the present value of 25 equal annual receipts of £50, if the first receipt is to be received just now, if the interest rate for the period is 8% compounded annually and if a terminal bonus of £2000 is to be received with the last receipt of £50.

### Exercise 14.5

Find the present value of an amount of £3500 to be received in 10 years' time if the interest rate is 16% per annum compounded:

(a) quarterly,
(b) monthly,
(c) daily,
(d) continuously.

### Exercise 14.6

What size of loan would require 12 equal quarterly payments of £300, with the first payment being made in one quarter's time, if the quoted annual interest rate were 16% per annum compounded quarterly?

## Exercise 14.7

A firm is considering the purchase of a new computer that is expected to produce annual net savings in labour costs of £8000 in each of the 6 years of its operational life.

The computer has an initial cost of £30000, and annual maintenance costs of £1000. All savings and maintenance costs accrue at the end of each relevant year.

The company has access to funds at the current market interest rate of 14% per annum, compounded annually, and wishes to decide whether the purchase of the computer is a worthwhile investment.

(a) By calculating the NPV of the proposed expenditure decide whether the computer should be purchased.

(b) If the market rate of interest fell to 8.5% per annum would the decision reached in (a) above be altered?

(c) In an attempt to finalize the sale, the computer salesperson offers the firm a 'trade-in' after 6 years, the terms of which guarantee a £7500 reduction in the price of a replacement computer. Would such an offer alter the decision reached in (a) above (i.e. at the 14% interest rate)?

## Exercise 14.8

A firm wishes to acquire a new photocopier, but has to decide whether it should purchase the item outright or lease one from a leasing company. It intends to keep the photocopier for 3 years and employs a 12% discount rate in all of its investment projects. The relevant expenditures for the alternative acquisition schemes are given below.

  A. Purchase of photocopier:

$$\text{Purchase price} = £5000.$$

    Service contract for maintenance, service, repair, etc. (payable at the start of years 1 and 2) = £200.

    Resale value of the photocopier after 3 years = £3500.

  B. Leasing scheme

    Annual lease (payable at the start of each year for a minimum of 3 payments) = £1000. Maintenance costs and resale value = 0.

(a) Which of the two schemes should the firm choose?

(b) Suppose that because of the cash flow situation the £5000 for the purchase of the photocopier would have to be borrowed from the bank at an interest rate of 12%, and repaid in equal annual instalments at the end of each of the 3 years. What difference does this make to the choice of schemes?

(c) If the borrowing rate demanded by the bank is increased to 18% and the repayment method is as in (b), what difference does this make to the choice of scheme?

## Exercise 14.9

Reconsider Exercise 14.8.

Prepare a worksheet that can compare the net present values of the purchase and the leasing scheme for discount rates between 0% and 15% in steps of 1%.

What conclusions can be drawn?

## Exercise 14.10

Reconsider Exercise 14.7.

Calculate the IRR of the proposed purchase of the computer, both with and without the 'trade-in'.

Should the computer be purchased if the current market rate of interest is 7% per annum?

## Exercise 14.11

A whisky manufacturer has just completed a production run of 10000 barrels of whisky at a unit production cost of £400 per barrel. The whisky must be matured for 5 years before it can be sold and this will impose storage costs of £10 at the end of each of the next 5 years.

Bottling and labelling a mature barrel of whisky will cost £4 per barrel.

The current selling price of a barrel of this whisky is £500, but this is expected to increase, on average, by 10% per annum in each of the next 5 years.

Calculate the internal rate of return of this investment, and decide whether it is worthwhile if the current market rate of interest is 11% per annum.

## Exercise 14.12

A forestry enterprise has just planted an area of land with 100000 saplings at a cost of £11 per tree, £1 of which was planting costs (the remainder being purchase cost).

The trees will be ready for cutting after 10 years at the earliest, and during the maturing period grow at an annual compound rate such that the value of usable wood increases each year by 20% of the initial purchase cost of each tree.

During the maturing period the annual cost of tending the plantation is expected to be equal to 1.5% of the value of the plantation at the start of that year, payable at the start of the second and all subsequent years. (The first year's tending costs are included in the planting cost at the start of the first year.)

Calculate the IRR of this investment if the forestry enterprise decides that all of the trees are to be felled as soon as they mature, and if the cost of this felling is 5% of the value of trees felled.

## Exercise 14.13

A shipping company has just taken delivery of an £8 million cargo vessel. The payment terms imposed by the shipyard are that 25% of the amount due must be paid immediately, but that the outstanding balance can be repaid in five equal annual instalments. The shipyard will, however, charge an annual **flat rate** interest charge of 10% of the incurred debt for each year that there is any debt outstanding.

(a) If the first instalment is to be made one year from now, calculate the size of the five equal payments that will have to be made by the shipping company and the APR on this loan arrangement.

(b) Funds are also available from the shipping company's bankers at a rate of 10.5% per annum compounded annually. This would mean that the outstanding debt to the builders could be borrowed from the bank and cleared off immediately.

   Which of the two loan arrangements should the shipping company use in terms of offering the lowest APR?

(c) In addition, however, suppose that the shipyard offered the shipping company a deal whereby (after the initial 25% payment) no interest was charged and no further payments were due until 2 years after the ship was delivered, would this make any difference to the decision reached in part (ii) above?

## 14.8 **Solutions to the exercises**

### Solution to Exercise 14.1

Use Workbook 14.1 and change the entry in B3 to 500. Then alter the step value for *t* from 2 to 1.

   Finally, enter values of 1%, 2%, 4%, 8%, 16% and 32% to the B4:G4 cells.

   The results will be calculated and graphed automatically (although you will have to change the value in the graph title from £1000 to £500 manually).

### Solution to Exercise 14.2

Use Workbook 14.1 and change the entry in B3 to 2000. Then enter 11% to the B4 cell.

   The present values of a **single** amount of £2000 after 1, 2, 3, 4 and 5 years are contained in B7:B11 respectively. Consequently the present value of the stream of five future payments of £2000 is given by

$$=SUM(B7:B11) = £7391.79.$$

## Solution to Exercise 14.3

The appropriate PV function is

$$=PV(11\%,5,2000,0,0)$$

and this evaluates to £7391.79.

  Remember that the last argument value should be set to 0 since the first payment is to be received one year from now.

## Solution to Exercise 14.4

The appropriate PV function is

$$=PV(8\%,25,50,2000,1) = £868.47.$$

That is, the terminal bonus is included as the fourth argument, and since the first payment is received just now the last argument is set to a value of 1.

## Solution to Exercise 14.5

All that needs to be done is make the appropriate entries in Workbook 14.2 and the correct results will be obtained. These are:

(a) $B1 = -3500, B2 = 16\%, B3 = 10, B4 = 4$ giving PV $= £729.01$.

(b) $B1 = -3500, B2 = 16\%, B3 = 10, B4 = 12$ giving PV $= £714.15$.

(c) $B1 = -3500, B2 = 16\%, B3 = 10, B4 = 365$ giving PV $= £706.88$.

(d) Use any cell to contain:

$$=3500/(EXP(0.16*10))$$

  This gives an answer of £706.64.

## Solution to Exercise 14.6

The size of the loan is calculated from

$$=PV(16\%/4,4*3,-300,0,0) = £2815.52.$$

Notice how the repayments on the loan are regarded as comprising 12 quarterly instalments, each of which is discounted at a rate of $16\%/4 = 4\%$ per quarter.

  Alternatively, the same result can be obtained by making the following entries to Workbook 14.3:

$$B1 = 0, B2 = -300, B3 = 16\%, B4 = 3 \text{ and } B5 = 4.$$

Finally, this result can be confirmed from the PMT function as follows:

$$=PMT(4\%,12,2815.52,0,0)$$

| | A | B | C | D | E | F | G | H | I |
|---|---|---|---|---|---|---|---|---|---|
| **1** | | Labour cost | Maintenance | Purchase | | | | | |
| **2** | Year | Savings | Costs | Cost | Net revenue | | | | |
| **3** | 0 | 0 | 0 | -30000 | -30000 | | | | |
| **4** | 1 | 8000 | -1000 | 0 | 7000 | | | | |
| **5** | 2 | 8000 | -1000 | 0 | 7000 | | | | |
| **6** | 3 | 8000 | -1000 | 0 | 7000 | | | | |
| **7** | 4 | 8000 | -1000 | 0 | 7000 | | | | |
| **8** | 5 | 8000 | -1000 | 0 | 7000 | | | | |
| **9** | 6 | 8000 | -1000 | 0 | 7000 | | | | |
| **10** | | | | | | | | | |
| **11** | Discount rate | 14.00% | | | | | | | |
| **12** | Net Present value | -£2,779.33 | | | | | | | |
| **13** | | | | | | | | | |
| **14** | | | | | | | | | |

Sheet1 / Sheet2 / Sheet3 / Sheet4 / Sheet5 / She

**Workbook 14.6**

A result of −£300 will be obtained, and indicates that 12 quarterly repayments of £300 are required to pay off a debt of £2815.52 that is incurred just now at an annual interest rate of 16% compounded quarterly.

## Solution to Exercise 14.7

(a) The relevant costs and returns are illustrated in Workbook 14.6. Load this file now from the online resource centre.
The entry in E3 is: =SUM(B3:D3), and this was copied into E4:E9.
The entry in B12 is: =NPV(B11,E4:E9)+E3.
Being negative, the NPV figure of −2779.33 indicates that the project is **not viable** at the discount rate employed.

(b) Change the discount rate in B11 to 8.5% and it will be found that the NPV has risen to £1875.11. The project has become viable as a result of the reduction in the implied cost of credit.

(c) The £7500 'trade-in' means that an extra income item after 6 years is to be received. Add this to the existing entry in B6 (so that it becomes 15500), and then notice that even with a 14% discount rate the effect of the 'trade-in' has been to make the NPV on the project positive (£637.58 to be exact). The project is now viable at a 14% discount rate, but **only** because of the 'trade-in'.

## Solution to Exercise 14.8

(a) Worksheet 14.7 tabulates the relevant costs and revenues for both the purchase and the leasing scheme.
The relevant formulae are:
In E4: =SUM(B4:D4) copied into E5:E7.
In B11: =NPV(B10,E5:E7)+E4
In B12: =NPV(B10,F5:F7)+F4

| | A | B | C | D | E | F | G | H | I |
|---|---|---|---|---|---|---|---|---|---|
| **1** | | Purchase | Purchase | Purchase | Purchase | Lease | | | |
| **2** | | Resale | Service | Purchase | Net | Annual | | | |
| **3** | Year | Value | Contract | Price | Revenue | Lease | | | |
| **4** | 0 | 0 | | -5000 | -5000 | -1000 | | | |
| **5** | 1 | 0 | -200 | 0 | -200 | -1000 | | | |
| **6** | 2 | 0 | -200 | 0 | -200 | -1000 | | | |
| **7** | 3 | 3500 | 0 | 0 | 3500 | 0 | | | |
| **8** | | | | | | | | | |
| **9** | | | | | | | | | |
| **10** | Discount rate | 12% | | | | | | | |
| **11** | Purchase NPV | -£2,846.78 | | | | | | | |
| **12** | Lease NPV | -£2,690.05 | | | | | | | |
| **13** | | | | | | | | | |

**Workbook 14.7**

As can be seen, the leasing scheme has a **less negative** NPV and is therefore to be preferred.

(b) The three equal annual payments to repay the loan of £5000 can be obtained from

$$=PMT(12\%,3,5000) = -£2081.74$$

These can then be included as cash flow items as shown in Workbook 14.8.

Clearly the situation is unchanged as a result of the new arrangements. This should have been expected since if the firm applies a discount rate of 12% to the project, then this is effectively **charging itself** an interest rate of 12% for the use of the funds. Since this charge is the same as that made by the bank there will be no change in the NPV of the project.

(c) It would be possible to go through arithmetic if necessary, but really there is no need, since we can reason as follows. The increased bank lending rate, means that

| | A | B | C | D | E | F | G | H | I |
|---|---|---|---|---|---|---|---|---|---|
| **1** | | Purchase | Purchase | Purchase | Purchase | Lease | | | |
| **2** | | Resale | Service | Purchase | Net | Annual | | | |
| **3** | Year | Value | Contract | Price | Revenue | Lease | | | |
| **4** | 0 | 0 | | | 0 | -1000 | | | |
| **5** | 1 | 0 | -200 | -2081.74 | -2281.74 | -1000 | | | |
| **6** | 2 | 0 | -200 | -2081.74 | -2281.74 | -1000 | | | |
| **7** | 3 | 3500 | 0 | -2081.74 | 1418.26 | 0 | | | |
| **8** | | | | | | | | | |
| **9** | | | | | | | | | |
| **10** | Discount rate | 12% | | | | | | | |
| **11** | Purchase NPV | -£2,846.77 | | | | | | | |
| **12** | Lease NPV | -£2,690.05 | | | | | | | |
| **13** | | | | | | | | | |
| **14** | | | | | | | | | |

**Workbook 14.8**

| | A | B | C | D | E | F | G | H | I |
|---|---|---|---|---|---|---|---|---|---|
| | | Purchase | Purchase | Purchase | Purchase | Lease | Discount | Purchase | Lease |
| **1** | | Resale | Service | Purchase | Net | Annual | Rate | NPV | NPV |
| **2** | | | | | | | | | |
| **3** | Year | Value | Contract | Price | Revenue | Lease | 0% | -£1,900.00 | -£3,000.00 |
| **4** | 0 | 0 | | -5000 | -5000 | -1000 | 1% | -£1,997.01 | -£2,970.40 |
| **5** | 1 | 0 | -200 | | -200 | -1000 | 2% | -£2,090.18 | -£2,941.56 |
| **6** | 2 | 0 | -200 | | -200 | -1000 | 3% | -£2,179.70 | -£2,913.47 |
| **7** | 3 | 3500 | 0 | | 3500 | 0 | 4% | -£2,265.73 | -£2,886.09 |
| **8** | | | | | | | 5% | -£2,348.45 | -£2,859.41 |
| **9** | | | | | | | 6% | -£2,428.01 | -£2,833.39 |
| **10** | Discount rate | 12% | | | | | 7% | -£2,504.56 | -£2,808.02 |
| **11** | Purchase NPV | -£2,846.78 | | | | | 8% | -£2,578.24 | -£2,783.26 |
| **12** | Lease NPV | -£2,690.05 | | | | | 9% | -£2,649.18 | -£2,759.11 |
| **13** | | | | | | | 10% | -£2,717.51 | -£2,735.54 |
| **14** | | | | | | | 11% | -£2,783.33 | -£2,712.52 |
| **15** | | | | | | | 12% | -£2,846.78 | -£2,690.05 |
| **16** | | | | | | | 13% | -£2,907.94 | -£2,668.10 |
| **17** | | | | | | | 14% | -£2,966.93 | -£2,646.66 |
| **18** | | | | | | | 15% | -£3,023.83 | -£2,625.71 |

Sheet1 / Sheet2 / Sheet3 / Sheet4 / Sheet5 / She

**Workbook 14.9**

the annual repayments on the loan will be higher, which, with a 12% discount rate means that the NPV of the loan scheme will become more negative. Now since the leasing scheme was preferable **before** the NPV of the purchase scheme became more negative, it follows that it must be **even more preferable** now. Consequently, there will be no change in the choice of schemes.

## Solution to Exercise 14.9

The solution is shown in Workbook 14.9.

The crucial formulae are located in H3 and I3, and are

$$=NPV(G3,E\$5:E\$7)+E\$4 \quad \text{and} \quad =NPV(G3,F\$5:F\$7)+F\$4$$

These were then copied into H4:I18.

When the G4:I17 range is graphed as an XY scatter graph, using the first column as the horizontal axis, then Figure 14.4 is obtained.

This clearly shows that the purchase scheme is superior to the leasing scheme (less negative NPV) for discount rates that are less than about 10.5%. Thereafter the leasing scheme is superior.

## Solution to Exercise 14.10

Load Workbook 14.6 (W14_6.xls).

Use B13 to contain the formula.

$$=IRR(E3:E9,0.1)$$

When formatted to two decimal places a value of 10.55% will be returned.

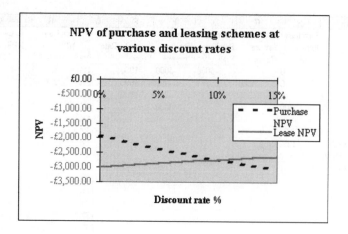

**Figure 14.4**

To calculate the IRR when the 'trade-in' is included, change the value in B9 to 15500, and the IRR will increase to 14.7%.

With a current market rate of interest of 14% the fact that the IRR with the trade-in exceeds this figure means that the project is superior to the alternative of placing the funds on deposit. Notice that this confirms the conclusion that was obtained on the basis of NPV analysis.

## Solution to Exercise 14.11

The selling price ($P$) of a barrel of whisky in 5 years' time will be

$$P = 500(1.1)^5 = £805.25.$$

The storage, production and bottling costs per barrel, and the eventual income give rise to the stream of costs and receipts indicated in Workbook 14.10.

The IRR per barrel is calculated in B10 from the formulae

$$=IRR(F3:F8,0.1)$$

| | A | B | C | D | E | F | G | H | I | J | K | L | M | N | O |
|---|---|---|---|---|---|---|---|---|---|---|---|---|---|---|---|
| 1 | | Storage | Production | Bottling | Gross | Net | | | | | | | | | |
| 2 | Year | Costs | Costs | Costs | Income | Income | | | | | | | | | |
| 3 | 0 | | -400 | 0 | 0 | -400 | | | | | | | | | |
| 4 | 1 | -10 | 0 | 0 | 0 | -10 | | | | | | | | | |
| 5 | 2 | -10 | 0 | 0 | 0 | -10 | | | | | | | | | |
| 6 | 3 | -10 | 0 | 0 | 0 | -10 | | | | | | | | | |
| 7 | 4 | -10 | 0 | 0 | 0 | -10 | | | | | | | | | |
| 8 | 5 | -10 | 0 | -4 | 805.25 | 791.25 | | | | | | | | | |
| 9 | | | | | | | | | | | | | | | |
| 10 | IRR | 12.98% | | | | | | | | | | | | | |
| 11 | | | | | | | | | | | | | | | |
| 12 | | | | | | | | | | | | | | | |

**Workbook 14.10**

| | A | B | C | D | E | F | G | H | I | J |
|---|---|---|---|---|---|---|---|---|---|---|
| **1** | | Value of | Gross | Purchase | Planting | Tending | Felling | Net | | |
| **2** | Year | Average tree | Revenue | Cost | Cost | Cost | Cost | Revenue | | |
| **3** | 0 | 10.00 | 0.00 | -10 | -1 | 0 | 0 | -11.00 | | |
| **4** | 1 | 12.00 | 0.00 | 0 | 0 | -0.18 | 0 | -0.18 | | |
| **5** | 2 | 14.40 | 0.00 | 0 | 0 | -0.22 | 0 | -0.22 | | |
| **6** | 3 | 17.28 | 0.00 | 0 | 0 | -0.26 | 0 | -0.26 | | |
| **7** | 4 | 20.74 | 0.00 | 0 | 0 | -0.31 | 0 | -0.31 | | |
| **8** | 5 | 24.88 | 0.00 | 0 | 0 | -0.37 | 0 | -0.37 | | |
| **9** | 6 | 29.86 | 0.00 | 0 | 0 | -0.45 | 0 | -0.45 | | |
| **10** | 7 | 35.83 | 0.00 | 0 | 0 | -0.54 | 0 | -0.54 | | |
| **11** | 8 | 43.00 | 0.00 | 0 | 0 | -0.64 | 0 | -0.64 | | |
| **12** | 9 | 51.60 | 0.00 | 0 | 0 | -0.77 | 0 | -0.77 | | |
| **13** | 10 | 61.92 | 61.92 | 0 | 0 | -0.93 | -3.10 | 57.89 | | |
| **14** | | | | | | | | | | |
| **15** | IRR | 16.50% | | | | | | | | |
| **16** | | | | | | | | | | |

Sheet1 / Sheet2 / Sheet3 / Sheet4 / Sheet5 / She

**Workbook 14.11**

and returns a value of 12.98% when formatted to two decimal places. The fact that this exceeds the cost of borrowing funds (11%) suggests that the project should be carried out.

## Solution to Exercise 14.12

The value ($V$) of an average tree on maturity will be given by

$$V = 10(1.2)^{10} = £61.92.$$

The associated costs and revenues give rise to the stream of amounts shown in Workbook 14.11.

The important formulae are:

| | |
|---|---|
| In B4: = B3*1.2 | this computes the value of the average tree in each of the years, and was copied into B5:B13. |
| In C13: =B13 | this translates the value of the average tree into gross revenue once felling takes place. |
| In F4: =1.5%*-B4 | this computes the tending cost as 1.5% of the value of the average tree and was copied into F5:F13. |
| In G13: =5%*-B13 | this calculates the felling cost of the average tree as 5% of its final value. |
| In H3: =SUM(C3:G3) | this calculates the net revenue as the gross revenue less all costs, and was copied into H4:H13. |

Finally, the IRR of the stream costs and revenue is calculated in B15 from

$$=IRR(H3:H13,0.1)$$

and returns a value of 16.5% when formatted to two decimal places.

Consequently, the forest is a worthwhile investment as long as the market rate of interest is less than 16.5%.

| | A | B | C | D | E | F | G | H |
|---|---|---|---|---|---|---|---|---|
| 1 | Cost of ship | | 8 | Bank loan Equivalent annual rate (EAR) | | 10.50% | | |
| 2 | Deposit | 25% | | | | | | |
| 3 | Balance | 6.00 | | | | | | |
| 4 | Flat rate | 0.10 | | | | | | |
| 5 | Number of repayments | 5.00 | | | | | | |
| 6 | Size of repayments | -1.80 | | | | | | |
| 7 | | Scheme 1 | Scheme 2 | Scheme 3 | | | | |
| 8 | Year | Repayments | Repayments | Repayments | | | | |
| 9 | | 0 | 6.00 | 6 | 6 | | | |
| 10 | | 1 | -1.80 | 0 | 0 | | | |
| 11 | | 2 | -1.80 | -1.80 | 0 | | | |
| 12 | | 3 | -1.80 | -1.80 | -1.80 | | | |
| 13 | | 4 | -1.80 | -1.80 | -1.80 | | | |
| 14 | | 5 | -1.80 | -1.80 | -1.80 | | | |
| 15 | | 6 | | -1.80 | -1.80 | | | |
| 16 | | 7 | | | -1.80 | | | |
| 17 | | APR | APR | APR | | | | |
| 18 | | 15.24% | 10.97% | 8.59% | | | | |

Sheet1 / Sheet2 / Sheet3 / Sheet4 / Sheet5 / She

**Workbook 14.12**

A more general model for this problem is contained in Workbook 14.11A (W14_11A.xls).

Load this now and then use it answer the following supplementary question.

With the data as given in the original question calculate the minimum required rate of growth of the trees if the project is to yield an internal rate of return of 20%.

The answer can be obtained from the Solver with a target cell of B19 (the IRR) and a target cell value of 20%. The changing cell is B1 (the growth rate of the trees). When these settings are made and the Solver run a solution value of 23.6% will be returned (when formatted to two decimal places).

## Solution to Exercise 14.13

(a) The solution is shown in Workbook 14.12, where the size of the five equal annual repayments is calculated from

$$(6 + 5(0.1)6)/5 = 9/5 = £1.8\text{million}.$$

The formula in B6 is therefore

$$=(B3+B5*B4*B3)/B5$$

(b) The APR of the builder's first scheme is calculated in B18 from

$$=IRR(B9:B14,0.1)$$

and returns a value of 15.24%.

This is clearly greater than the annual rate of 10.5% charged by the bank and so the bank loan is to be preferred.

(c) The effect of the moratorium on the repayments to the builders is displayed in column C of the worksheet, and the APR of this scheme calculated in C18 from

=IRR(C9:C16,0.1).

Clearly the effect of the moratorium has been to reduce the APR on the debt to the builders to 10.97%, but this is still not **quite** enough to make it preferable to the bank loan. However, it is an easy matter to confirm that if an extra year's moratorium were offered then the APR would fall by enough to alter the decision as to which scheme should be chosen. The calculations for this have been entered into column D of the worksheet, and the new APR (8.59%) calculated in D18 from

=IRR(D9:D16,0.1).

Clearly the builder's scheme with the 3-year moratorium now has a lower APR than the bank loan.

# ■ INDEX